CROSSING THREE WILDERNESSES

MAP OF CAMBODIA

STUNG TRENG

RATTANAKIRI

ATIE

● **Sambor**
● **Kratie**

Mekong
River

MONDULKIRI

⑥
⑤
⑧ ⑨
⑦

MPONG
HAM

SVAY
RIENG

❶
❷

1 Thlok, where U Sam Oeur was born

2 Svay Rieng City, where U Sam Oeur
   was educated

3 Factory at Koh Kong

4 East Bodhibreuk: first forced labor camp

5 Prek Ta Am: second forced labor camp

6 Boh Leav: third forced labor camp

7 Sre Pring: fourth forced labor camp

8 Chrawlk Marah: fifth forced labor camp

9 Sampoch: sixth forced labor camp

10 Area where U Sam Oeur gave speeches
   on behalf of PRK government, 1986

CROSSING THREE WILDERNESSES

A MEMOIR BY U SAM OEUR

WITH KEN McCULLOUGH

COFFEE HOUSE PRESS
MINNEAPOLIS

COPYRIGHT © 2005 by U Sam Oeur and Ken McCullough
COVER DESIGN Linda Koutsky   BOOK DESIGN Allan Kornblum
COVER PHOTO © Getty Images   AUTHOR PHOTOS © Theodore D. Hall

Coffee House Press is a nonprofit literary publishing house. Support from private foundations, corporate giving programs, government programs, and generous individuals help make the publication of our books possible. We gratefully acknowledge their support in detail in the back of this book.

Coffee House Press books are available to the trade through our primary distributor, Consortium Book Sales & Distribution, 1045 Westgate Drive, Saint Paul, MN 55114. For personal orders, catalogs, or other information, write to: Coffee House Press, 27 North Fourth Street, Suite 400, Minneapolis, MN 55401.

LIBRARY OF CONGRESS CATALOGING-IN-PUBLICATION DATA
U Sam Oeur, 1936–
Crossing three wildernesses : a memoir / by U Sam Oeur ;
with Ken McCullough.— 1st ed.
p. cm.
ISBN-13: 978-1-56689-167-7 (alk. paper)
ISBN-10: 1-56689-167-1 (alk. paper)
1. U Sam Oeur, 1936– 2. Cambodia—History—1975–1979.
3. Cambodia—History—1979–
4. Cambodia—Officials and employees—Biography.
I. McCullough, Ken. II. Title.
DS555.86.U16.A3 2005
959.604'2'092—DC22
2005016116

FIRST EDITION | FIRST PRINTING
1 3 5 7 9 8 6 4 2
Printed in Canada

"Lift Every Voice and Sing," from *Lift Every Voice and Sing: Words and Music* by James Weldon Johnson, illustrated by Mozelle Thompson, copyright © 1970 by Hawthorn Books, Inc. Used by permission of Dutton, a division of Penguin Group (USA) Inc.

Author Acknowledgments

We would like to thank the following people for their generosity and kindness: Clark Blaise, Cyndi Bishara, Taufiq Ismail, Rowena Torrevillas, Peter and Mary Nazareth, Maggie Hogan, Carol Harker, Wally Chappell, Marlene Perrin, Greg Smith, Ginny and the late Mike Duncan, Hua-Ling Engle and the late Paul Engle, Lucksmann Kim, Mom Ven, The First Mennonite Church of Iowa City, especially Pastor Firman Gingerich and Hobart Yoder, Kathleen and Edward McAllister, Nakry and Voha Chuon, Chan Ny, Vi Houi, Pheany Chey, Smith Leng, Phuon Roeung, Loeng Chang Vang, Joyce Brabner, Dr. Lise Strnad, Kim Tuoy Khu, Sim Um, Sarem Neou, Samreth Kim, Measkoy Kim, Lang Leang Kulen, Robin Martin, Todd Lieber, Fred Woodard, Jim Gilmour, Mary Ellen Will, Steve Clary, Jean Feraca, Michael Dennis Browne, Mark Bruckner, Mary Beth Easley, both the Iowa City and Minneapolis casts of *The Krasang Tree*, the people of Taos, including Rose Gordon, Catherine and Stephen Rose, Lorraine and Ron Ciancio, Phyllis and Sy Hotch, and especially Charley Strong and Mag Dimond (who have helped in so many ways), Hannah Lee and Barbara Morford, Dinitia Smith, Bob Holman, William Golightly, Sr. Anita Beskar, FSPA, Sharon May Brown, Catherine Filloux, Tom Beller, Brian Builta, Michael E. Young, Esther Wu, Thi Nguyen, Mark Larson, Allie Shah, Brian Bonner, Jerome Christenson, Benjamin Spillman, Kat Garrison, Erin Hemme Froslie, Britt Robson, Dave Carlson, Julie Smith, Yos Roeun, Em Proum, Ann and Steve Coleman, Kathe Davis, Leslie Tung, Ann Struthers, Carolyn Collins and Shannon Hanzel, the late Hale Chatfield, Jim Cihlar, Mark Nowak, Mike Amato, Daniel Bourne, Ed Folsom, Daniel Weissbort, Ray Heffner, Julie Englander, Ron Kuka, Jim Autry, Rachel Weintraub, David Hamilton, Kevin Benson, Katherine Meyer, Ray and Stella Young Bear, Jim Harris, Paul Ingram, Rick Rotert, Stavros Deligiorgis, Lynn Nankivil, the late Willy Nolledo, Mr. and Mrs. Sim Um, Jocelyn Cullity, Jill and Dr. Daniel Christian, Glenda Potter, Toby Thompson, Mary Ross Hostetter, Laura and John P. Douglas, and David Chandler. Thanks to Allan Kornblum for all his hard work and astute questions, Chris Fischbach for his careful reading, and to the staff of Coffee House Press. Each of these persons deserves a separate chapter, spelling out the manner in which they helped—maybe that will be Volume II.

Thanks also to The Dashiell Hammett and Lillian Hellman Fund for Free Expression, the St. Paul Companies, The Bush Foundation, PEN, St. Anthony's Bread (administered by St. Mary's Roman Catholic Church, Iowa City), The Martin Foundation, the International Writing Program of the University of Iowa, the Office of International Studies at the University of Iowa, Winona State University, all the colleges, universities, high schools, and communities who sponsored readings and presentations, The Center for Victims of Torture, Poets in Need, The Pangea World Theatre, The Douglas Corporation, the Spring Green Literary Festival, the Khmer Buddhist Society of the North Bronx, The Buddhist Temple of Flower Mound, Texas.   —U.S.O. and K.M.

In addition to those listed above I'd like to thank the Iowa Arts Council, the Witter Bynner Foundation for Poetry, and the Jerome Foundation. Special thanks to my wife Lynn Nankivil, who has been a vigilant reader and steady source of inspiration during the writing of this book.
                                                    —K.M.

CROSSING THREE WILDERNESSES

PREFACE

U Sam Oeur, whom I've never met, springs to life in the pages of this full-blown, inspiring memoir. He is an accomplished poet and a born writer. He has absorbed enough experience for several lifetimes. As a Cambodian who survived the Khmer Rouge years, he is lucky to be alive at all.

He was born on a farm in Svay Rieng Province in eastern Cambodia in 1936. As he tended his father's water buffalo in the closing years of French colonialism, he could never have foreseen what lay ahead for him or for his country. Luckily, his father was prosperous enough to send him to school. Sam Oeur's abilities as a student took him to Phnom Penh, where he completed high school (as very few Cambodians did; there were only a handful of high schools in the country) and studied industrial design.

In 1961, the U.S. government, as part of its aid program to Cambodia, awarded him a scholarship to study in the United States. Sam Oeur was engaged to be married just before he left; neither he nor his fiancée Yan imagined that he would be gone for seven years.

Sam Oeur's encounter with America in the 1960s was bewildering at first, but confusion soon deepened into love. He crisscrossed the country, and as part of his English-language training he memorized the Gettysburg Address, parts of the Declaration of Independence, and hundreds of lines of his favorite poet, Walt Whitman. After he earned a degree in industrial design in California, his own talents as a poet came to the attention of Dr. Mary Gray, an almost legendary figure in the Asia Foundation at that time. Dr. Gray recommended him for a scholarship at the prestigious Writers' Workshop at the University of Iowa, where he earned an MFA and met several other writers, like Ken McCullough, who became his friend for life. By 1968 Sam Oeur was anxious to come home. His fiancée, almost unbelievably, had waited for him for seven years—they married shortly after his return. In the closing years of Prince Sihanouk's one-man rule in Cambodia, Sam Oeur avoided politics. He chose, instead, to start a family while he managed a fish cannery, very competently, in the remote western province of Koh Kong.

In March 1970 a bloodless coup removed Sihanouk from power. The Khmer Republic, led by General Lon Nol, was pro-American and anti-Communist. So was U Sam Oeur. The coup makers promised to install liberal democracy in Cambodia, and Sam Oeur, like many others at the time, hoped for the best. He joined the army (never firing a shot), becoming a political officer. In 1972, he was elected to the Khmer Republic's National Assembly, and served as a delegate to the United Nations. Offered several chances to leave the country (or to stay in the United States), he patriotically refused. In the meantime, Lon Nol's poorly trained, badly led army proved no match for the Vietnamese Communist and Khmer Rouge forces arrayed against them. By 1974 the government, mired in corruption, controlled only a few urban centers and was totally dependent on aid from the United States.

In April 1975, the Khmer Rouge swept into Phnom Penh and drove its two million people, including Sam Oeur and his family, into the countryside. An adroit survivor, he shepherded his family toward the northeast of the country, where they endured over three years of hardship, including the tragic deaths, at birth, of his twin daughters, at the hands of a midwife who was under orders to kill all newborns.

For over three years U Sam Oeur kept his head down, concealed his background, and relied on reawakened peasant know-how to withstand the rigors of the regime. When he was alone, he lifted his spirits by reciting Walt Whitman's poems and John F. Kennedy's inaugural address. His immediate family also survived, he tells us, because an array of guardian spirits was always there to help them. But after the fall of the regime, in 1979, he discovered that twenty-three members of his family, including his parents, two sisters, three brothers, and fifteen nephews and nieces had been killed or died of overwork and starvation in the Khmer Rouge period.

In 1978, the Khmer Rouge regime foolhardily declared war on Vietnam. When Vietnamese armies invaded Cambodia at the end of the year, the country broke open like an egg. The Vietnamese soon established a friendly Cambodian government in Phnom Penh, The Peoples' Republic of Kampuchea (PRK), and stationed over 200,000 troops in the country. Cambodia was dependent on Vietnam until 1990, when the collapse of the Soviet Union, and the end of Soviet assistance, forced the Vietnamese to withdraw their forces. The PRK officials remained in place, but quickly ditched Marxism-Leninism as an ideology.

Sam Oeur's description of his life in the 1980s is in many ways the high point of the book. After a few months of scavenging in the skeletal city of Phnom Penh, Sam Oeur found some work in the Ministry of Foreign Affairs, and later was put in charge of a bicycle factory before rising inside the PRK's Ministry of Industry—probably the first and last Cambodian poet to climb as far in such surroundings. He gives vivid glimpses of a decade when, as he tells us, he "hoped to stay alive and to serve [his] country." Having done both, he lost his government job in 1990, in part for writing some subversive poems. For a few months, vividly described, Sam Oeur drifted into alcoholism at the margins of society. At a time when readers might assume that he was losing his mind, his guardian spirits were working overtime. In 1991, his luck changed (yet again) when he was hired by the newly established U.S. diplomatic mission on an informal basis, to gather intelligence for the ambassador. Not long afterwards, Sam Oeur's literary friends from his Iowa City days obtained a new fellowship for him at the University of Iowa, supposedly for three months. Sam Oeur has remained in America ever since.

Crossing Three Wildernesses closes, aside from a brief epilogue, at the airport in Cedar Rapids, where Sam Oeur is met by his friend Ken McCullough, picking up threads that had been dropped nearly a quarter century before.

It's an honor for me to introduce a book that has taught me so much and has given me so much pleasure. Newcomers to Cambodia's history will find themselves in the hands of an alert, courageous, sensitive participant and witness. Old Cambodia hands will delight, as I did, in the refreshing insights and new information that Sam Oeur imparts. But the book is more than the story of one man's entanglement with history. It is a moving and persuasive account of a tumultuous life that has taken U Sam Oeur from the rice fields of Svay Rieng, to America, and back again, coming to bask at last in the pleasures of being a grandfather, here represented at the height of his powers, perhaps as his guardian spirits had always intended.

—David Chandler, May 2005
author of *A History of Cambodia*

This book is dedicated to my son, James Bonya Ou, his wife April McAllister-Ou, my grandsons Edward, John, and Daniel, and to my loving wife Sim Syna. And to the people of Cambodia, and to all our sons and daughters.

In memory of Dr. Mary Gray
In the spirit of Walt Whitman
In the name of Peace
Freedom and Democracy

CAMBODIAN NEW YEAR

The Cambodian New Year begins on April 13th and lasts through the 15th. On the 13th, at seven in the evening, people go the pagoda to pray, and to recite the Five Precepts of Buddhism, which are the injunctions not to kill, steal, commit adultery, lie (gossip, bear false witness), or drink alcoholic beverages. People then formally invite the monks to chant the Dhamma *(blessing). This opening ceremony is followed by games such as tug-of-war and also informal dancing. Cambodians continue to use hand gestures from traditional ritual dance, even when the music is rock and roll. A traditional game that is usually played at this time is* Col Jhoong, *which involves tossing a ball made from a knotted-up checkered scarf, the* krama. *The game resembles Western dodgeball. Another game is called* ankgunh, *kind of like aerial bowling: a round-flat nut, two inches in diameter, is pitched through the air at five other nuts placed strategically on the ground. The object is to hit as many of the nuts as possible. Some of the games are specifically for teenagers, such as hiding-the-napkin: young people sit in a circle, alternating gender, and the person who is "it" walks around behind the circle until he or she deposits a napkin down the back of a person's shirt—a person of the opposite gender. The object, then, is to get back to one's place and be seated before the other person tags you. The boys usually have an advantage, but they sometimes lose just to get in good with the girl who does the chasing.*

Early on the morning of the second day, people offer breakfast to the monks. This consists of rice porridge with salty fish or pork, ansam jrook *(round cakes of sticky rice as big around as one's kneecap),* nom gom *(sticky rice flour wrapped around a core of green beans), bananas, and a wide range of other fruit, and cookies. Lunch is offered to the monks at 11:00 a.m.—the fare is similar to breakfast.*

The monks then chant the paticca-samuppada *(dependent origination) to transfer the essence of four requisites (clothes, food, shelter, and medicine) to the spirits of deceased relatives. After lunch, men and women (young and old) play games again on the grounds of the pagoda.*

During the evening of the second day, old people of both genders go to the pagoda to receive blessing prayers and to listen to two monks recite a formal call-and-response dialogue about the history and traditions of the New Year celebration. This lasts about half an hour. Young people, who are excused from this ceremony, stay at the village, dancing and playing popular games, as on the afternoon of the first day.

On the morning of the third day, old people offer breakfast to the monks, and at lunch, people both young and old put rice in the monks' bowls; this ritual is called daak baat. *These bowls are of various materials and shapes, but serve the same purpose as the begging bowls one sees among Hindu monks. People bring* ansam jrook *(pork)* ansam cek *(bananas wrapped in sticky rice), and* nom gom *to offer to the monks. The monks, then, offer this feast to the spirits of deceased relatives. After lunch, people bring water to shower the Buddha images and to clean them meticulously. Young people also shower their parents and elders to ritualistically wash away any residual bad luck from the year that has just ended. This is again followed by popular games and dancing, until 3:00 p.m., when the celebration ends. There is not really a closing ceremony, but this brings to a close the events at the temple. The secular celebration continues in the village for an indeterminate time, from another three days up to an entire month.*

CHAPTER ONE: APRIL 1975

SEEKING REFUGE

"April is the cruelest month." That's the way T. S. Eliot begins "The Waste Land." Eliot, of course, was writing about the promise of spring, and his loss of faith in that promise. In Cambodia, April doesn't mean spring—it is already unbearably hot. For me and for millions of other Cambodians who lived through the events of 1975, Eliot's statement is frighteningly poignant. In our country, April will remain forever the cruelest month indeed.

As a child I had herded water buffalo, keeping them out of the rice fields. But, by April 1975, I was no longer a simple farmer's son. I was a National Assemblyman; I had been educated in the United States; I knew Cambodian history; I had knowledge of the strengths and weaknesses of the Cambodian government and armed forces; I had influential friends who gave me sound advice; and my guardian spirit had warned me in dreams. Nonetheless, nothing could have prepared me, or anyone else, for the cataclysm that overwhelmed our homeland.

Although Cambodia is now a modest-sized country—about the same dimensions as the state of Missouri—in the middle of the thirteenth century it encompassed almost all of what is now called Indochina, including much of Thailand, Laos, and Vietnam. But by the time the French forced King Norodom to sign an agreement making Cambodia a French protectorate in 1863, our neighbors had extended their borders at our expense, after several hundred years of warfare.

When the colonial era began to come to a close in the 1940s and 1950s, rebel factions gathered small armies in the countryside. The European powers, along with the United States, first backed the French colonial government, and then backed the often corrupt governments that took power when the French left in 1953-54. Meanwhile, in Laos, Vietnam, *and* Cambodia, the communist rebels sought and received help from either the Soviet Union or China. Since other rebel factions never received any financial or military backing, the communist factions inevitably became the dominant rebel force. We had hints that the Cambodian Communist Party, the Khmer Rouge, was somewhat different from the communist movements in other Southeast Asian countries, but of course no one knew how different they would prove to be.

After being educated in the United States, I believed passionately in democracy. I knew the governments of Prince Sihanouk and Lon Nol were corrupt, but I served as an official of the Khmer Republic because I thought I could work with others to bring democratic principles to my country. Unfortunately it was not meant to be.

About my guardian spirit: much is made, in current guidebooks and sourcebooks, of the fact that "animism" is still a strong element in Cambodian culture. But the books give you the impression that this kind of worldview is perpetuated primarily among the peasants, and that—as in the West—educated people have left behind such beliefs and regard them as antiquated relics of the past. But many educated Cambodians like myself continue to consider spiritual entities to be an ever-present part of daily life.

My guardian spirit had told me, in a dream, to wear the clothes of a farmer—to dress as I had in my childhood and youth. Accordingly, I had a Chinese tailor make me two farmer vests with large hidden pockets inside. They were made of simple cotton, in a floral pattern—one was green and white, the other, blue and white. I tucked them away for safekeeping.

Of course, even without dreams, current events were alarming enough. On April 1, 1975, President Lon Nol, weakened by a stroke, and by then without any remaining credibility as a government leader, fled Cambodia for the United States.

On April 5th, while I was walking along the sidewalk toward my office at the National Assembly in Phnom Penh, a mini-jeep pulled up to the curb next to me. It was my classmate Kethavy Kim—we had attended school together in Cambodia and at California State-Los Angeles. He offered to take me to the u.s. Embassy, and from there, out of the country. But I told him I was going to stay to fight the Khmer Rouge. He told me that they already had the city surrounded, but he could not convince me. In hindsight, I imagine he must have thought I spoke with absurd bravado.

On April 8th, the United States Ambassador, John Gunther Dean, also left Cambodia.

On April 12th, I accompanied Chhay Yat, another friend, to Pochentong Airport. A few months prior to this, the World Anti-Communist League had held its conference in Brazil; Chhay Yat and I were the two delegates from the Khmer Republic selected to attend, although, because of the deteriorating situation, we never actually went.

Chhay Yat understood the ramifications of our situation that April, but I was still operating in some kind of delusional state, thinking that it was all going to blow over. Just before he got on the plane, he finally convinced me. We agreed to rendezvous in Bangkok on April 27th, and leave from there for Brazil. As it turned out, I was not to see him again until 1992. Both he and Kethavy Kim now live in Long Beach, California.

April 13, 1975 was the beginning of our three-day New Year's celebration. Close to forty people had come to my home to share in our traditional dinner. We lived in a modest but roomy house on stilts right on National Highway 1, the main route east, toward Vietnam. Our house, Number 38, was in the ramshackle suburb of Chbar Ampeou (which means *sugarcane field*—a name it took on under the French), just across the Monivong Bridge from Phnom Penh, where the Tonle Sap, Mekong, and Bassac Rivers converge. My wife and I had moved in with her mother and father when we married in 1968.

Her father, Dy Sim (last name first), was a successful self-educated designer of temples and public monuments. When you go around Phnom Penh and its environs these days, a number of these structures are on the map as tourist attractions. Born in 1900, he had recently turned seventy-five, and had lost the use of his legs. But he still had beetling eyebrows, the intense eyes of a cobra, a pointed nose, and very long earlobes. He was a quiet, meditative man. Even though I was a member of Parliament and my father-in-law was a successful architect, my mother-in-law, Sum Yoeun (I called her *Me,* meaning Ma, or Mom), was considered, as is usual in Cambodian society, the head of the household. She was strong, thoughtful, and hardworking. She was unusually light-skinned and fairly tall, the same height as my father-in-law.

My wife, Dy Yan, was slender, beautiful, and soft-spoken with a sparkling personality. In other words, she was, by Cambodian standards (and especially my own), a perfect woman. My son Bun Nol was a solid, talkative, happy child (*Nol* means robust).

In Cambodia, a National Assemblyman is obligated to welcome anyone who comes to New Year's dinner—hence the large crowd. We sat on the floor, which was covered with two rows of reed mats of several colors, with no distinction as to rank or position. My wife and my mother-in-law prepared thin noodles with mixed vegetables and steamed pork. When everyone had been served, I proposed a toast:

> Dear Big Brothers and Big Sisters,
> Little Brothers and Little Sisters,
> The Year of the Bull has left us—
> enter, the Year of the Tiger.

We are all brothers and sisters here—
let us enjoy this New Year's feast
as we greet the Year of the Tiger
in hopes we will work together
to bring back peace to our land!

May I propose a toast to
solidarity
peace
freedom
and democracy!
Please enjoy our feast!

From the manner of their dress, I assumed that most of my very hungry guests were predominantly farmers. I did recognize Em Sen, the son of my second cousin, who had come with one of his friends. We consumed ten kilos of thin noodles, but the guests kept eating, so my wife ordered another ten kilos from a nearby shop.

Our guests enjoyed the feast until about four-thirty in the afternoon. At that point, Em Sen asked permission to scout around to see if the Khmer Rouge had reached Prek Pra or not. (Prek Pra is located about two miles from my house, along the Bassac River, south of the Monivong Bridge; we knew they would be coming from the south.) Other guests began to slip off one by one. At around six o'clock, one of them returned and told us that the Khmer Rouge had closed off the bridge to Phnom Penh, and had surrounded the city.

Upon hearing this report, I put on my military uniform (I had been a captain—more on that experience later), strapped a P.A. Colt .45 to my hip, took up my M-16, and strode over to a command post three hundred meters northeast of my house. On my way there, I saw weary soldiers from Lon Nol's army trudging along in front of my house, heading east. At the post itself, I observed a captain tossing away his AK-47. Then he ran to his house and threw all his uniforms onto a rubbish fire burning in the alley. I stood watching him, out of curiosity. He loaded some bundles hastily onto a cart and took off, towing it eastward along National Highway 1, following the human river. I threw away my own rifle but kept the pistol, and returned to my home.

As I was climbing the steps, Em Sen shouted at me: "The bridge is closed! The bridge is closed!" We were all frantic. I paced back and forth from the living room to the kitchen. Night fell; I saw flashlights everywhere. As I threw my pistol into the well by the west window of our house, I heard heavy artillery that sounded as if it were right in our backyard.

I looked out our back window and, indeed, an artillery battery *had* been positioned there! I heard riflemen shouting signals to each other, then the *pak pak pak* of their weapons. Then 82 mm fire: *Bong! Boong!* After the shelling, the Khmer Rouge began evicting people from their houses. People swarmed into my basement to hide. The Khmer Rouge called them by name: "Tith! Heng! Phon! Out of your house! Leave the door open—Angkar will take care of your wealth, don't worry! Out! Out!" The soldiers knew us by name; obviously they were quite familiar with the neighborhood and who we were.

I was shaking. *Pang! Pang!* The tenant of my guest house next door was shot sitting at his dinner table. He was drunk and had the temerity to object when they ordered him out. Then it was dark. Bombs were dropping everywhere around us; we were in a dreadful panic. Following the lead of the captain I had seen, I threw my military uniforms and the rest of the guns I owned into the well. Even if we wanted to escape, it was too late now.

I called my wife to bring our son to me. I hoisted him up into the attic, and my wife followed. Although we said nothing to each other, my wife and I understood that we would, in all probability, be burned alive if a shell hit our roof. Meanwhile the heavy artillery continued from my backyard, zeroing in on Chamkar Mon, the presidential residence in Phnom Penh, some three miles northwest of my house.

We wrapped ourselves in a bamboo mat, waiting for death. Only days before, my wife and I had taken a vow that if we had not done our share toward bringing democracy to our people and toward helping human beings in general, then a bomb should drop directly on us. Although several unidentified planes flew over, they continued to Phnom Penh.

My boy whispered: "Mom, pee." She said "Go ahead, right here." My son, then four years old, was completely toilet trained; consequently, he couldn't urinate or defecate unless it was in his portable toilet. But we told him that this time was different.

By midnight, the sounds of the artillery had died out. We slept in the attic that night. At one point my wife woke me and told me the dream she'd just had, "I saw a ball of light flying from the southeast. When it came close to me, it became small and entered my mouth." I told her that it was a good omen. I told her I thought it meant that Lon Nol would seek help from President Suharto, and that Indonesia would rescue Cambodia. (This help would not come until 1987, when the Tripartite Government— the remnants of the Khmer Rouge, and two other factions— finally met with the ruling government of Cambodia for peace talks at a conference that became known as the Jakarta Cocktail.)

We stayed wrapped up like that until 10:00 the next morning. I climbed down to take a look outside; the street was deserted. There was an unearthly pall compared to the intensity of the overnight shelling. I called my wife to bring our son to me. I was terrified. My father-in-law, Ta Sim (Ta means grandfather) was still in his room. He told us to get going, even though he couldn't leave because he was a cripple. I experienced great apprehension about leaving him, but all of us revered him and did not question his decision. I met my mother-in-law's eye and she signaled me to hurry up.

The day before, I had overheard one of the Khmer Rouge telling someone that we had to leave for three days, because the Americans were going to bomb the city at any moment. We lived on the outskirts of the city—would Ta Sim survive the bombing? My wife and mother-in-law planned to take turns carrying little Nol. I was so shaky that I couldn't even find a pair of old shorts, so I tore the legs out of my trousers, making them into shorts. Once in the apartment downstairs, I spotted a bunch of soiled diapers forgotten by a frightened neighbor. I picked up the sodden mass, balanced it on my head, and stepped out into the street, half naked. I was hoping to look like a peasant carrying a bundle of soiled laundry.

I thought I was well-disguised until a Khmer Rouge soldier with an M-16 pointed upward snickered at me, "Take light things along with you, like clothes, then go straight east to the liberated zone, Nhom! Don't worry about rice." (*Nhom* is the term a monk uses when speaking to laypersons, meaning something like aunt or uncle. It can be used as a title of respect, or an insult, depending on inflection. In this instance, I was obviously being insulted.) The soldier thought I was carrying rice! Realizing how foolish I looked, I threw down my bundle. But I ignored his directions.

Almost out of my mind, I gathered my wife, son, and mother-in-law and led them through the swamps north of National Highway 1. I was trying to reach Phnom Penh, but we kept running into Khmer Rouge soldiers directing us away from the city. Lon Nol's Khmer Republic forces had three helicopters left in operation, and they deployed them over this area, spraying bullets indiscriminately from above. They were trying to hit the Khmer Rouge soldiers who were digging trenches, but they wound up hitting civilians. We were caught in the midst of this hail of bullets.

Noticing our dilemma, some Khmer Rouge soldiers instructed us how to evade the bullets—when a helicopter fired from the east, we ran east; when firing came from the south, we ran south. We played this game for half a day, then the helicopters flew away. All of us were terrified. There was no time for discussion, complaint, or fault-finding. Our actions were conducted in silence— the herd instinct had taken over.

In a recent dream, my wife had heard soft voices saying "When the enemies enter the city from the south, proceed eastward."

Sure enough, the soldiers ordered us eastward, just as in Yan's dream. They told us that B-52s were going to bomb at any minute, and they herded us ahead, like a flock of frightened animals. I didn't know whether to believe them, although I had heard reports about towns east of us being bombed heavily. Not knowing what else to do, we continued along National Highway 1.

On the way to nowhere, about a mile from my house, I saw milled rice spilled all over the street. I filled my pockets as best I could, for our next meal. The sun was high and intensely hot. I came across one of my cousins, Ros Ket. His belly had been cut open and his intestines were hanging out. I was carrying my son, and turned his head so that he could not see. Ket begged me to help him. I asked a Khmer Rouge soldier where the nearest hospital was. The soldier pointed his finger to the other side of the highway—corpses lay everywhere. I told my cousin that there was nothing I could do, but if I found a cart I would come back for him, then I blessed him. (We heard later that the Khmer Rouge had thrown people from hospital windows, including the disabled and pregnant women, then run over the bodies with tanks and bulldozed them into mass graves.)

By the time we returned, on the 18th, it seemed as if the Khmer Rouge had driven out virtually all of the 2.8 million residents overnight. The image has been overused, but is nonetheless accurate: Phnom Penh had become a ghost town.

The asphalt was so hot that my son couldn't step on it. I picked up a pair of old slippers, which someone had discarded, and tied them to his feet. Nol, my poor sweet boy—how confusing this was for him.

There were so many people on the road that we couldn't make any progress. It was almost noon—my son was crying for rice, and in our confusion we hadn't brought any food with us. My mother-in-law begged a clump of cold rice for my son from an old woman. He gobbled it down, but of course he was thirsty too, and we didn't have any water.

We kept going until almost sunset, and finally reached Prek Eng, seven miles southeast of our home in Chbar Ampeou. We met some of our relatives and Madame Yen (a medium, and a close friend of our family—we called her Auntie), and her lover, Choeun. We trusted Auntie Yen's intuition, so during the next few days we followed her lead as to where we would go next. We spent that night sleeping on the ground. On the second day we tried to double back toward our home, but it was apparent that we'd have to wait until the Khmer Rouge gave us permission to return. Then, on April 18th, they finally allowed us to go home.

On the night of the 14th, we'd heard a rumor that our house had been burned down; we steeled ourselves against the possibility that Ta Sim had been burned alive, but the next day we heard that the house was safe. When we reached the house we found him in his room, somewhat agitated but in good spirits. Two of his nieces, who had returned almost immediately, had brought him water every day and cooked rice for him. These nieces were poor and seemingly immune to fear. I admired them for that quality.

Ta Sim was agitated because many women and several officers had filled our house. Children had taken my books and scattered them all over the place. Our immediate reaction to the presence of these squatters was outrage, but I took my wife and mother-in-law aside and told them that we had lost the war and that we'd best just keep our mouths shut. A few once-elegant ladies were reclining on my bed. Trying to maintain their sophisticated demeanor, they asked me where they could get ice for a cold drink. They told me that their husbands, generals and colonels, had been recruited to serve Angkar. Although I had been hearing the word for several days, at that time, I still didn't know what the word *Angkar* meant.

Knowing that war was coming, I had stockpiled twenty sacks of rice, totaling two tons—enough for two years. But when I checked, I discovered that the rice had all but disappeared. It wasn't the loss of material goods that made me feel this way, but at that moment, I felt I had indeed already lost the war.

*   *   *

While I was at home, I wandered around during the daytime. I met three of my cousins and several more distant relatives who were heading to their native village. It was the last I was to see of most of them. I met a previous acquaintance, Lady Keam Reth with several of her friends—all women of high social status—sitting on the ground at Roeussei Sros Temple a mile northeast of my house, helpless, with their children, waiting to return to Phnom Penh. Lady Keam Reth begged me for fifteen kilograms of milled rice. I returned home and scrounged up ten kilos, which was all I could carry. By the time I lugged the rice back to her and her friends, twice as many people had gathered there. I trudged back, full of sorrow.

Eng Soth (vice chairman of the National Assembly) and his family arrived at my house as they were evacuating Phnom Penh. His daughters wept day and night, because they had "lost everything." Born to wealth, they had not yet learned how to do without.

Many National Assemblymen came to my house seeking advice from Eng Soth. Should we surrender or remain incognito? His advice to everyone was the same: we should surrender; he told me "Good politicians must be courageous. As losers, it is appropriate for us to surrender."

Consequently, many assemblymen did just that when the Khmer Rouge set up a recruiting site down the street from my house. Next to a simple table and chair, they had placed a green chalkboard with the following message:

HIGH-RANKING OFFICERS
from Majors to Generals
Please sign up to help Angkar!
Support our revolution!

Taking Eng Soth's advice, I dutifully went to this primitive recruiting site and declared that I had been a major, and that I wanted to join the revolution. Although I had only been a captain, I had seen that some of the assemblymen who had joined Angkar had received generous amounts of food and were driving jeeps, so I thought, in the chaos, that I would give myself a promotion.

The Khmer Rouge cadre at the desk was in his early forties. Wearing the ubiquitous black pajamas, he had the comportment of a schoolteacher. He gave me the once over from head to toe, grinned, and said, "Old man, Angkar does not need you. Go to the liberated zone!" It was clear to me that he did not believe a scrawny bird like me could have been an officer—he thought I was lying. And even though this fellow was older than I (I was thirty-nine), he considered me an old man. I felt insulted by his tone and his remarks, but I returned home without a word. By then, all our female "guests" had left for points unknown, replaced, this time, by a collection of men, all acquaintances. We had all been top officers, and here we were, waiting in vain for a reprieve from our life in stasis. My wife prepared one meal a day for these men, and otherwise, except for special cases, they were on their own. My mother-in-law was busy looking after Nol, and I occupied myself by trying to learn as much as I could from our guests. But all any of us could do was speculate about our future.

The next day, there was a new message on the chalkboard:

> All officers ranking from
> Under-Lieutenant to Captain
> May join the revolution
> To rebuild our country!

I approached the recruiting site again. There was a different fellow seated there. I told him I had been a captain (the truth this time), but he also dismissed me.

On the third morning I saw yet another message:

> Civil Servants
> Noncommissioned officers,
> corporals, privates
> teachers—
> Join the revolution!

This time the cadre was a woman. She was beautiful and charming, and, like the others, wore black pajamas. I said to her: "Comrade, I'd like to join the revolution and serve Angkar!" She fixed me with a stare, then scolded me with a vengeance: "Stupid old man, why don't you pack up and get out! Go! Go quickly!"

I told her "No, I am not an old man—I am an assemblyman, a high-ranking official."

"Are you crazy? I know you are crazy!" she said. "Do you want to die now? Go grow rice!" *(Bangkaw bangkeun phawll)*. Again I was devastated and returned to my house crestfallen. I later learned that that young woman had taken pity on me and saved my life. It turned out that those officers who were recruited wound up in one of several mass graves. I thought I recognized her—had she been a teacher?—perhaps that is why she spared me.

I started to burn all papers with my picture, and all copies of the World Anti-Communist League booklet that included my biography. I'd never taken pride in seeing images of myself, but as some of those photos went up in flames, I realized that this physical destruction of pieces of my past was more than symbolic.

Then I carried my most important books, and my amrita crystal, my most important talisman, up to the attic. We normally kept the crystal in a vase full of water. I wrapped the crystal in cloth, and then poured some water from the vase into a plastic container, knowing that the water was imbued with the same powerful properties as the crystal. I planned to bring the amrita water with us for protection. I assumed I would recover the vase when we returned, hopefully within a month.

Next, I packed three suitcases with milled rice, gathered some clothes and a few important documents, two pots (one for soup, one for rice), a frying pan, a small scrap-metal oven so we could cook off the ground in rainy weather, petroleum (five liters), enameled iron plates, a big knife, spoons, an ax, a hoe, a mattock, fish paste (a sauce used in almost every Cambodian meal) in three small plastic containers, and enough mustard to last us a year. I put on one of my special vests and stashed the other one.

We loaded everything onto a hand cart, which I had constructed on the spot, then I covered as much of the load as I could with a plastic military tarp. My stockpile of rice had dwindled to almost nothing, but I still had 50 kilograms. I decided to lock the suitcases I had filled with rice. We took just a few mementos, leaving all the rest, including my library of several thousand books.

My son climbed on top of our supplies and I hoisted my father-in-law up next to him. Before leaving the house I tried to catch our calico cat, but she ran back into the house and looked down at us from a window as we departed. Calico cats are said to bring good luck, and this particular cat had come all the way from New York City, brought by an American friend.

By this time, I had almost lost my mind. It was eleven o'clock at night; the moon was full and was rising over the tops of the trees. Now that I think of it, almost every important event in my adult life has taken place during a full moon. I stood there and took a long last look at my house. In my mind and soul, I chanted these words:

O, home! home! the sacred ground where we lived happily,
the heritage built, bit by bit, by my father,
O, the naga *fountain with its seven heads,*
preserving our tradition from days gone by.

O, Monument of Independence! O, library! O, books of poetry!
I can never chant the divinely inspired poems again!
O, quintessential words of poets!
O, artifacts I can never touch or see again!
O, Phnom Penh! O pagoda, where we worship!
O, Angkor Wat, sublime monument to the
aspirations of our ancient Khmer forefathers.
Ah, I can't see across those three wildernesses:

I'll be nowhere,
I'll have no night,

I'll have no day anymore:
I shall be a man without identity.

(Let me explain a few of these images: When I referred to my father, I actually meant my father-in-law, the builder, who had designed many important monuments, pagodas, etc., and one in particular, a fountain of a sacred cobra *(naga)* with seven heads. This fountain is part of the Monument of Independence in downtown Phnom Penh, which was built in 1957 to commemorate the departure of the French colonial government. The reference to the "library" was to my own books, of course, but also to libraries in general, as repositories of knowledge. I wasn't aware of the extent to which Pol Pot intended to completely eliminate our entire traditional culture, but I had a deep, visceral dread of what was to come. The three wildernesses represented death by execution, by starvation, or by disease, which almost all Cambodians faced during Pol Pot's regime, although at this point I could only imagine what was in store.)

But I couldn't gaze at the moon all night. I began towing the cart eastward, with my son and father-in-law on top, and my wife and mother-in-law walking behind. After a short distance we turned north, toward the home of my father-in-law's older sister, in Boeung Ta Lao, a little over a mile northeast of our house.

When we got there, my father-in-law told us that he wanted us to leave him at the local meditation center. His older sister and other relatives still occupied their houses nearby, and he knew some of the old men and women who spent their time at the center. We assumed that these farmers on the outskirts of Phnom Penh would not be evacuated. After my father-in-law and his relatives discussed the particulars of his stay with them, we started the seven-mile trek back to Prek Eng to join Auntie Yen, because in the confusion of the moment, it seemed as good a place to go as any.

I had become very close to Ta Sim, closer than to my own father, and I had apprehensions about leaving him there. But it was our duty to honor his wishes. In our tradition, men often take an ascetic path in their later years, so such a decision was not that unusual. Of course in this instance he knew that he would be a burden to us because he could not walk, and he wanted the family to survive. My mother-in-law cried, but she knew that she could best help the family if she stayed with us. I can still see his face—such a vibrant man. As it turned out, it was the last time I would ever see him.

We started forward with sorrow and a sense of foreboding. After all, confusion reigned everywhere we looked. But even though we had just left my father-in-law, as far as we knew, everyone in our family was alive, most of my immediate family was still together, and we were relatively healthy. The real nightmares were yet to come.

ON THE BACK OF A WATER BUFFALO

The sixth of ten children, I had three sisters and six brothers. With the exception of my two older sisters, we all lived and were educated under the French system. Until 1954, the French colonial government ran the country, and the schools were all conducted in French. I should explain that my older sisters were not educated because my father, like other farmers, felt that if they learned to read, they might write love letters to their boyfriends.

Though we came from a somewhat humble background, several of my siblings rose to positions of importance. My oldest brother, U Sa Em, attained the rank of deputy governor of our native province, Svay Rieng. Of my other brothers, U An was a banker, U Sam Ok was a veterinarian, and U Sam Ul a chemist; all were killed by the Khmer Rouge, along with two of my sisters, who were housewives.

As of the turn of the millennium, I have three surviving siblings— my older sister U Touch, who lives in the village where we grew up; my little brother U Sun Ly, who retired as a factory worker and now has a farm outside Sihanoukville; and Un Buntha, the baby of the family, who, as of 2005, serves as the vice minister of commerce. Buntha, like many others, took a different surname in 1979, distancing himself from his previous identity, and, I suspect, from our family history.

How could a peasant family produce so many children who rose to positions of prominence? I don't have a simple answer for that. Both my parents were intelligent, but had no formal education. Some of our relatives in Svay Rieng City were Chinese, and from backgrounds that held formal education in higher esteem.

They always supported me and my brothers and sisters when we went there for school, and they let us stay with them.

I was born and raised in the village of Thlok, fifteen miles north of Svay Rieng City, the provincial capital; Svay Rieng Province is in the southeast corner of Cambodia. When I was born, in 1936, Svay Rieng City was a dusty town of about 15,000 people. The population has grown to 40,000, but its character is much the same. Located about fifty miles west of Vietnam, Svay Rieng City has a large central market, with nothing to distinguish it from any other substantial agricultural trading center.

During my childhood years, the town seemed to be dominated by Chinese and Vietnamese merchants, and French military personnel; the native Khmer people stayed in their villages, farming rice according to centuries-old traditions. During World War II, the Japanese had an occupational force in Svay Rieng City, but I don't remember ever seeing them. They arrived in 1943 and surrendered in 1945. I remember hearing that several of the commanding officers committed hara-kiri rather than surrendering.

Svay Rieng Province is dominated by the Vaiko River, which meanders slowly through the countryside, all the way to Saigon, (now Ho Chi Minh City). The annual flooding of the Mekong and Tonle Sap rivers is a major event; when the Vaiko floods, it's scarcely noticed. The river was wide and the channel was deep back then, but erosion has silted it so that it is now quite shallow. In the old days, my grandfather U used to load his large boat with paddy rice and take it to Saigon himself, where he could get the best price.

Our house was built on stilts high enough so that the water buffalo could walk under it. The floor was made of rough planks. The house was fifteen feet wide and thirty-six feet in length. We had a nine-by-eighteen foot room at the rear of the house where we stored rice. My father eventually built a sizable barn for rice storage when he enlarged his paddy fields to five hundred acres.

Our *phum* (property) was composed of a grove of several kinds of fruit trees, several ponds, a vegetable garden, cotton fields, a savanna area, and mulberry trees. This was surrounded by moats and bamboo thickets at the perimeter, which acted as fences. Our phum was on the bank of the Vaiko River. In April, my father and I would cut bushes and bamboo to stick in the river to make a fish trap—about seven yards wide and three hundred yards long. Each June, we caught fish to put in the ponds for our own food supply, and to trade during the rice transplanting season. Meanwhile my mother made a year's supply of *prahoc* (fish paste).

When we needed to bathe, we bathed in the river, soaking our entire bodies, usually during daylight hours. The only exception was after we'd pestled paddy rice all day long—then we'd bathe at night.

We grew guavas, mangoes, bananas, grapefruits, jackfruits, and blackberries. Wild fruit could be found all over my father's property; palm fruit, for instance, hung from the tall sugar palm trees. If you are not familiar with them, the fruit have a tough green skin around a fibrous layer containing three white pods. These pods are edible when they get soft; they have the consistency of hardened jelly. We would pick the fruit off the ground under the trees. They didn't have much taste, but we ate them like candy. Many people boil the unripe fruit with rice—it's called sugar soup.

My father was a prosperous rice farmer with a herd of sixteen water buffalo (my primary responsibility as a child). He was considered a peasant, but we certainly lived above subsistence level. I was not as close to him as I was to my mother, but I can still see him in front of me, tall, dark, and very strong, working in the sun without a shirt or vest. He always spoke in a booming voice, which scared me when I was little. His voice carried so well that he could shout from one bank of the river to a village 200 yards away and the villagers could hear him clearly. When he came home from working in the fields, I would often run and hide, and then sneak a peek at him from my hiding place. When he drank too much rice wine, he'd tell stories of his own childhood. He had trained to be a monk when he was young, and one of my favorite early memories is hearing

him chant scriptures as he worked in the fields. I'm sure this expo-
sure made me receptive to poetry later in life. My father was fair-
minded but not particularly patient.

My mother and I had an excellent relationship. She was a lovely
woman, who moved with the carriage of a dancer. Khmer people
often laugh about the strangest things—even while talking about
their children dying during the Pol Pot regime, they will punctu-
ate their tale of woe with laughter. But unlike most Khmer people, my mother didn't smile very often, which made her look very
serious. I remember her rising early to weave mats of sugar palm
leaves, on which we dried the paddy rice. Usually, by the time I
had awakened, she had already completed one of those large mats
(about two-and-a-half square yards).

She was a loving mother, but she never let us take on airs. Once,
when I was a grown man and had just returned from six months in
New York City as a U.N. delegate and apparently quite full of myself,
my mother decided to take me down a few pegs by telling my wife
the following story. "When I was pregnant with Oeur, I was miserable. Three months after his conception I went to the soothsayer.
He told me that my boy was satanic; when he grew up, he was going
to overthrow the king. So he exhorted me to abort the baby—he told
me to eat prahoc with chopped-up lemongrass. When Oeur was
born he was so tiny that I forgot the date of his birth."

I was a runt through most of my childhood years. I sometimes
wonder if my mother had taken the soothsayer's advice, and
eaten lemongrass and prahoc. Was that what stunted my growth?
Despite being teased because of my small stature, I have fond
memories of my early years.

In May, after the rainy season begins, there is an abundance of
crickets in Cambodia. Many children of my village went looking
for them. They'd catch a bunch of them, spray them with a little
salt water, then dry-fry them and eat them along with rice. But
my brothers and I preferred watching them fight. We'd dig a hole
in the ground, about five inches in diameter and three inches

deep; then we'd put our crickets in the hole and brush their tails with grass that had burrs on their tips. The crickets would chirp loudly and bite each other.

One day, when I was five, I followed one of my older brothers (without his knowledge), as he led our water buffalo herd to the prairie. I was curious about the horizon. It was so blue! I thought it was the edge of the world. Of course when I ran to catch the horizon, it only retreated farther and farther. I heard my father's voice calling me: "Oeuy, Uk! Oeuy, Uk! Please, Little Boy! Please, Little Boy! Where are you? Come home . . . there are lots of mad dogs out there!" But instead of answering, I wandered further, into some thorny bushes. I was mesmerized by a flock of vultures and black crows eating the corpse of a dog. Those vultures were taller than I was; I was terrified. Fortunately my brother finally happened upon me, and took me home to my distressed father.

I remember being given the responsibility of supervising my younger brother and sister while we were transplanting rice, later that year. My brother was three-and-a-half, and my sister was less than two, and when they got hungry, they started crying inconsolably. I tried to soothe them, but they wouldn't let up. I was only five myself, and before long, I wound up joining them. There we were, the three of us, sobbing together. Soon my mother arrived and breast-fed my sister, and that was the end of it. You may question putting a five-year-old in charge of two infants; but that was our way of doing things. Hearing that we bathed in the river might make our village seem primitive; but that, too, was part of Cambodian farm life—and it was a good life.

When I was eight years old, my chore was herding the water buffalo. When it rained hard, I submerged my body in the water to keep warm. We didn't have anything like sheets of plastic in those days, or raincoats or umbrellas. Actually, most Cambodian kids didn't wear much clothing until they turned ten, and I was no exception.

As I mentioned, we had sixteen water buffalo in our herd—
quite a responsibility for a youngster. I used to ride on an old
grandma water buffalo named Hing. She was very kind to me; she
grazed only on grasses—even when there was grass growing
among the rice shoots, she never ate the rice. One day I drifted
off, while lying on her back, until I suddenly realized the sun had
set. When I slipped off her back to lead the herd home, I ripped
my scrotum on one of her horns. I fell unconscious, lying in the
water on the footpath. A Vietnamese neighbor stepped on me,
then ran to call others to light torches and come see the big snake
he had found. When he discovered it was me, lying half-dead, he
got my father, and the two of them transported me to the hospital in Svay Rieng City. At least that's how the family story goes—
I was barely conscious. The only thing I remember is my father
crying, "Oh, son! My son is dead!"

This was in 1944, during World War II, when the Japanese
occupied the city. As a result, no lights or medicine could be
found. A distant relative, Pheng, helped track down a nurse.
They held me down by my hands and legs while they poured
heated alcohol on the wound. I felt no pain at all. My brother
An, who was studying in Svay Rieng City at the time, took care
of me while I convalesced. It took me a month to learn to walk
again.

It remains a mystery to me how I survived my early years.

One night, in a dream, I saw three single-engine planes flying in
the direction of my house. The plane in the middle had guns
mounted under both wings. It sprayed bullets all over the place
when they buzzed my house. The following morning, when I was
alone, I tried to make a toy that looked like the airplane in my
dream. Using my father's machete, I cut down a perfectly healthy
guava tree. As I was hacking away at the fallen trunk, trying to
shape the fuselage of the plane, my father returned home. After
he pounded me on the head with a coconut shell, I scrapped the
idea of making the airplane.

Any Cambodian hearing this story would naturally speculate on the meaning of such a dream. Most of us continue to believe that dreams foretell the future. In this case, those planes fit the exact description of three French planes that shot up Unalom Temple near the end of the war, because of a rumor that Japanese troops were hiding there. Many of the Japanese soldiers shaved their heads, and, of course, so did the monks. And several of them wore monks' robes as disguises. As it turned out, there were no Japanese soldiers in the temple at the time, but a number of monks were killed.

My eldest brother, Sa Em, was a high school student in Phnom Penh at this time, but my brother Sam Ok was studying at the Thlok elementary school only five hundred meters from our house. I sometimes took Ok's notebooks along with me when I was herding the water buffalo. They were written in French, and I liked to pretend I could read them. Meanwhile the other herders liked to pretend that they were listening to me read in French. Of course it's entirely possible that I held the notebooks upside down—I had no idea what I was really looking at.

One day I went to school with my brother, and his teacher allowed me to sit in on the class. There were three grades in one room: first, second, and third, with the first-graders in front.

But on that particular day the French superintendent was coming to inspect the school. When the teacher heard the sound of the superintendent's car approaching, he ordered the tallest student to pitch me out the north window, because I was too young to be there; the French colonial authorities wouldn't allow a shrimp like me to learn. I was terrified of the French. I ran off and submerged myself in the nearby pond up to my nostrils and listened to the superintendent and the teacher babbling at each other in French. Finally I crawled out into the bushes and hid, sneaking a look at the superintendent standing next to his white Citroën. Cambodians called the car "tortoise." I was amazed that our teacher could converse with the superintendent in that

language, which was nothing more, to my ear, than a staccato barrage. From that day forward the teacher refused to let me into his
classroom. I became a full-time cattle herder.

I didn't start school until I was ten. By that time I was three years
older than the rest of my classmates, but my parents said that I
was seven, and no one ever questioned it—we had nothing like
birth certificates. I actually maintained this fiction until I was in
graduate school, which sometimes confused people when I talked
about events in my childhood that could only have happened
before the year when I was supposedly born. In any event, once I
did start school, new doors were opened, but I didn't realize that
I was starting on a path that would eventually take me far from
the simple rural life I had known and loved.

THE FULL MOON IN NOVEMBER

On the occasion of the full moon in November, Cambodians celebrate several events simultaneously, and among them are Sampeah Preah Khe *(Salute to the Full Moon),* Awk Ambuk *(Eating Flat Rice), and the Boat Racing Ceremony.*

The story behind Sampeah Preah Khe is as follows: once upon a time, the Boddhisattva was reincarnated as a rabbit. One November night when the moon was full, the Boddhisattva Rabbit thought: "If anyone wants to eat my flesh, I shall donate my body to him." The Boddhisattva Rabbit walked around, obsessed with this idea of sacrificing himself for the benefit of someone.

Meanwhile, at Tavatoneungsa, the Second Heavenly Realm, Indra was sitting on his throne. He was restless, and could not sleep. Indra spotted the Rabbit and was able to read his mind. So Indra descended to earth, disguised himself as an old Brahmin, and said to the Rabbit, "I haven't eaten for days. I believe I will die almost immediately if I can't get food to eat."

The Boddhisattva Rabbit told the Brahmin to make a fire so that the Rabbit could jump in and prepare himself to be the Brahmin's meal. Indra immediately made the fire and the Rabbit hopped into the conflagration without hesitation. As soon as the Rabbit entered the fire, the fire disappeared.

Indra then soared up into the sky and, with limestone, drew the Rabbit's silhouette on the surface of the moon as a reminder to everyone that selflessness is to be honored. Therefore, Cambodians have saluted the full moon in November every year since then.

To celebrate, Cambodians observe Awk Ambuk, which means to throw flattened rice into the mouth. The three-month rice is harvested a week ahead of its normal harvesting time, so that it is still moist. It is fried (ling) whole, without oil or water, and then flattened with a pestle. The rice is then cleaned in a flat basket (cang-e) and thrown in the air to get rid of the husk. It resembles Quaker Oats at this point. It is harvested for just this purpose. Observants take a small handful of flattened rice, turn their faces to the full moon, and describe, especially for youngsters, the features of the Rabbit—especially its ears. Then, they pitch the flattened rice into their mouths and chew it. (It is tasty, but not a gourmet's delight.) Then they offer prayers of thanks to the full moon.

The Boat Racing Ceremony commemorates the naval victories of Javaraman VII over Champa, which took place from the year 1177 to 1181. Not many years after this, a warlord from the Khlang Province introduced this ceremony as a reenactment. Khlang Province is now part of South Vietnam. The warlord chose the day of the full moon in November to celebrate this event, and it has remained on that day ever since.

The race occurs on the day after the full moon. The boats are traditional crafts, meant to mimic the style of the Angkor period. The purpose of the race is, in part, to celebrate the glory of that era. The race begins at the Chroy Changvva Bridge and the boats race downriver to the Royal Palace, where the King sits, watching the finish.

Originally this event took place at Angkor Wat, but when the capital was moved to Phnom Penh, the ceremony was also moved. I suspect smaller versions of it happen in other cities and towns, though I have never witnessed it outside of Phnom Penh.

CHAPTER THREE: 1946-1950

ÇOINÇ TO SCHOOL & PLANTINÇ RICE

My parents gave me the name U Sam Oeur when I entered school after World War II. We didn't have birth certificates in those days, so there was no reason, until then, for me to have an "official" name. Up to that time they had called me *Ok-Ok* (little boy). I started school in 1946, the year after the end of World War II. Our school year ran from early October to mid-July with a break of almost a month in April to participate in our traditional New Year's celebration.

I've heard and read about the excitement and anticipation surrounding the "first day of school" in the Western world, but I don't remember going through that kind of anxiety. Perhaps it was because school seemed to slip seamlessly into my daily routine. Or maybe I didn't get excited because I didn't get any special clothes to wear to school. In fact, no girls attended, so all of us boys came to school naked; it was not unusual in Cambodian villages at that time.

I was ten—masquerading as a seven-year-old—a half-time student and a half-time herder, except on Thursdays and Sundays when school was closed. My first-grade teacher was a Buddhist monk, who taught us the Khmer alphabet and the vowels. First grade was a long time ago, but I do remember that we had to make chalk for the blackboard out of white clay, and since I had found a good place to quarry it during one of my long walks, making chalk became my regular assignment.

Our class met in the morning. We used a palm tree near the school as our sundial; when its shadow fell on a certain mark (we called it *sun-at-the-top-of-the-palm-tree*) we knew it was time for class to begin. Everything we did at this point was rote repetition. The class repeated after the teacher, then one of us was called to the front to read and the class repeated after him. We made such a din that no birds ever came close to the school. We had a break from this routine on Saturdays, when we learned various handicrafts.

Before heading in to class, I would tie up my three oxen so they could graze near the school. I took them with me because everyone else at home was occupied with other work. Each ox had a primitive halter—a braided rope *(kanluh)* made from three strands of sugar palm fronds that ran through its pierced nostrils and was tied through a loop behind its horns. Attached to the kanluh, by a toggle device, was a long rope of up to twenty meters, known as a *khse*. The khse could function as a lead rope or a tether, or a rider could slide it up the side of the kanluh and use it as a single rein. I'd tether each ox to a bamboo stake; during recess, I'd move them to a different site. At 11:30, class was over, and I returned home for lunch. During the rice planting season, I often picked up snails on the way home. I'd eat them boiled and served with rice, or sometimes I had dried fish and rice. During the dry season, I dove in the river to catch crayfish, a real delicacy.

I remember one day in February when, during our lunch break, I came upon a muddy spot in the fields. I reached both my hands into the mud to catch a fish I saw lolling there. Of the many kinds of fish that lived in those waters, I happened to grab hold of a catfish, and one of its barbels stabbed the palm of my hand. As I threw it away, a sharp throb of pain extended all the way up to my armpit. The elders had told me that anyone who is stung by a catfish must stay away from his house. If not, he would surely die. I believed it. I sat outside under a banyan tree until the pain faded. I still remember how hungry I was, when I finally thought it was safe to go home. To this day, I have no idea what the basis for that superstition is.

After lunch, I'd release the water buffalo from the stall under the house and lead them, with my oxen, to the savanna. I should mention that the water buffalo were kept in stalls because, unlike oxen, they retain some of their wildness and balk at being tied up. The dikes between the paddy fields were narrow, and to keep the water buffalo from eating rice shoots I would muzzle them. The old bull would lead the way, while I, mounted on the back of the old female, would bring up the rear. Our savanna, on the bank of the Vaiko River, wasn't really big enough for all our cattle to graze there. One shrewd female always swam across the river to graze on the other side. I was too little to handle the swift current, so I just stood there and cried. But we had lots of relatives on the other side of the river, and one of my uncles would bring the errant water buffalo back to my father.

Flocks of brown and black birds (two varieties of *sari ka keo*, which are about the size of a Western mockingbird) would settle on the water buffalo and pick off the lice on their backs. Leeches could always be found on water buffalo. We would pick them off and feed them to the red ants.

*   *   *

Mid-July was the end of the school year for us. We were given two-and-a-half months furlough to work in the rice fields. In many ways, the procedures involved in the cultivation of rice have been the one stable element of the Southeast Asian experience for more than a thousand years. Changes in transportation and communication have put us in touch with the Western world; Bangkok, Phnom Penh, and Ho Chi Minh City are not that different from cities in other modern nations. But in the villages, where most of our people still live, planting rice provides not only our "daily bread," but also an enduring link to our past. I hope the following description of the planting season will give the reader a feel for a way of life that may yet change in the near future, but that for the moment still dominates our landscape.

The rainy season usually began in early May. By mid-May, the farmers began to plow the paddy fields, although if the rains came late the plowing didn't start until June. This first pass through the fields was known as *dah* (to wake up the earth).

Rice germination took place in a *thnal* (seedling bed), which measured, on the average, thirty by sixty feet. My father had ten thnal, spread across a five-mile area, which necessitated hauling quite a bit of fertilizer. All kinds of excrement were used on the seedling bed (and the paddy fields): chicken, duck, pig, cattle, and human. Although we did not use human excrement in the thnal near our own phum, I often observed people defecating right in their thnal or paddy field, digging a hole then covering the excrement.

Between May and June, rain covered the fields with water two to three inches in depth, contained by earthen dikes. Two weeks after the first pass through the seedbed, the farmers plowed again. Then they harrowed the fields, and shaped the mud into even furrows with one to two meters between them. We call these ridges "turtlebacks."

After this, the rice seed—soaked the night before—was sown in the thnal. Typically, this task was done by women, who carried the damp seed in a deep, round bamboo basket, balanced against the left hip. With her right hand, a woman scooped out a handful of seed, and cast it along the turtleback with a sweeping gesture. When that area was spread evenly, she stepped backwards and repeated the process. Most of the seed wound up on the ridge, but some found its way into the furrows.

While the shoots were growing in the thnal during June and July, the paddy fields had to be prepared. This meant plowing every day, rushing to get done before the earth hardened. Our paddy fields, for example, were so extensive that it would take a whole day to walk from one side to the other. This work was communal, of necessity—we all traded time in order to get ready for transplanting. We always woke at the third crowing of the cock to plow the fields. It was hard enough for me to get up, but then I was faced with the prospect of dealing with the water buffalo, all sixteen of them, sleeping in mud mixed with dung that came up to my waist. On top of that, it was cold outside in the morning. But when my father shouted, "Get to work!" I'd jump up as fast as a frightened dog. Each of us led a pair of water buffalo to the fields where we would wash them. As they walked they always swished their tails. When I let my mind wander, and I'd forget to keep my mouth shut, suddenly I'd discover dung spattering into my mouth.

We started to turn the earth and to harrow the newly plowed ground to make it soft and muddy, so that the women could transplant the rice shoots easily. This was known as *prè ach bam nah* (to plow upside down). We had five plows going at a time. These were wooden plows pulled behind cattle. The paddy fields were flat, with no furrows, and they were not irrigated or flooded.

By late July, it was time to uproot and transplant the rice shoots. It was my task to bring the bundles of shoots to spread out around the paddy fields where they would be transplanted. It was tough to keep up because my father used to hire fifteen to twenty women to work for him. I would lay out three bundles every five yards, each bundle containing as many as 500 rice shoots. Each woman would reach with the left hand to grab about 100 shoots and transplant with the right hand. She would start to her left, take a plug (referred to as a *gum*), which was usually five shoots, depending on their size, then poke them into the mud with thumb, index, and middle finger. Then, five inches to the right, she would repeat the process. And then again three more times, across in a straight line. This was dictated by what she could reach easily, stooped over from that one position. A woman with a long arm could plant six across, children might be limited to three—five was standard.

Having planted a row of five, she would step backwards one foot and repeat the process until she had covered the width of the paddy. Each row of five plugs was called a *muk*, which means front, or face. These women worked very fast and their rows were always perfectly straight. They'd transplant rice from sunup until noon and then, after a break, they'd return at 3:00 to help uproot the rice shoots from the thnal until dark. They were saturated with mud from head to toe. My father paid them thirty kilograms of paddy rice for three days work. Oh, God, what misery for them!

Harvest began in November and lasted until February, because my father transplanted one variety of rice that matured in three months from the day of transplantation and another that matured in six. The three-month rice was known as *srauv sral* (light rice), and the six-month as *srauv dhngorn* (heavy rice). The paddy fields for the three-month rice were shallow and on high ground. They dried up before November, when the dry season began. The six-month rice was transplanted in paddy fields where the water was knee-deep, almost like ponds. These fields were tilted toward the Vaiko River, so we could drain them at transplanting time in order to be able to see the ground well enough to plow in straight lines. These paddies were harvested when the rice was almost golden.

At harvest, we'd use sickles as cutting instruments. Each harvester would hold the sickle in the right hand, then bend over to gather three to five gums of rice in the left hand, cutting them around a foot and a half from the top. Five or so bunches of this sort would form a bundle. Then the person would cut two gums of rice at ground level, knot them together at the seed end, and use that to tie the bundle.

My job was to harvest in the morning and carry bundles home in the afternoon. I would place five bundles each in two woven baskets called *sangrek,* loop them over the ends of a pole, then place the pole across my shoulders and walk home. One year I got lucky—my father bought an oxcart for transporting the rice bundles, which meant that I could load 60 to 100 bundles at a time. The two harvests were of exactly the same duration and involved the same processes.

To me now, these days seem idyllic—yes, we worked hard, but the rhythms of life and of the seasons were predictable and we could depend on each other and our neighbors. Our lives and lifestyle were fairly typical.

*   *   *

But getting back to school; I remember when our teacher distributed the portrait of Sisowath Yuthévong, the leader of the democratic movement. I had never seen his picture before, but I had heard of him, and he fascinated me. By July, we were mourning his death from tuberculosis. Of course I had no idea what was going on at the time—I was only a second grader.

Our teacher used to order us to stand in two rows and sing democracy songs before our classes started. The first through third grades fit into one classroom. The teacher put me in the front row, which made me jealous of the kids who sat in the back, until I found out that all of them were lazy. Many of them received terrible punishments. After those beatings, some of them never came back to school again. Fortunately I stayed in the teacher's good graces, and was never punished.

Just before my second year of studies was to start in October 1947, the old school that had been built by the French collapsed, literally, as the result of termite damage. Since I was more prosperous than some of the other students, the teacher assigned me to be the foreman in charge of rebuilding our school. You might assume that this would be a community project, but in rural Cambodia at that time, parents were rarely involved in education in any way; hence, it fell on the teacher to oversee tasks of this sort—farmers had little free time to devote to such pursuits. Accordingly, I requisitioned my father's supply of bamboo and palm leaf thatch to use as building materials, which got me in plenty of trouble with him. But that was OK, because we once again had a school where we could gather and learn together. There were only ten of us at that time, because the poor families in our subdistrict needed their sons for chores such as gathering firewood and herding cattle. Although we studied informally in the shade of the mango trees during the dry season, the 1947-48 school year didn't count.

School started up again in the fall of 1948, but shortly after classes began, the Vietminh infiltrated our village. One late afternoon, around 4:30, while we were reading in our classroom, Vietnamese men, women, and children ran wildly around the subdistrict office near our school, and when we looked toward Kompong Thlok, which was next to my phum, we saw thick black smoke swirling in the sky. Many native Khmers in my village suspected the local Vietnamese of harboring Vietminh guerrillas, and went to their enclave and burned down most of their houses. The next day, our Buddhist teacher was afraid to come to school, and the school was closed for several months. Then I heard that our teacher had disappeared. A younger teacher, about twenty-five, with only a sixth-grade education, came to teach us.

During the school year of 1949-50, my father sent me, and my younger brother, Sam Ul, to Mreak Elementary School, five miles southeast of our village, on the other side of the river. We had to cross the river by the third crowing of the cock in order to get there on time, and we had to bring our lunches with us. Our lunch boxes were made of woven palm leaves. My brother and I had to swim across the river, each with our notebooks and lunch box held out of the water with one hand while we paddled with the other. Sometimes our lunches got soaking wet, but this was no problem—we simply dried out our lunch boxes by hanging them from one of the low branches of the two short *angkanh* trees in front of school. This "structure," consisting of three adjacent classrooms, was built on high ground with walls made of mud and rice straw.

My brother was in second grade, and having missed a year after the school collapsed, I was in third. Like all young boys, every day was an adventure for us. We walked through spooky thickets. Actually, we ran more often than we walked. We sprang along the dikes of the paddy fields as swiftly as sprites, then through more bushes, and we were finally at the school. Our cousins (on the other side of the river) admired us for our courage, but we were just having fun. After all we had been liberated from having to herd cattle, except on Thursdays and Sundays.

*   *   *

Of course there's more to an education than what takes place in the classroom. For a young boy from a farm village, going to the city can be an unforgettable experience. Sometimes just trying to get to the city was an adventure. One morning around 4:00 a.m., Sam Ul and I stole three chickens from my older sister, and put them in a cage. We ran a pole through the cage and off we went to sell the chickens at the market in Svay Rieng City.

After we had walked about a mile, we met a middleman who said he'd give us twenty *riels* for our plunder. But we didn't sell them to him—we knew we could get more than that. By the time we had walked about three miles, the day started to break. I told my brother that we'd never reach Svay Rieng City because it was too far, and we wound up selling the chickens for fifteen riels to the next guy who came along. I felt sorry for my little brother because he wanted to see Svay Rieng City so badly, and we both wanted to see our older brother Sam Ok, who was boarding there as a sixth-grade student.

When we were kids, the city always captured our imaginations. One day I woke up early in the morning with an overwhelming urge for adventure. I led my water buffalo and oxen to the southern perimeter of our land, and left them there to graze. I was so excited, I ran along the sandy road to the city. At first, I counted the distance poles along the road, but I was so amazed by the groves of magnificent palm trees, mango trees, and others I didn't recognize, as well as the huge paddy fields, that I forgot to keep count. Then I saw houses, and people climbing up into the tops of the palm trees. All this was new to me—I forgot that I was tired and that I had chores to do. I walked and ran, walked and ran. I even forgot that I wasn't wearing any clothes.

When I finally arrived at the city, I sought out my brother Sam Ok, who was staying with our Chinese relatives. I was certain I would remember the house because I'd stayed there to convalesce. Sure enough, I found the house; luckily my brother hadn't yet left for school. I was so hungry that a simple bowl of rice tasted great. Then he gave me a glass of ice water. I'd never had ice water before. I couldn't drink it because it somehow felt hot, and when vapor rose from the ice, I thought it was smoke, which further convinced me that it would burn my mouth.

My distant cousin Kei pointed at my genitals and said something and he and his five buddies all laughed at me. I knew he had told them about my wounded scrotum. Since they spoke Cantonese, I couldn't understand a word, so I just pretended that I hadn't heard what he'd said.

When my big brother went off to class, I decided to walk around the market, which had been built by the French colonial government. It was on open-air structure, with a red-tiled roof, and a brick floor. The merchants, who were all Chinese, set out their produce in rows of bins. For some reason, I wasn't wanted. Some of them shouted, "Go away, you little brat," and others muttered, "Get out of here, goblin!"

In the middle of the market, cardsharps were looking for country bumpkins to trick. One of them flipped over three cards: the king, queen, and jack. He showed us the cards, turned them over and had us bet on which was the queen. The setup was that if you guessed right, he'd give you back triple the amount you'd bet. I put down five riels on the card I knew was the queen and won! But he refused to pay me, saying I was too young to play. He made me take back my money and told me to go home.

It was afternoon when I decided to leave the shade of the market and start home. Suddenly I realized that there were six roads leading into the market; I hadn't paid any attention to which one I'd traveled on. Five of them looked exactly the same, but I knew I'd come in from the north so I took that route. After I'd walked for a while I was met by French soldiers carrying guns. I knew I was near their fortress, where I wasn't supposed to be, and I thought they might arrest me. I didn't run away, I just turned around and went back to the market where I took a different road; *now* I was proceeding northward. I came to a fork in the road, one paved, the other sandy. The sandy road was obviously the one to take. Convinced that this was the road to my village, I started to run, because the sun was starting to set. I started to run like an elf. Since my legs were so short, each stride probably didn't cover much more than a foot in distance. I was certainly making the sand fly in the slanting rays of the twilight, and I was getting frightened. No one was on this road. Then I thought of my cattle—what had happened to them? Maybe thieves had stolen them. All those fears prompted me to run faster.

It was dark when I finally got home; luckily I had taken the right road. And there were my water buffalo, safe and sound under the house. I counted them—all there. I felt an enormous sense of relief. Everyone asked me where I had been the whole day. I told them that I'd been hanging around the herd. They said that the herd had returned before sunset—where had I been? I told them that I had gone off trying to catch frogs for dinner in the paddy fields. I knew, before I'd left, that they would question me, so I'd hidden a giant frog in the yard and had already brought it in with me as evidence. On my way home I'd picked up a beautiful cigarette lighter I found in the middle of the road. No one in my entire village had one of these! I gave it to my mother a day later. When she asked me where I'd gotten it, I told her the truth about my trip to the city. My mother never scolded me about this misadventure, though. Later, I told my little brother about life in the city in minute detail—this was, after all, why we'd stolen the three chickens.

*   *   *

The give-and-take of friendship is another part of one's education, and although I was a bit of a loner, there were three boys I spent much of my time with. My friends—Seng, Than, Suon—and I were obsessed with a game kind of like baseball. It involved placing a stick in a hole about five inches deep, with a forty-five-degree incline. You'd rap that stick up into the air with a larger one, and bat it out toward your playmates. If you hit it over their heads you scored points. I wish I could look up those childhood friends, but they were all killed during the Pol Pot years.

*   *   *

Slowly but surely we began to get glimpses of the future. From time to time our family had to hide in the swamps when Khmer Vietminh began slaughtering people at night. Once, I woke up and discovered the house was empty; I was terrified. Had the family gone into hiding and forgotten me?

My "cousin-in-law" was the chief of the subdistrict of Thlok, so I decided to head over to his office, about a mile-and-a-half south of our house, in Kompong Suong. As I walked through the door, I saw two men lying on the floor in a pool of blood. They were *Khmer Issaraks* who'd tried to kidnap a young Chinese girl. The Khmer Issaraks called themselves *Free Khmers* as if they were freedom fighters, but in actuality they were mostly bandits. My cousin had thrown a grenade at them. He'd wounded the two men on the floor; the others had escaped. I stayed there until daybreak. At the age of fourteen, this was the first time I had witnessed casualties of this sort. Given that I'd grown up in that part of the world, I'd led a sheltered life.

When I returned home, I found out that my family had gone into hiding when they heard what they thought were gunshots. And they were laughing at me because they thought I'd slept through it all like a log. I told them about my trip, that the noise was actually a grenade, and I told them about the two Khmer Issaraks, who were lying in their own blood, groaning like pigs.

My parents were furious. "You fool, why did you dare to go so far in the middle of the night?" my mother shouted.

"Why not?" I answered, with the bravado of youth.

*   *   *

One morning near the end of the school year, while Sam Ul and I were running along the dike halfway to school, we met our uncle, Hem Thong (my mother's little brother), who had a huge knife suspended from his right shoulder. He was yelling at everyone on their way to class that if they didn't turn around and go home he would chop off their heads. Hem Thong was about five years older than us; hence, much bigger, so we did an about-face and went to the home of another uncle, Hem Tim, where we played with our cousins until late afternoon before returning home. The next day I heard that Hem Thong had been punished by our teacher. Hem Thong was lazy; he didn't want to go to school that day and this was his way of canceling classes.

*   *   *

In the French educational system as it was structured in Cambodia, elementary school lasts three years, and final exams are required to graduate. In June of 1950 I took those exams— arithmetic, composition, dictation in French, and dictation in Khmer—all required for graduation. I remember hopping up behind my friend on his bicycle to go to the test. First, we had a twenty-mile ride just to get there; then the test lasted all day. It was so long that I felt as if I were in a slow-moving dream. When I was done, I realized I had no memory of having taken the exams, and had no idea of how I had done. But for the moment, I was done with school. At that time, in our part of the country, it was considered prestigious just to have completed third grade.

Incidentally, before I took this test my father had to go to Svay Rieng City to buy a birth certificate for me. On it, he indicated that I was born in 1940 (not 1936), thereby making me the same age as most of my classmates. Given that I had started school at a later age than usual, and then lost an additional year when our school collapsed, my father reasoned that this ruse would make it possible for me to get several more years education than I would if the French authorities knew my actual age.

The day I heard about the results of my exam, I was literally moving our house. Most Cambodian village homes were built at a distance from whatever road they lived near, leaving room for gardens and fruit trees, unlike the Vietnamese, who invariably build their homes in clusters. But from the point of view of a colonial government that wanted to be able to drive along the road in a jeep and see what was going on, our customs were an impediment to security, and our privacy was the least of their concerns. So in 1950 the French authorities, worried about Vietminh activities, began a process of relocation; they ordered villagers throughout the country to dismantle their homes and move them close to the road. The term for this was *pramoal* (to gather). This pattern persists to this day—in other words, the villages of my childhood no longer exist.

We all had to help out, of course. My assignment was to transport the columns we used to support the roof, using an oxcart. The columns were made of *pcoeuk* (teak)—very heavy and hard as iron. I mounted the back of my bull ox named That Thom, and he started to pull. When we arrived at an irrigation ditch, I fell off the cart, and as I fell, the light seemed to take on an odd greenish cast. There were five columns on the cart, more than a ton of weight; that and the oxcart would have been enough to pulverize me. I now believe that it was a *breay*, a kind of spook, often surrounded by a greenish light, that had pushed me. But that day, in a state of distraction, I continued working until I bumped into my father, who told me that he had just received word that I had passed the exam. "Son," he said, "now you are more educated than me."

Regardless of exams, though, it was the rainy season, and I was big enough to plow the fields by myself now. Sometimes I harrowed the mud. Then I had to transplant rice shoots. At noon, I'd lead the cattle to the savanna. This was my daily routine for the next three months, and it could have been my routine for the rest of my life.

But in September of 1950 my father brought me to Svay Rieng City to stay with my Chinese cousin Ung Koy, to attend the Svay

Rieng Middle School. My father was a simple man who wore simple clothes, but even though I could have helped the family by working in the fields, he brought me to the city to go to school. He may not have been able to give me any money, but he gave me a chance to learn. And I was very excited by the move to the city, and eager for the next stage of my education.

MY "OATH OF ALLEGIANCE"

During the school year 1950-51, I stayed with my distant cousin Ung Koy, who was part of the Chinese side of the family, through my father. Koy was forty-five, married, with a daughter named Sao Yoeung (twenty-five), and a son named Ung Kei, who was ten. (It is the Chinese custom that daughters do not take the last name of the father.) They were a typical Chinese family: they rarely talked in loud voices and never seemed to get upset. They had a general store on the ground floor of a building. The store consisted of one long narrow room with the merchandise on shelves along both sides, such as dishes, soy sauce, incense, candles, dried fish, salt, eggs, and sugar cane. There was a sizable sleeping loft divided into rooms at the back of the store, where all of us slept. Later in life, when I was in Chinatown in San Francisco, I saw many shops exactly like this. Koy smiled a lot and was fond of gambling with his neighbors. In those days it seemed that most Chinese men retired at the age of forty-five, and he had shifted the pace of his life in that direction. They always fed me well and treated me as a genuine member of the family, and every Chinese New Year, Koy gave me fifty riels (fifteen dollars), which was a staggering sum to a country boy in those days.

I was now a fourth grader. My teacher was a tall man, who approached every class with enthusiasm. Our lessons were in math, reading in French, composition in French, biology, history, geography, civic instruction, sport, and handcrafts. I was particularly good in math, so two of my classmates, a boy and a girl, liked to study with me at my relatives' house. But my Chinese friends teased me every time the girl came, so she stopped.

My school shared a fence with the French Officers' Club. When the officers got drunk they made a lot of noise without worrying about consequences because they were the masters. We acted like monkeys around them: when we stood to look at them, they chased us, and we ran away, frightened.

My father came to visit me after a week and bought me a pair of French white shorts and a short-sleeved shirt, a kind of uniform worn by my classmates—now I was as urbane as they were. None of us wore slippers or shoes—for some reason this was considered insolent at that age. But I walked about in a haughty fashion, proud of my attire, and happy to be away from the routine of my village. This was to be the only time my father visited me while I was in school there.

It was understood that I would make a contribution to the household where I was now living, and that contribution would come from my strong arms and back. My cousin sold soft drinks in a twenty-four-bottle wooden case, along with perishable goods, and he also distributed ice to retailers in the market, which was 300 yards from his shop. He had ice trucked in from Phnom Penh on a regular basis—each block a yard-and-a-half long and a half-yard wide.

When the ice arrived, he would saw the blocks into four smaller blocks, which weighed about fifteen kilograms each. Before I went to school, my job was to carry five of these blocks—each wrapped in jute and hoisted onto my shoulder—to different retailers nearby. This meant five round trips. One of my cousins, who was seven years older than me, also worked for Koy. He did not go to school, so he had to carry twenty of these blocks! Once in a while a truck loaded with merchandise—jars of fish sauce, dishes, etc.—came right at lunchtime and we had to unload the truck before we had lunch. On those days I nearly starved because I was in the habit of never eating breakfast.

The governor's office was across the street from my school but we never dared to walk close to it, perhaps because the prison was next door. The prisoners worked for the French authorities, and they pocketed every penny the prisoners earned. Prisoners were beaten every day; we could hear them bellowing like bull oxen as we went to school.

Using those prisoners, and other arbitrarily conscripted Khmer workers, the French "built" National Highway 1, which ran from Phnom Penh to Saigon. Well, they may have supplied the reinforcement rods and paving supplies, but the Khmer workforce supplied all the labor, including moving the earth with shovels and oxcarts. Not only were the workers not paid, they weren't even fed.

There is a running debate among former "colonized subjects" as to which colonial power was the cruelest. I don't believe the French would be pleased to know how competitive they are in this "contest."

Our family, like many, had a personal experience with these enlightened representatives of Europe. A man named Khat, who lived next to us in Thlok and later became a relative by marriage, was once accused of armed robbery by the French authorities. As I heard it, one evening a Chinese man biked from Svay Rieng City carrying 10,000 riels on his person. At a secluded place along the dirt road, with a sugar palm tree on the left where the road curved a bit, a thief was waiting with a big curve-bladed knife. When the Chinaman reached this spot, the thief jumped out from behind the tree, kicked over the bicycle, and attacked his victim with the knife. But a number of the Chinaman's friends were following, and when the thief saw them, he took off running. And his path took him right through Uncle Khat's property. When the victim's friends got to Uncle Khat's house, they broke in and dragged him to the police; he was lucky they didn't kill him. Fish sauce was forced through his nostrils to make him confess, but even the French could tell that his confession was meaningless. After they kept him in prison for a year, they let him go, and the crime remained unsolved. A man named San, the real perpetrator, told me this story himself many years later.

*   *   *

School started in early October and the days became a kind of blur for me, because my life was now geared to an urban pace. I don't remember many details until April, when we celebrated the traditional New Year and school was closed, as usual, for fifteen days. Before leaving for vacation, we celebrated at school by cooking duck eggs. I brought white salt and put it in small bowls to go along with our meal. We invited our schoolmates from the fifth and sixth grades to join us. Since I was the only one who had a family connection with the Chinese community, my teacher assumed that I was rich. He was mistaken, but to keep up appearances, I stole ice, soda, the duck eggs, and the salt from my cousin's stock. I stole so much that I lost track of it all. But it was worth it—we had a great time at school. A boy from fifth grade, who didn't know salt from sugar, thrust a spoonful of it into his mouth. I was looking at him out of the corner of my eye. His mouth was so dry, he couldn't spit it out. Then he noticed me looking at him, and swallowed (with a grimace) in order to save face; then he guzzled some soda to wash it down.

Back in my village—as a fourth grader from Svay Rieng City— I was given the royal treatment by the boys and girls my age and younger. And my brothers An and Sam Ok came home from Phnom Penh. People said we had grown like bamboo shoots, a Cambodian saying that means that we would surpass our father, as new bamboo shoots are always superior to old ones. The New Year celebration began on April 13th and ran through the 15th, as always. None of us boys imbibed alcohol as part of the celebration. My father probably drank enough for all of us.

I remember an incident, four years earlier, when my father had gotten himself in trouble while celebrating the success of one of his sons. It was in June—my brother An had gotten his secondary education diploma. My father went to Svay Rieng City to visit Koy. They had an impromptu party at which Koy offered my father several kinds of French liquor. My father was used to rice wine only, so he got pretty drunk. As he was making his way home, he passed

near the French fortress on National Highway 1. He was minding
his own business, but singing at the top of his lungs—he was
really sailing. Several French policemen came out and arrested
him for being "drunk and disorderly." I guess he argued with them
and pushed back when they grabbed him to take him in. Koy sent
a messenger to say that my father had been arrested and would be
in jail for thirty days. I was too young at the time to understand
what had happened. I do recall that my father returned in a chas-
tened mood and we were told not to ask him questions. From that
day forward the topic was off-limits. The French did not tolerate
locals challenging their authority.

But as of that April, 1951, my father realized that his four sons had
more cumulative years of education than any other family in the
district, maybe even the whole province. To celebrate, he hired a
Vietnamese to butcher an ox and a 110-kilogram pig. My father
didn't have the skills to take on this task, and he wanted it done
right, so he hired a professional. I remember that the pig was
roasted until it was crispy—perfect! I can still remember how it
tasted these many years later. My father was so happy.

On the evening of the 13th, we went to the pagoda to listen to
the monks recite Dhamma. We walked across the dikes of the
paddy fields in single file, and the dust we stirred up looked like
mist in the moonlight. We returned home at midnight feeling
blessed. My brothers and I made a lantern out of translucent
paper—white, green, red, yellow—and hung it on a pole in front
of our house so that it could be seen from the road.

On the evening of the 14th we played a traditional game of tug-
of-war, the girls at one end, the boys at the other. We continued
under the full moon, out in the road in front of my house, almost
until midnight, laughing and clowning. The game continued the
next evening. Then, at noon on the 15th we held a final game of
tug-of-war at the pagoda. After the New Year celebration had
been completed, my brothers and I left to return to school, with
only a month left before final exams.

After vacation, my teacher reviewed everything we'd covered up to that point, to make sure that we understood the material. We didn't have daily lessons on which we were graded; the system dictated that if you flunked the final exam, you flunked the subject. I studied hard, passed all the tests, and went home for the transplanting season to plow the paddy fields again.

That June the weather was very refreshing—the rain fell gently, the grass was green, and gusts of wind frequently blew mangoes off the trees. We ran to pick them up as they fell—there was plenty to eat that month.

During the day, while I was herding water buffalo alone, I sang stories about the birds and the trees, imitating an opera I'd attended two years earlier, during the dry season. The Vietnamese community had hired a Khmer opera group to come to our area to perform. In those days the community was more integrated than it is today, and the Vietnamese and Chinese often collaborated with us on projects, and showed support for our culture. That particular opera, the epic of Preah Leak Sin Vong, took a whole month to perform in its entirety. Up to that point, I had never seen anything remotely like it. I was very impressed, and attended every night, in part, perhaps, because it was free. I sat on the ground with some family members, and every night I'd eventually fall asleep, only to be awakened by the final applause. Dosakandha was the main character and star of the show. *Dosakandha* means superpower, and he *was* a superpower as a commander of troops, as the possessor of superior weapons, and of wealth. Those melodies stayed with me, and to this day I can still sing a few of them.

As I mentioned before, during plowing season our families took turns working for each other. The well-to-do families got the use of fifteen to twenty plows for one morning from sunrise until noon. Poor families used maybe five plows because it was an expensive proposition—the host family had to offer a meal and wine to their neighbors who helped them.

At these meals, each farmer would boast about the effectiveness of his respective plow and his skill in making it.

They also boasted about the strength of their water buffalo. They worked the earth in silence, but during the two or three hours following the communal dinner, they made up for lost time.

This particular rice transplanting season was peaceful. We worked the fields in the usual manner, but my three brothers who were in Phnom Penh did not come home to work with us. Even though it was between school sessions, all three of them were occupied taking private classes in preparation for their exams. Under normal circumstances we might have celebrated the fact that my little brother Sam Ul had passed his final exam and was heading to the fourth grade, but he was so smart that we expected perfection.

In September everyone returned home to celebrate Phjom Ben, which lasted from the waning moon to the new moon—fifteen days. Cambodians believe that the God of Death releases their deceased relatives to share in the feast during this holiday. The souls of these ancestors roam in search of their descendants, looking in seven specific pagodas. If they don't find their descendants paying homage in any of those pagodas, they go back to the Land of the Dead hungry and weeping. One of the traditions of this holiday requires everyone in the village to cook food for the monks. In fulfillment of another tradition, the old people bring groceries to the nearby pagoda and stay there for the whole fifteen-day period, cooking both early-morning and midday meals to offer the monks.

Three days before the new moon that year, our entire family gathered for a big reunion. There was an enormous amount of food to eat, people to talk to, and prayers to be said, but I still had to spend part of my time at my old job, taking care of the water buffalo. After Phjom Ben, the five of us siblings who were in school elsewhere left for classes.

The school year of 1951-52 was appreciably harder. Every lesson we studied was completely new material. In French this was called *cours deuxieme année*. I was the marshal of the class, which meant that I was responsible for making sure all the supplies were in order and also for keeping discipline. By now I was becoming homesick, so I asked my father for a bicycle. When he got one for me, I started biking home every day after school. My little brother, however, stayed on in the dormitory. He was always a straight-A student, so he was given a scholarship and his room-and-board were covered.

During my lunch break I'd go to my Cousin Koy's house. One day, Ung Wang, another one of my cousins, told me that my big brother U An had left Phnom Penh and had joined the Issaraks at Phnom Dang Rek. This was the first openly democratic movement, led by Son Ngoc Thanh. He was the leader of the Issaraks, as opposed to those bandits, the Khmer Issaraks—groups with completely different intentions. My cousin gave me money to take the bus to Phnom Penh to ask my big brother U Sa Em whether the news was true or not. At that time there was only one real road to Phnom Penh. Wang told me to get off the bus at the Slaughterhouse Market, and that my big brother's house was south of the market.

Once I reached Phnom Penh, I did as he had instructed me, and as I looked about I asked people along the road if they knew my big brother Sa Em. When I saw a woman who was making cakes over a grill, I raised my hands, palms pressed together above my forehead, in the traditional gesture of supplication, and she pointed out the way. I found my brother, related what Cousin Wang had told me, and asked him what the story was. Sa Em told me there was nothing to it. We had dinner, and he saw me off to school the next morning.

When I got back, I told Cousin Wang what Sa Em had told me, but Wang was convinced Sa Em had lied to me. I felt sad, because An had taken care of me when I'd been wounded, and now he'd disappeared. I learned later that many of the students at Lycée Sisowath had left for the jungles, and it was mostly the children of the middle class who remained.

That year, 1952, was the first time I heard the word *jati* (nation) on the radio. We were struggling for independence from France,

but being a farm boy, I felt isolated. I didn't have a clear understanding of the political situation. I knew that we had once been
a proud, glorious people, but we seemed to have lost everything,
including land, leadership, and even human dignity.

This sadness I felt compelled me to take, what I came to refer
to later, as my "Oath of Allegiance." Early one morning, in planting season, I went to the bank of the Vaiko River, and made this
vow, chanting to the Heavens:

If I am a rake	let me not survive.
If I'm just a weight on the earth	let me drop dead.
Let me sink with the sun	if I'm noncommittal
to this land of Kok Thlok.	

I shall never betray you	Oh my Motherland!
I was born from your womb,	and I shall pay my debts
to the shade under which I've rested,	the shade of the thlok tree,
under which Gautama once sat.	

But if my lot is	to make no contribution to society
may my body	be swallowed up by Mother Earth
before I've grown up.	Do not let me weep
in sorrow for my motherland.	

(see note at end of chapter)

Then I burned three sticks of incense and raised both my hands
to God and cried out: "Why are my people always mistreated, living in a broken homeland? Who has cursed this little nation?" I
cried out for peace for my people. I was fifteen years old at the
time. This was a vow brimming with the idealism of youth. I
didn't realize the significance that it would have in the grand
scheme of my life. How could I? Now, fifty years later, I believe
that I have honored this vow, and will try to do my best to continue to do so.

That fall our sixth-grade class moved into the recently abandoned French Officers' Club next door. It was almost symbolic, because even though liberation movements in Cambodia and Vietnam were in the process of bringing an end to colonial rule, we still studied French, among our other subjects. And the following June, we again had our final exams. Once again I passed, and once again I went home to help my family by working in the fields.

Upon completion of this level of schooling, one could apply for any job, ranging from teacher to secretary to civil servant. There was a particular shortage of civil servants at that time, and they were encouraging applications. Despite this shortage, it was nevertheless still important to know someone influential, or to "grease someone's palm."

I applied to take the entrance exam for high school, which was still being administered by the French colonial civil service system. The entrance exam took place before the school year started. We were tested on our abilities to read in Khmer and in French. The subjects to be discussed were written on separate slips of paper and put in a box. The candidates were called from our tables one by one to draw our assignments from the box. When my turn came, I drew my slip with my eyes closed and presented it to the examiner. It was Ronsard's sonnet, *"A sa maitresse,"* which begins: *"Mignonne, allons voir si la rose / Qui ce martin avait été déclose . . ."*

The questions were pretty basic, and the exam lasted for about fifteen minutes; I passed without any difficulty, and was given a scholarship of thirty riels toward living expenses. There was no tuition fee. Given my future studies at the University of Iowa Writers' Workshop, and the importance poetry has played in my life, it seems appropriate that I would have to interpret a poem for my high school entrance exam. But at the time I was more interested in agriculture, industry, politics, and philosophy.

I was also beginning to exhibit a typical adolescent impatience with life in my village, and with my parents. At home, it seemed as if life had frozen. In a way, I was being unfair. I knew my father read newspapers, spoke of events around the country, and believed in democracy. But he didn't mention my missing brother's name anymore. And my mother seemed to be indifferent to politics. In fact, *no one* mentioned An around the house any longer.

Of course as a teenager, I couldn't keep my mouth shut. I told my parents that in order to have an effect on politics we had to pursue higher education! We had to be open to the exchange of new ideas! We had to reach out to other nations! Since no one ever listened to me, however, we never got into any arguments.

Confused by the transition in my life and the changes going on in the country, I took to brooding. And I started to develop an interest in girls, although I merely fantasized about them—I was too shy to do otherwise. But it was the season for transplanting rice. I worked in the fields, and bided my time until high school started.

Notes on "Vow of Allegiance": Gautama: The Buddha's surname. Legend has it that the Buddha and his cousin Ananda once traveled through ancient Cambodia. The country was, at the time, uninhabited. The two of them stopped and sat in the shade of the thlok tree for their noon repast, which consisted of food from Heaven; i.e. food that materialized from the etheric plane. The thlok, incidentally, bears fruit that resembles the kiwi, but it has a big nut inside. During times of great privation, Cambodians have lived on this fruit. This is not, however, what the Buddha and his cousin were eating. As they ate, a *trakuot* (large lizard) came down the tree and begged for food. Since the lizard could not talk, it merely gestured toward the food with its forked tongue. The Buddha gave some of this magical food to the lizard and told his cousin that future inhabitants of this land would always, like the forked tongue of the lizard, have words that incorporate two aspects; for example, Cambodians say *muuch tduk-phuok*—*muuch* is a verb meaning to bathe and *tduk* means water, while *phuok* means mud. Hence, when Cambodians submerge themselves in a pond or river, they immerse themselves in water as well as mud, because the water is, by nature, murky.

PHJOM BEN

Every September we celebrated Phjom Ben—our equivalent of Thanksgiving, but with an element of Halloween, in that the King of Death released dead souls to roam the temples. During the fifteen-day celebration, my mother prepared innumerable cakes for the festivities—always two kinds, ansam and tien. An ansam cake looks like a cylinder about eight or nine inches long and about four inches in diameter. It's made of sticky rice mixed with green beans and pork, and wrapped in banana leaves. Tien cake (nom gom) is made from sticky rice flour wrapped in a banana leaf also, but in a pyramid shape. Some are eaten, and some are brought to the temple as an offering through the monks to the dead souls. It took a day and a half to cook them all because each cake weighed about two pounds. These cakes showed that we were prosperous—other families made cakes that weighed only half a pound and had no pork inside; others wrapped the sticky rice in palm leaves, which were smaller. Ansam represents the male generative organ and tien cake the female. (If a man says, "I'm really hungry for nom gom!" It means he wants to have sex.) Cambodian people always prepare both—my wife does so to this day. I remember asking my parents why we bothered to prepare two kinds of cakes, but no one seemed to be able to give me a good answer. I told them that I thought it was because everyone was supposed to go to Phjom in couples. This made them laugh.

LIBERATION, & MORE EDUCATION

I attended Preah Suryavong Junior High School in Svay Rieng City. Preah Suryavong was the king who built most of Angkor Wat. There were two sections of our seventh grade class (A and B) during the 1953-54 school year, with fifteen students in each section. We did exactly the same work. The lessons were easy—mostly a review of what we'd learned the year before. Having become a *collegien*—one of thirty in the two provinces of Svay Rieng and Prey Veng—I was held in high regard by almost everyone. I've since learned that education is regarded differently within different cultures: some hold it in disdain, some distrust it, some view it as a means to money, and others view it as the path to enlightenment. Traditionally, Cambodians regarded education as the province of monks and royalty. The elite, who did learn, studied Cambodian religion, history, and customs, while the villagers learned to plant rice. Since world history has left its mark on our country, however, attitudes about education have begun to change.

History was marching through Cambodia throughout my childhood, although I was only vaguely aware of it. Emerging as the central figure at this time was Norodom Sihanouk. Cambodia had had a king since the beginning of our history as a nation. But unlike European monarchies, succession didn't automatically flow to an oldest son. After a king died, the entire royal family would meet to consider the abilities of the late king's brothers, sons, and nephews, before selecting a new ruler. After the French became our colonial masters in the middle of the nineteenth century, they "assumed" the right to select a replacement when a king died. And in 1941, when I was just five years old, King Sisowath Monivong died. The French government of that day—the puppet "Vichy" government that collaborated with the Nazis when France was overrun by Germany during World War II—plucked nineteen-year-old Norodom Sihanouk from a French school in Saigon, to be his successor. The colonial authorities probably decided he was the least likely member of the royal family to make waves.

I began school shortly after World War II, when the new French government was busy trying war criminals, trying to recover their economy, and trying to keep their colonies. As it turned out, their colonies didn't want to be "kept." While I was learning to read and write, political parties formed in Cambodia, each with its own vision of what independence should look like. The democratic party wanted a form of representative government, with a strong national assembly, an elected prime minister, and a ceremonial king. Another was—in all but name—a royalist party, which wanted a powerful king, and a ceremonial assembly composed of the elite, somewhat like the British House of Lords. And of course there was a Khmer communist party, along with troops of North Vietnamese soldiers—the Vietminh—who conducted raids on French outposts and on Cambodian villagers, when they got hungry. In some cases, the parties developed factions that splintered off the main branch because of differences in ideology, or personality conflicts. In addition to these parties, Sihanouk himself was acting on his own, looking for an alliance with anyone who promised to help keep him in power.

Finally, in October 1953, as I was settling into seventh grade, Sihanouk negotiated an agreement with the French government that began the end of our period as a colony of a European power, and at a Geneva conference in the summer of 1954, the terms for our independence were finalized. As called for in the agreement, French soldiers and administrators departed for Europe, while most of the Vietminh troops left for North Vietnam. Although only a few educated people in Cambodia bothered to learn French during the colonial period, the Vietnamese essentially adopted it as a second language. As a result, the French colonial administrators had hired Vietnamese to fill the lower- and medium-level civil service jobs during most of their ninety-five-year occupation. When the French pulled out, the Royal Government didn't have enough trained people to take their place, so many civilian Vietnamese stayed in the country and continued in their previous positions.

And just as many Vietnamese civilians remained, a number of French civilians who had worked in Cambodia for a substantial portion of their adult lives, also decided to stay on, including the director of my school. Every culture has its own variation of the phrase: the more things change, the more they stay the same, but every time history seems to prove the proverb true, things really do change.

Sometimes small changes are a sign of more to come; in my case, I began to wear shoes to class. Our school's campus was roughly rectangular, and took up about 200 square yards. Two two-story buildings faced each other, with the seventh and eighth graders in the south building, and the ninth and tenth graders in the north building. A bit further away stood an apartment building for the teachers. The school has since grown into a thriving campus with a new library, but even today, those two old classroom buildings are still in use. The French tamarind tree in front of these buildings, which was a mere stick at the time, is now a venerable giant.

They didn't use corporal punishment at this level of education, which took some pressure off, even though in my six previous years at school I'd received only three beatings. We were tested more frequently at this level, and our marks were calculated more rigorously, but the work was still just rote memorization; we were not required to think or to apply what we were learning. On my vacations I still worked in the paddy fields or helped my parents sew palm leaf thatches to be sold in town.

I started eighth grade in the fall of 1954, shortly after the Geneva conference that called for elections in 1955. The people's hopes were riding high; the political parties' hopes were riding on their candidates for the National Assembly. I was pro-democracy, and my youthful political enthusiasm was unrelenting. I explained to all the people in my village how wonderful it would be if Cambodia became a republic—they looked at me as if a crow were cawing at them.

We weren't very far into the campaign when King Sihanouk pulled an unexpected power play. In February, for no apparent reason, he called for a national referendum, asking the people to approve his efforts to gain independence. People had to choose between a white ballot with Sihanouk's picture on it, or a black one with the Khmer word for "no." Needless to say, he won the referendum. Then things got stranger. Shortly before my nineteenth birthday, in March 1955, he abdicated the throne in favor of his father, and launched his own political party, so that as a prince, rather than as king, he could run for prime minister. His party was called Sangkum Reastr Niyum, which some have translated as People's Socialist Community; well, the people I knew called them by their rightful name: Society People First. Sihanouk twisted arms to get key members of the Democratic Party to defect to the Sangkum, and within a few years, our dispirited Democratic Party simply decided to dissolve itself. With all these tumultuous events going on, it was hard to stay focused, but I was still in school. That year new subjects were introduced: algebra, geometry, biology, history, geography, and reading—all in French. I memorized my lessons meticulously. I was embarrassed to study at my cousin's house. On the one hand, I was afraid that my constant repetition aloud would give them ammunition to tease me, and on the other hand, I was afraid I would keep them awake at night. So I started to memorize my lessons while biking home, and then repeated them the next day while biking to school. Math and reading didn't call for that kind of memorization, however, so I could go to my cousin's house and study those subjects in relative silence.

My little brother, U Sam Ul, who was now sixteen, applied for the School of Pedagogy (which was adjacent to my school), and again received a scholarship that enabled him to stay in the dormitory on campus. He was a very bright student but was so painfully shy that I never walked anywhere near his dormitory, so as not to draw any attention to him. I didn't make many friends myself—I was obsessed with knowledge, searching for Truth. Unlike most teenagers, socializing was the last thing on my mind. My geography professor, a Frenchman, told us in class that geography was the Truth, but I could never quite accept his vision of the nature of life and reality.

I was pretty independent at this point in my life—there were days when I might go to work in the fields or stay home to study instead of going to class. Yes, I memorized all my lessons, but I had very little understanding of what it was that I was memorizing. Even when it concerned the human body, I didn't have the slightest idea what the heart, lungs, or any of the other internal organs were like. I couldn't apply my book knowledge to the physical world, but my good memory kept me afloat.

At the end of this school year I got permission from my father to go to Phnom Penh to study math in the French *Prend Cours* or *Cours Privé*. They taught math during vacations. Anyone who was a competent math student could pass the exams with ease. Math was worth 4 units, so, if a student got 16 out of 20 on the exam, he'd receive 16 x 4, or 64 points; this would give him extra time to study other subjects.

While I was taking math, I stayed with my big brother U Sam Ok in his dormitory, south of Chamkar Mon. He was interning as a veterinarian. I was supposed to spend a month studying math but I got bored. I left Phnom Penh for Kompong Chhnang Province, where my brother-in-law was training to be a policeman, but I didn't stay there very long either. Next, I went to the

Kang Rei mountains to get training in stickfighting and boxing. It was easy to get around in those days; the Vietminh ran the ferries across the rivers and the boats up and down the rivers, and they charged next to nothing—outside of the cities, it was basically free public transportation.

I stayed with my Aunt Hong, my father's younger sister, who lived nearby in Sam Rong, a village of about 200 families, where the foothills became the mountains. My cousin Duc and his buddies admired me because I was a collegien, a high school student—none of them had learned to read or write. I remember that my Aunt Hong was getting ready to bring a lawsuit so that she could obtain a plot of land belonging to her deceased husband. All her children had to grow corn and green beans so they could get enough money to bribe the judge, but she never did get the land. That's the way things worked back then; I guess they still do to a great extent.

While I was there studying stickfighting, my master told me to drink a potion made from extracts of several kinds of tree bark. He told me that after seven pots of the stuff that my skin would become so tough that I could not be cut. He demonstrated by letting my cousin hack at him with a sharp ax—it bounced off his arm as if his skin were made of rubber. I wonder what was in that potion?

During the evenings we attended shows, which were similar to the military reenactments in the United States. The dialogue, which was pretty minimal, was in Vietnamese, and most of the people in the audience were Vietnamese. I found the spectacle engaging; I wasn't there, after all, for the subtleties of the story, if, indeed, there were any.

I stayed with Aunt Hong for two weeks. I was coming to the realization that acquiring crocodile skin and learning to kill people was not what I wanted. Like many young men, I had once imagined a future as an officer in the army, of mastering the martial arts, or of even becoming King of the Thieves. This sojourn helped put all those boyhood fantasies in perspective. I was, I concluded, obsessed with the life of the mind. To find Truth I knew that I had to study more, to learn English, to read book after book, and to understand philosophy. I promised myself, accordingly, that I would study in Canada. I knew of Canada because it was a member of the International Commission of Control in Cambodia. Other than that, I didn't really know a single fact about Canada, or about the United States either, for that matter.

With what was left of my vacation, I returned home to help my parents work in the fields again. It was rice transplanting season. This was a year of distress and frustration for me; my brother had disappeared to fight in the jungle and we had not heard from him. I seemed to be walking around in a daze, half-asleep, half-awake. Maybe this was just a side effect of the hormonal changes of adolescence.

From time to time, I'd visit my distant relatives in Moeun Chey, the village on the east bank of the Vaiko River. I met a girl named Chey Son there. She cooked meals for me, unfolded her special mat and set out an embroidered pillow for me. This meant that her parents willingly accepted me as her fiancé. It was assumed that if she didn't love me, she wouldn't prepare meals for me and set out a special pillow—this was Cambodian tradition. I visited her often, by day and night, but we never had sex. To be a life partner one couldn't have sex before marriage in our culture; one remained a virgin until the honeymoon—no playing around. So we held hands as we walked, and snuggled on occasion. But our attraction was strictly on a surface level; we never let it go too far. We rarely discussed anything of consequence. We were entranced by each other in this way for almost a year before we drifted apart, both of us realizing that the relationship was nothing more than infatuation. But for a time, even seeing the roof of her house from a distance, or hearing her dog bark was comforting to me. We were both so innocent that the overwhelming urges of sexuality never entered our relationship. We lived in a kind of dream world.

Two years later, my big brother Ok surprised me by asking for my permission to marry her. Of course I told him our affair had been brief, and had long been over, and granted permission. They were married during my tenth-grade year, after I had moved to Phnom Penh. Although my brother was killed by the Khmer Rouge, Chey Son escaped, and wound up living in Columbus, Ohio for a while. She moved back to Cambodia just a few years ago.

During tenth grade (1955-56), the intent of our studies was to prepare us for the junior high diploma examination. If a person passed and got a diploma, he or she was eligible for almost any job available in the country at that time.

My professors were French. I remember that when I was taking my midterm history test, my classmate Tith San, who sat behind me, looked over my shoulder to copy what I'd written. M. Jean Brun, the professor, spotted him doing this, collected our tests, and failed us both. At noon, I asked San to accompany me to talk to M. Brun in his study room at his residence. No student had ever dared venture near the French residence. I had a knife in my hand and stepped right into the residence, up to the second floor. I confronted M. Brun: *"Monsieur! Monsieur! Pourquoi vous m'avez donné zero?"*

"Parce que tu as laissé San copier la composition quoi." he answered.

"Non, monsieur, je n'ai su rien. Donnez moi 06 points n'est pas, si non je vous poignarde dés maintenant!" I growled. Mr. Brun said he'd give me six points and San zero. San whispered to me "Tell him to give me three points, Oeur." but I was finished negotiating. I bowed before my professor and said *"Merci! Merci! mon professor!"*

"Au revoir, Oeur."

When I came downstairs, his wife, who was Vietnamese, was visibly shaken. My classmate Sun Seng, who would later become a helicopter pilot, asked me "How could you do that, Oeur?" I told him "I just wanted to get the grade I deserved, that's all." That was the first time I'd spoken French to a French professor outside the classroom. Maybe he gave me six points because I'd conversed in French with him.

Tith San always followed me around. This made me uncomfortable, because I didn't want anyone to know how I studied, that I was so vigilant. If he'd heard me repeating my lessons ad nauseam, he'd have seen that I was no genius. At night I'd light sticks of incense and memorize my lessons by their glow. I'd go out under the sugar palm trees, far from anyone else, because I recited in a loud voice, over and over, until I'd memorized my studies: history, geography, biology, recitation (of literary texts), chemistry, physics. At this level of education we needed to get a 5.0 average or better (out of a possible 8.0). I earned a 6.0, but didn't think I had what it took intellectually to advance. Yet I didn't know what else to do, because I was still a minor and the government wouldn't accept my application for work. I dreamed of becoming an agricultural agent.

By then I was wearing tee-shirts with human images and words written in the English language on them; I'd buy them in the market in Svay Rieng City; they astonished everyone who saw them. I wore long trousers and had a pair of leather sandals, until my big brother Ok threw them away—it seems I was always picking up hand-me-downs from my brothers, which were always too big. I rarely looked at myself in a mirror so I never knew what I looked like—I didn't care anyway. I guess my brothers thought I looked like a French wannabe, but I didn't look much different from the other kids in Svay Rieng City.

Then, in ninth grade, we were introduced to the English language. My professor was from India. I discovered it was easier for me to learn English than French—there aren't as many tenses in English. Our text was entitled *Anglais Vivant de l'Angleterre*.

At the end of the school year I went to Phnom Penh to take a math class. I was admitted free of charge because my math teacher was a member of the democratic movement. The name of the school was Chamroen Vija (To Increase Knowledge). I learned much later that that high school had been owned by Lon Nol. This was when he began calculating his political move, all the way back in the early 1950s—he figured that if he could get in good with students, they would become part of his future power base. The math class lasted a month, after which I returned home to work the fields again.

By this time my academic achievements had earned me the admiration of the entire village, which actually wound up turning me into a bit of an outcast. The boys and girls of the village respected me so much that they stopped playing and dispersed whenever I wandered by to join them. But I was too self-absorbed at the time to notice this dynamic. I still enjoyed helping herd the water buffalo with my younger brothers because I could read books while sitting up on the back of our faithful old female.

That year one of my eldest brothers came home. Sa Em had gotten married to a woman who'd been educated in Phnom Penh. This raised my parents' status as high as the highest sugar palm tree. We had a marvelous feast for them.

At that time of my life I didn't know how to drink. In fact I detested alcohol, probably because my father always assigned me to carry a twenty-liter bottle of rice wine to sell from a shop set up in front of our house. It was our practice to bring a 200-liter jar up the river from Svay Rieng City on our boat, unload it, then divvy it out into twenty-liter jars. The plan was to make a little money, but he always drank most of it himself before we could make a profit. Secretly, this made me happy.

One night my father drank so much rice wine that he passed out, and when he came to, he noticed that all his water buffalo had vanished. They had been stolen by the Issaraks, the Khmer version of the Vietminh. We kept our water buffalo in stalls next to the main road, but while my father was snoring away in a rice wine stupor, the thieves led them away undetected.

One of my distant relatives was a ruffian named Uncle Yee. His skin was tough as leather—maybe he had drunk the same concoction as my stickfighting master up in Sam Rong village. All thieves were afraid of him. He always wore his sword hanging over his shoulder. He didn't talk much but if he ever smiled at anyone that meant he was going to kill that person—at least that was the local legend. My father assigned Yee to track down our water buffalo and he found them in short order, once the Vietminh knew who was on their trail.

Just to get things straight, the Vietminh were the North Vietnamese communist troops; the Viet Cong were "underground" South Vietnamese communist troops; at this time the Cambodian communist factions were operating under many names—it would be years before they came out in the open as the Khmer Rouge. It was about this time that the Viet Cong were starting to become very organized. I remember that a Vietnamese in my village—a young guy about my age who spoke Khmer with the same accent as the rest of us—told me that Cambodia would become part of Vietnam someday. I didn't respond to him, I just listened. He was working on me, trying to convert me to his way of thinking. I went away to school soon after that, and lost track of him; I assume he went to Vietnam to support the Viet Cong cause.

After Phjom Ben we all left for our respective pursuits. I was proud that I'd come this far in school. Given my level of education, I would have been eligible for a position as an agricultural agent, but my birth certificate indicated that I was just fifteen years old; hence, not yet eligible. So I went back for the last year of schooling I could get in Svay Rieng City: grade ten, or *classe de troisieme*, in the French system.

We had two sections on the second story of the school, Classes de Troisiemes, A and B. Finally I was considered advanced enough to be placed in Classe A. M. Bijien, the director of the school, also served as my math professor. Later, when I returned from the States in 1968, I saw him at the Grand New Market, in Phnom Penh, but it was only from a distance. We waved a greeting to each other and I never saw him again. I also had classes in French, biology, physics, chemistry, history, and geography. A Khmer language class had still not been introduced into the curriculum. I remember going out at night and sitting with my back against the trunk of a sugar palm tree while I memorized my lessons.

When the time came, in June of 1957, I went to Phnom Penh to take the exam for the secondary diploma. The test was administered at College Norodom, on Norodom Boulevard, east of the Grand New Market. I stayed at my big brother An's apartment half a mile west of the market—within walking distance of the exam site. The exam took two full days to complete.

After the exam, I returned home. As far as I knew, there was no more schooling available to me, but according to that birth certificate I was still a minor and could not apply for any civil service jobs. So I asked my parents for permission to sightsee a bit. I took a bus from Svay Rieng City to Phnom Penh with nothing particular in mind. On the ferry at Neak Luong, I met Thong Saradang, my classmate, who told me that the School of Arts and Trade was recruiting student engineers. At that time I didn't have access to a radio or newspapers, so any news I received was by word of mouth. If I hadn't had a guardian spirit to guide me, I wouldn't have gotten this news. As it was, I knew nothing of the School of Arts and Trade. When I reached Phnom Penh, I asked a policeman where this school was; he pointed his index finger to the sky in a northerly direction. I knew he meant that it was on the far northern edge of the city.

The next morning, I biked along the Tonle Sap until I reached the School of Arts and Trade. I remember being fascinated by a floating village of Vietnamese houses that I saw along the way.

At the gate of the School of Arts and Trade, there was a poster recruiting students, so I bought a sheet of eggshell white paper from a nearby stand and wrote the following:

Le 25 August 1957

Je, sous signe U Sam Oeur, Titulaire de Diplome Secondaire du College Preah Soryovong Svay Rieng.

Ai l'honneur de venir auprès Monsieur le Directeur de l'École des Arts et Metier pour souhaiter devenir un etudient a cette École.

Veuillez agreer, Monsieur le Directeur, mes sentiments distingués.

Signe
U Sam Oeur

I included my address at home, folded my note, and dropped it in the box. Within a week, I received an official letter that I had been accepted. My immediate destiny was set, at least for the next four years.

GRANDMOTHER PENH'S HILL

There was a great flash flood in Laos in 1378 that washed everything in its path downstream, including a huge kaki tree. If you want to see a good example of this kind of tree, go to Phnom Penh today and you will find a large kaki tree in front of the Royal Palace. The wood of the kaki, incidentally, is a hardwood used for boat building.

This particular tree wound up at the location of the four affluents of the Mekong. Two four-faced Buddha images, each the size of a human knee and carved of emerald, had been placed in the tree at some point, probably for safekeeping, and the wood of the tree had grown around them. They were, in effect, embedded, in the same way the strangler figs at Ta Prohm have embraced the structures there. This kaki tree was trapped in an eddy where it had been swirling in circles for seven days.

At that time there was a woman named Penh running the nearby Lanka pagoda. When "Grandma Penh" heard about this strange tree adrift in the river, she ordered her servants to row out and observe it. Then she herself came up next to the tree and tried to remove the Buddha images, but she could not dislodge them.

Grandma Penh sought out the assistance of the abbot of Wat Preah Dharma Lanka, a clairvoyant. The abbot informed her that the images could not yet be removed by human hands, but that he would help her find a way to release them from the grasp of the kaki tree. The abbot then invited a group of musicians to perform traditional pin peat music for seven days. After that, he tied a thin thread to the tree and towed it up to the Bangkang (Lobster) River, at the northern edge of present-day Phnom Penh, where he plucked the images from the tree.

The abbot gave one of the four-faced images to Grandma Penh and he kept the others. Grandma Penh persuaded the local people to build a phnom (mountain) in the swampy area where the kaki tree was first brought to the shore of the river. Once the mountain was built, she erected a temple to house and honor the four-faced Buddha image. Not long after that, she had a facsimile carved of kaki wood, and hid the original so that no one would be tempted to steal it. To this day, one can still see the facsimile in the temple atop Grandma's Hill, but no one is sure what happened to the original made of emerald.

Phnom Penh, then, is Grandmother Penh's Mountain. It is the symbolic heart of the village that grew into the capital city of modern Cambodia.

MOVING TO THE CITY

When I started vocational school in October 1957, I began the life of a genuine city-dweller. Although I had been to Phnom Penh several times by then and considered myself a seasoned traveler, I was still somewhat anxious about finally living in this new environment. So along with one small suitcase, I got on the bus to our nation's capital with a fifty-kilogram bag of pestled rice as my food supply for six months. I stayed with one of my older brothers, An, who rented an apartment west of the Grand New Market. U An, you may recall, had disappeared into the jungle when he joined the Democratic Movement, but when the French withdrew, in 1954, he and his protégés came out of hiding as the Democratic Party to run their candidates for Parliament. I biked to my new school, the School of Arts and Trade, every morning at 6:00 a.m. and back at 5:00 p.m., following the Tonle Sap River. The distance to school from Grandmother Penh's Hill, where we lived, was about four miles.

Vocational school was a long haul—a full four years. The first year (1957-58) provided an opportunity to become acquainted with a range of vocations, including auto mechanics, general shop, electricity, metal shop (which included welding), wood-working, blacksmithing, and drafting, in addition to general studies. We spent a month in each of these areas to acquaint us with all vocations. The blacksmithing class was problematic for many of us. Mr. Sou, our instructor, gave each of us a steel rod four inches in length. We put these rods in the fire and went outside to chat, but when we returned the rods had disappeared! Not a single trace. We accused the instructor of stealing them, but he explained that the fire had eaten them; we, of course, didn't believe him. He then demonstrated this process, to our amazement. I spent the entire year familiarizing myself with the technical curriculum. Many of the other students already knew the material, so this gave me the opportunity to catch up. When I completed the coursework I passed on to the second year.

But before I went home at the end of the school year, my parents and many of my relatives came to town for a wedding: my brother An married a teacher named Long Van Thet. This was the first time that my mother had ever visited Phnom Penh and she was a handful. At the wedding feast, she didn't like the food—a menu of Chinese dishes, including stirred vegetable chicken, chicken sour soup, beef salad, and fried rice. After the meal, while some were dancing, I overheard many of my relatives dropping hints to each other that they were freedom fighters involved in the Song Ngoc Thanh Movement. During the middle of the night, my mother woke me up to have me accompany her to the butchering market, for rice soup (white rice porridge)—some "decent" food. The end of school, the wedding, the reception, the food, and my mother—everything seemed to hit me at once. I was exhausted.

After the wedding, all of us returned home to Thlok. My father told me that most of our relatives lived in Koh Norea, a mile-and-a-half northeast of Chbar Ampeou, on the south bank of the Mekong. He suggested that I look up his cousin named Dy Sim, the youngest son of his great-uncle Dy, who lived in Chbar Ampeou, right on National Highway 1. This was all news to me—I never knew that I had so many relatives.

When I returned to school for my second year (1958-59), I went to look for my Uncle Dy Sim in Chbar Ampeou. In the process, I came upon my distant relative Tith Pheng, who had opened a salon for styling women's hair at the Chbar Ampeou market. Meeting him changed my plans; instead of heading further down the road, I wound up visiting my other relatives in Koh Norea. When I went to Tith Pheng's house, I met my great-uncle-in-law Khieu (son-in-law of Grandpa Dy), who told me about Kralahom (General) Kong, and the revolt against the French back in the 1890s. He told me that we had gone up against the French with swords, bows and arrows, and were mounting a successful attack until they started firing their cannons, which caused the mango trees around our soldiers to collapse. When the trees fell, our troops scattered, and the battle was over. After that, I often visited Uncle Khieu. His wife Thor had passed away some years before, but his daughter (my cousin) still lived with him, and on holidays I helped her plant corn from seed. It was the first time I'd ever planted corn—we planted rice and leafy vegetables at home.

The second-year curriculum consisted of math, electricity, drafting, English, French, mechanics, technology, and a major in automobile mechanics. By this time, three other students—Leng Mith, Meng Hing, Ny Bun Heang (who all live in California now), and I—had rented an apartment north of the school within walking distance. All of us received scholarships which were worth thirty riels a month. In 1958, a dollar equaled thirty-five riels on the foreign exchange market, but in Cambodia those thirty-five riels had more buying power than a dollar. Our rent was only five riels each month. We usually ate soup. Sometimes we could get dried fish free to add to the soup, but normally we would pay one riel for a handful of those fish. Also, for one riel, we could buy enough fish paste to bolster our soup stock for an entire month. Thirty riels wasn't much, but at that time and in that place it was enough for us to manage at a subsistence level.

I studied hard to get good grades, but because I was a farm boy I didn't have much affinity for auto mechanics, or drafting (front view, top view, right side view, left side view—all the drawings appeared flat to me). But I understood the material in the other classes readily and always got A's. I later found out that the city students thought I had become a teacher's pet. Their jealousy kept growing; some muttered that I smelled bad, and several of them actually said they'd like to kill me and dump my body in the Tonle Sap River.

Considering that all I had to wear was one pair of shorts and a khaki shirt given to me by a soldier who was about to discard it, I probably did smell bad, but I didn't realize it at the time. I was still just a country boy. I went to school with an empty stomach— I never had been in the habit of eating breakfast. On occasion one of my classmates would buy me something to eat during our morning break. But then he wasn't around any more; he had joined the Royal Khmer Marines. Most of my generous class-mates eventually disappeared. Jobs were plentiful during this period, and many of them joined the workforce, attracted by decent salaries. The school year was fast slipping away and before we knew it, those of us who were left were looking forward to our third year, later that fall.

At the end of the school year we threw a big party on campus. The campus was pretty small anyway, and was surrounded by a sub-stantial barbed wire fence. I contributed thirty riels toward the celebration and on the appointed night I made my way to the feast. Even though I didn't dance—I was still afraid of girls—I had a great time. The following week everyone left school for their homes; I went back to my brother Sa Em's cabin at Tuol Kok, which was then in the suburbs. Now it's been absorbed into the southwest section of Phnom Penh, a victim of urban sprawl.

One day during the break a cousin of mine named Suos showed up at the cabin. My brother didn't stock much in the way of food, so we decided to go searching for Uncle Dy Sim. My father had told me that Uncle Sim was a mason and his front yard was full of sculptures made of cement (I would soon learn that he was indeed much more than a mason). We biked to Chbar Ampeou and found a house that had lots of sculptures in the front. We parked our bikes at the gate then went down the embankment, where we were confronted by a woman holding on to a girder of her house with her left arm.

"What is the nature of the business you young men have come here for?" she asked. She assumed we were there to buy sculptures, but actually we were just two starving youths who hadn't eaten anything for a solid day.

"Is this Uncle Sim's house?" I asked the woman as politely as I could.

"Yes, what do you want of him? I am his wife," she said, rather brusquely.

I told her who I was and said that I'd wait for him. Suos, by now, had gotten frightened and had run off. When my uncle returned from work he invited me into the house, and my aunt ordered her niece to unroll a multicolored mat a yard wide and two yards long, at the northwest corner of the house. I sat there alone in silence. An hour later the niece, whose name was Khmao, brought me a bowl of rice and a bowl of boiled brown trout, which was delicious.

I spent the night at my uncle's house but couldn't get to sleep because the bedbugs bit me all through the night. When day broke I made a beeline for the market where I purchased a can of roach killer. I sprayed every crack in the planking of their house. This also gave me a chance to get into my cousin's bedroom, which was dark and teeming with bedbugs. My relatives were quite grateful when the work was done.

My uncle's house consisted of three adjacent rooms that were roofed with dragon scale tiles (a sign of the middle class). The house had a wooden frame and walls made of bamboo. I stayed on and off at their house for some time. On holidays I would clean the house for them and even built them a fortress of a latrine.

Uncle Sim's daughter, Yan, was sixteen years old at the time. She neither looked at me directly nor spoke to me. At this time, in a dream, a black bird placidly perched on the back of my hand. I asked my brother-in-law, Ou Yim, who was married to my older sister, and good at interpreting dreams, what it meant. He told me that the bird was Yan, and that the dream meant that she would, in most likelihood, be my life partner. This seemed far-fetched at the time, but the possibility was planted in the back of my mind. Incidentally, Yim is still alive and well in Thlok.

The full moon day of November was Samdech Auv's (the traditional term for the father of independence) birthday, and we had a break from school at this time. Everyone had to fly the flag on the shoulder of the road in front of their houses. Their flagpole was quite high, so I leaned the ladder against it and climbed up to attach the flag. Just then an old man stopped to ask me where Wat Nirodha was. To be polite, I started down the ladder to answer him but my sarong got caught on the ladder and I pulled over the ladder on top of myself, hurting my knee. When I stood up, the old man was gone.

That evening, my Aunt Yoeun, Yan, and Khmao wanted to go to the palace in Phnom Penh to see *ayai* and the brightly lit boats in a procession passing by, and to be part of the bustling crowd. Ayai are question-and-answer poems that are chanted—a female poet chants the questions, a male poet chants the answers. In the evening chill my knee swelled and hurt terribly. The next day I went to school and a traditional healer treated my knee with ginger soaked in alcohol and wrapped it with the skin of a black hen. It took a week to heal.

One holiday, I helped my uncle build the stand for the cremation of King Suramarith, Sihanouk's father. The stand was sixty yards high and the cremation platform was five yards square. My aunt and Yan visited us and brought us lunch. Yan had gotten over her initial shyness, and was now quite an animated conversationalist. Anyone who knows her today would be surprised to hear that she was shy at one time. I was always invited along when the family would go on outings or to ceremonies, but Yan and I were always chaperoned, as tradition dictated.

My third year (1959-60) passed very quickly and when the year ended I stayed on at my uncle's house, sleeping near the kitchen, in the back. I worked with him as an apprentice, but didn't really learn much beyond making rudimentary shapes out of wood,

CROSSING THREE WILDERNESSES   91

which my uncle used as armatures for his impressive traditional sculptures.

While I was attending the School of Arts and Trade, Prince Norodom Sihanouk, the head of state of Cambodia, was becoming an increasingly autocratic leader. Every six months he assembled a handpicked "popular congress" made up of officials ranging from the subdistrict level to the ministry, in order to criticize, demote, or discharge officials he didn't like. In November, at one such congress, Ny Bun Heang and Pheany Chey took the podium. They were naive fellow students who stepped forward to protest the piddling amount of our scholarships, which were barely enough to pay room and board. They demanded that the amount be doubled to sixty riels a month. The popular congress took place at a square usually reserved for cremations, north of the Royal Palace, in front of the National Museum. While Ny Bun Heang was speaking, Kou Run, minister of national security, broke in on the speech yelling, "They have a guru, they have a guru!" His implication was that either the communists or the Khmer Rouge were behind our demands. Accordingly, police grabbed Ny Bun Heang around the neck and arrested him and Pheany. I was then at the west side of the meeting grounds, talking with an ex-classmate, Chan Tabot. Chan instructed me to keep my mouth shut because the audience was filled with military people and officers of the secret police. Chan told me to fade away before they arrested me; I walked to the nearby market and disappeared into the crowd of customers, then took a taxi back to school. Pheany Chey was released in a few days because his brother was a district chief and popular among those of the Royal Court. Ny Bun Heang, who had no connections, remained in custody for three months.

As you may have gathered, the government kept a tight rein on us; looking back, I'd say that we didn't exist in a totalitarian state yet, but we were quickly approaching that status. Of course everything is relative; that world certainly looks more positive to me now, after surviving the Pol Pot years. By this time, the Democratic Movement, the Song Ngoc Thanh, had moved to South Vietnam. They were supported there by the Eisenhower administration.

Actually, during my fourth year (1960-61), my main concern was less about schoolwork and more about paperwork. I learned that I had an opportunity to spend two years in the United States as a teacher trainee. In May 1961 a group of us were sent to an intensive English class and were given seventy dollars a month—I was rich! My brother An handled this exchange for several of us and got us forty riels per dollar—the low end of the black market rate, but better than the bank rate. Flush with my recent success, I asked my parents to ask for Yan's hand in marriage. My mother refused because she was from a farming family and Yan's parents were Phnompenhards. American readers, even if you imagine that my mother lived on an Iowa family farm and my future mother-in-law was a New Yorker who lived on the Upper East Side, you might not realize the gap between our families. In Cambodia in those days, upward mobility was so rare that the concept didn't even exist. But I assured my mother that I had discussed the subject with Yan and her parents, and they had given their consent. Yan and I had become quite close, and her outgoing nature had helped draw me out socially. Our affection for each other had grown and ripened over time, and it seemed logical to both of us that we would join our lives. Neither of us had ever contemplated marriage before, but filled with the confidence of youth, we were both prepared to proceed undaunted.

A full Cambodian wedding is quite elaborate and takes as many as four days to perform all the rituals. But time was short, because I was also getting ready to leave for the United States. So we had what is called a half-wedding. My parents agreed to participate in the formal ceremony, which involved offering presents to Yan and her family. The gifts were presented, followed by a party with about 120 guests. Then we, the bride and groom, were allowed a private wedding night together. Happiness and contentment filled our hearts, even though we were about to be parted. But after two years of training in the United States, I planned to return and we would conduct the complete ceremony. Legally, we were considered married—we could have sexual relations, and Yan could travel as my wife and any children we might have would be legitimate. Prior to the half-wedding, though, we could not even touch without incurring the wrath of Yan's guardian spirit. We were committed to each other as marriage partners, but we would refer to each other as fiancées until the full ceremony took place. We had no idea that this would be the first of two unbearably long separations.

My ticket, passport, and papers were all prepared by the United States Agency of International Development (AID). AID threw a big party for all the students just before we left Cambodia. It was September 1961—a full moon. In the first chapter of this book, I mentioned that almost all the important events of my life have occurred during a full moon. My mother, my mother-in-law, my new wife, and my brother Sam Ok accompanied me to Pochentong Airport. We were all upbeat and excited, but none of us had the slightest idea about the experiences awaiting me, nor did we speculate about it much. Yan and I held each other's hands, like schoolchildren. I looked in her eyes and she in mine, and this brief moment gave both of us confidence.

"Son, how can you have meals if the iron bird is in the sky?" my mother asked.

"They serve meals on the iron bird," I explained, even though I didn't have any idea what I was talking about. Then I embraced everyone and boarded the plane.

AMERICAN STUDIES: GEORGETOWN

We left by Pan Am to Hong Kong. While we were in the air I pretty much kept to myself. This was the first time I'd ever flown and, to some extent, I had to fight off motion sickness, altitude sickness, and general all-around fear. I can't remember how long the flight took, but for most of it, I was holding on tight to the armrests. I'd thought that Phnom Penh was a huge city, but when I encountered Hong Kong I was stunned. We stayed there overnight, then left the next morning for Honolulu, with a fuel stop in Guam. They let us stay in Honolulu for a few days to sightsee. We decided to go to a restaurant where we all ordered salad, but when it came out, we discovered that it was just mixed greens and other vegetables and did not contain strips of beef, pork, and chicken as we'd expected. Then we ordered soup, expecting big bowls of noodles, mixed, again, with several kinds of meat and fish, but this time all we got was flavored water that was too salty to eat. So we left and went to a grocery store. We must have seemed like hayseeds to the local people.

We arrived at the Baltimore airport. From there, we were transported by bus to Washington, DC, where we were to spend the fall semester improving our rudimentary English, and taking in some of the sights. There I was, in the capital of the United States. At this point in my life, I was a tabula rasa, a blank slate, with barely any understanding of the nature of human life. In a sense, my life was just beginning, but I didn't know that.

Under the auspices of the AID program, I shared an apartment overlooking Wyoming Street with two other Cambodian students,

Leng Mith and Meng Hing. Leng Mith and I became good buddies, while Meng Hing, who was more worldly, ventured off on excursions of his own. Our group went on field trips to the Tomb of the Unknown Soldier and to the White House, and Leng Mith and I would occasionally go to a small supermarket on Pennsylvania Avenue, but basically both of us stayed put because we were afraid of getting lost. Just to give you an indication of how clueless we were back then, we got into trouble with our landlord over a clause in our rental agreement forbidding pets—a clause we scrupulously honored. But at the supermarket, I noticed cans of meat that were cheaper than others, so I stocked up on them, and this meat became a staple of our diet. By now you've probably guessed that we were eating dog food—I'm sure my American readers are wincing, but over rice, with sauce, it tasted pretty good to us. We discovered my mistake when the landlord was visiting one day and upon seeing the empty cans, became agitated. Convinced we were hiding a dog, he accused us of violating the lease, and told us that there would be serious consequences. After a few back-and-forth calls with AID officials, he finally understood what had happened. Then we all had a good laugh, although when you come down to it, the laugh was at our expense.

In the fall of 1961, I was enrolled in an intensive English program at Georgetown University. We had three classes—phonetics, writing, and reading. In our phonetics class we had to stand at the back of the room and project each word, pronouncing it clearly. Each morning I articulated the same words in the shower: *girl, world, word, tray, train, dog* . . .

   In writing class, our professor let us write freely on whatever subjects we liked. One day I wrote about the beach in Kampot Province at a place called Kep. I got my paper back with the following note: "You seem to have been influenced by Walt Whitman. Please write more." I had no idea who Walt Whitman was, but this remark led me to read some of his poetry and to try to glean what I could, despite my sketchy knowledge of English.

Whitman, over the years, has become my mentor and my touchstone, in both what he said in his poetry and what he expressed in his essays, particularly on the subject of democracy. Some may find his thinking jingoistic and naive, but I still believe in the spirit of his words, not only in the context of his times, but also as they apply to the present. The Buddhist underpinnings of his poetry, influenced by the New England Transcendentalists, represent a possible bridge for Cambodian poets, who, if they were to read his work in translation, could use them to cross into the twenty-first century. Our traditional poetry, written in classical forms, is quite beautiful, but is no longer suited to expressing many of the horrible and incongruous experiences of contemporary life. The few poems of his that I read while I was at Georgetown were mostly beyond me, but even then, I felt as if something oracular was entering my consciousness. I wish I had kept what I had written about the beach at Kep—it would be amusing to see if my writing then bears any resemblance to my current work.

I clearly remember the assignment to memorize the opening of the Declaration of Independence: "We hold these truths to be self-evident, that all men are created equal, that they are endowed by their Creator with certain unalienable Rights, that among these are Life, Liberty and the Pursuit of Happiness. . . ." These words put me in a euphoric state. Again, I did not understand them completely, but it was as if they were a magic incantation. Although I had heard such ideas bandied about back home, hearing them in this context, in America, led me to believe that I was apprehending them on a much deeper level. I could not imagine the boldness of the passage ". . . whenever any Form of Government becomes destructive of these ends, it is the Right of the People to alter or to abolish it, and to institute a new Government . . ." In my years, I have seen many governments rise and fall, and obviously the Cambodian experience shows that not all change is for the better. But I firmly believe that someday our country will operate under some permutation of democracy. It won't be exactly like what exists here in the United States, but it will be free of the kind of strong-arm tactics that permeate Cambodian society today.

Next we memorized President Lincoln's Gettysburg Address: "Now we are engaged in a great civil war, testing whether that nation or any nation so conceived and so dedicated, can long endure. We are met on a great battle-field of that war." I can still recite these documents in their entirety, which is probably more than most Americans can say. Our professors sketched in, for us, the momentous events of the War Between the States, and the fact that we were in Washington made these words all the more dramatic. I have never been to Gettysburg, but I have perused several books of photographs, particularly those taken by Matthew Brady, so I have at least some sense of the ambience of those times. Eight years later, when I was back in Cambodia and we were in the midst of our own civil war, those words were constantly on my mind.

Now that the horror is over, Lincoln's words continue to resonate for me as I contemplate the past, and try to imagine Cambodia's future. This passage I find particularly haunting:

> The world will little note, nor long remember what we say here, but it can never forget what they did here. It is for us the living, rather, to be dedicated here to the unfinished work which they who fought here have thus far so nobly advanced. It is rather for us to be here dedicated to the great task remaining before us . . . that we here highly resolve that these dead shall not have died in vain—that this nation, under God, shall have a new birth of freedom—and that government of the people, by the people, for the people, shall not perish from the earth.

During the 1980s, when I visited s-21, also known as Tuol Sleng Prison, and also the "Killing Fields" at Choeung Ek, nine miles south of central Phnom Penh, I said these words aloud to myself: "I here highly resolve that these dead shall not have died in vain."

Both these sites are primary tourist attractions today and, in my mind, they should be kept as they are. The current prime minister, Hun Sen, and others have expressed the opinion that Tuol Sleng should be closed, and perhaps reconverted to a high school, which is what it was before the Pol Pot years. Hun Sen believes that we should move on and start living in the present. As far as I can tell, everyone pushing this agenda has Khmer Rouge ties.

Some say the old memorial, a stark wooden frame filled with heaped skulls, was a more effective display than the present memorial, which is eight stories high—you don't get the same overwhelming effect. As a display for non-Cambodians who want to vicariously experience the horror, and feel sorrow and guilt, the old memorial was more effective. But as a Cambodian, and as a Buddhist, I would prefer to have the skulls of my people who died there memorialized in a more reverent manner; hence, I am of the opinion that the new memorial is much more appropriate.

There's a similar division in Cambodia over the fate of those who have been imprisoned for their leadership roles in carrying out Pol Pot's policies: those with Khmer Rouge ties say we should forgive them and move on, while people who suffered under the Khmer Rouge want them punished. I myself say yes, they should be punished but not executed—we should forgive them to that extent, but we should never forget what happened, and we should be vigilant in sorting through the evidence, sketchy though it may be, so that no one can say "that was just unsubstantiated rumor."

If you spend any time in Cambodia, you will soon discover that rumor, innuendo, and gossip are part of the fabric of our culture. We don't have a monopoly on this national flaw; it seems to be one of the driving forces behind so many of the wars going on in the "Third World." The result of these wars is that old grudges are never put to rest—they keep resurfacing ad infinitum.

We do know, for example, that 17,000 people were imprisoned and "processed" at Tuol Sleng, and only seven survived. We do know that 8,985 people were buried in mass graves at

Choeung Ek, and that there are 8,000 skulls in the Memorial Stupa that has been built there. But many questions about responsibility remain. If we put those who are regarded as the key players on trial, and some semblance of the truth comes to light, then and only then will we be able to move on. When Pol Pot died (or was poisoned), I, for one, felt cheated. First, I regretted that he was not brought to justice, but I also wish that we could have had the opportunity to learn from him about how the minds of such men work.

But I'm getting ahead of myself. At this point in my life I had not yet seen such atrocities. When our class memorized President Kennedy's inaugural address, the idealism that rang through the entire speech moved me. Two passages in particular have stayed with me:

> The world is very different now. For man holds in his mortal hands the power to abolish all forms of human poverty and all forms of human life. And yet the same revolutionary beliefs for which our forebears fought are still at issue around the globe— the belief that the rights of man come not from the generosity of the state, but the hand of God.

And this paragraph:

> Let every nation know, whether it wishes us well or ill, that we shall pay any price, bear any burden, meet any hardship, support any friend, oppose any foe, to assure the survival and the success of liberty.

I loved these lessons; I memorized them by heart. Then, in February of 1962, our group was sent to California by train. That very next year, John Kennedy would be dead, and a decade of events began that would test the fabric of the democracy I was coming to idolize.

I have since seen newsreels of Kennedy delivering this speech and can still see his breath in the cold of that January day, and hear the pacing of his distinctive Boston accent. I was, of course, heartbroken when he was assassinated. If you consider everything that has happened since Kennedy's speech, and more recently, since September 11, 2001—his words sound as if they were uttered in another century—as in fact, they were.

AMERICAN STUDIES: CITY OF ANGELS

At the end of the fall semester in Georgetown, I went to say good-bye to my recitation teacher. "Oh, yes," she exclaimed, "when you came to my class, you didn't speak a word of English. Now you speak English quite well, thank God! I hope you have a pleasant trip to California." Being a dreamer, hence, prone to fantasizing, I'd developed a crush on my teacher. But lacking the vocabulary of love, I expressed my gratitude rather simply, and bid her good-bye.

The next day, in the afternoon, we boarded the train at Union Station in Washington. I still had no idea where Union Station was, and neither did any of my peers—actually, even the most adventurous of our group had only a foggy idea of how to get around the Washington area. Fortunately my advisor, Norwood Teague, took us to the station by taxi and put us on the train. I still wasn't absolutely sure what the mission of the USAID was, but up to that point it was evident to me that everyone involved in the program was dedicated to having our stay be successful and that, ultimately, we carry back to Cambodia new, modern skills, and a positive image of the United States.

That first semester in Washington studying English was a good idea, but to be honest, I still felt overwhelmed by the size, pace, and energy of the United States. I had a four-day/five-night non-stop train ride ahead of me, an incredible opportunity to see America, but I scarcely looked out the window. I felt as if I were lost in space. Cambodia—its smells, its colors, its food, and Yan, my fiancée, were always on my mind. (Because only half of our marriage ceremony had been completed, I still thought of her as my fiancée, not my wife).

Except for trips to the dining car for lunch and dinner, I sat in my assigned seat, trying to get oriented, and not quite succeeding. I ate most of my meals alone, but I did share my table once with an American couple. I showed them a ring given to me by Yan, and explained that she was my fiancée. We talked a little bit about Cambodia, but since I did not speak English very well at that time, there were many lulls in the conversation.

When the train finally pulled into Los Angeles, advisors were waiting to pick us up at the station and book us into our respective apartments. I was assigned to room with two other Cambodian students, Bun Heang Ny, and Meas Phanna, an old friend from home. It was comforting to deal with mundane matters like deciding who would get which bed, and storing our meager gear.

The next morning was registration at Los Angeles State College (in 1964 the name was changed to California State–Los Angeles). Everywhere my roommates and I looked we saw students lined up in front of tables at the registrar's office, signing up for classes. We made a mess of our registration cards, but an American student helped us through the process. Then we returned to our apartment and stayed there, like robots, waiting for classes to begin.

My goal, of course, was to bring useful skills back to my country. My plan was to major in industrial arts. At that time I did not understand the hierarchy—who was in charge of what—nor did I have any sense of what all the departments were for; our system at home was much simpler. On orientation day my advisor, Mr. Teague, took us on a tour of the industrial arts department. The drafting classroom, the electronics classroom, the graphic arts classroom, the metal shop, and the woodworking shop—I remember being bewildered by so much modern equipment, and impressed by how neatly it was arranged.

In addition to math, English, drafting, and other industrial arts classes, I also had a physical education requirement—I took archery and golf. We kept pretty much to ourselves, and didn't socialize. Most of us were serious about our studies, knowing that this was an important opportunity for us, and that if we didn't perform, we'd be back in Cambodia in short order. Of course our language difficulties made our studies that much more of a challenge.

I thought often of Yan, wondering what she was doing. It was comforting that I knew her routine. I could visualize her face, quick to smile, and her laugh, which was contagious. She was much more at ease with people than I—she had always lived in an urban environment, while there was still a lot of the country boy left in me. We wrote each other at least once a week—her letters were full of news about our mutual acquaintances, while mine were mostly reports about schoolwork. It was clear that she was devoted to me, and I to her. Although I knew other international students were undergoing the same experience, that didn't make mine any easier to go through. Part of me spent some of each and every day imagining what our life together would be like in the future, while another part attempted to grow a thick skin around these vulnerabilities.

Over spring break we went on a field trip, first to Sacramento, then out toward the coast. More adventures in dining awaited us. When we ordered steak, we were shown a buffet table with numerous side dishes. We had no idea how big American steaks were, so we wound up stuffing ourselves with those side dishes. When the steaks arrived, all we could do was look at them. Too bad we hadn't heard about doggy bags.

I had done well in the English classes I had taken in Cambodia, and I memorized the recitations I had been assigned in the class I took in Washington, DC. But real-world conversational English, with confusing idioms casually coming out of the mouths of Americans—well, that's a horse of a different color (to use a classic example). Outside of class or the apartment, I was always worried about getting lost, and not knowing how to ask for directions. Had I been more comfortable with the language, I would have appreciated the opportunity to see the zoo, the colorful Pacific coast, and most especially the giant redwood trees. Would that I had been aware enough to sit and meditate, surrounded by those ancient beings. A few years later, when I was at the University of Iowa, in the midst of daily campus political unrest, I heard Bob Dylan sing, "I was so much older then, I'm younger than that now." And I thought back to that field trip.

Somehow—perhaps with help from the spirit world—I passed that semester, and was allowed to continue. We had an intensive summer session that Mr. Teague arranged—a government class, for Cambodians only. I just went to class and sat passively at my desk, like a water buffalo hearing the bell hanging around his neck. The professor tried to explain the principles of the United States—checks and balances, the three branches, freedom and democracy—ideas that he said were very important for us to take back home, but because English was still so hard for us, we didn't absorb much of what he was saying. I'm sure he could read the confusion on our faces to some extent—it must have been just as frustrating for him. But it was a pass-fail class, and we all passed.

The fall of 1962 arrived, and I was enrolled, once again, for twelve units. And I studied *hard*. When I came home I sat down and did my homework immediately. Work! Work! Work!

Then, one morning in October, as we were getting up to go to classes, we looked at the Santa Monica Freeway—it was deserted. We crossed the bridge and went to campus—deserted. We hung around for a while; then we returned to our apartment and turned on the television. There was President Kennedy, quite worked up about Russian missile sites in Cuba. Then there were images of B-52s taking off from Strategic Air Command bases, darkening the skies. The commentators seemed to indicate that nuclear war was imminent. We, of course, were terrified, and didn't know what to think—we were just simple Cambodians.

The next morning we got up and noticed that traffic had returned to normal. We went to campus, tentatively. Everything seemed to have returned to normal there also. When we asked people where they had gone the day before, they told us that they had all gone to a bomb shelter in downtown Los Angeles! The fact that no one attempted to contact us didn't register with me immediately. I was so naive.

Campus life seemed to return to the way it had been before the Cuban Missile Crisis. I moved to a different apartment, which I shared with another Cambodian student and an American guy named Don, an English teacher at Southgate High School. He wasn't around much, usually returning just before he went to sleep. I wish I'd asked him for help, but a sheep doesn't know how to speak. Don did wonder why I always stayed home and worked so late. How could I explain that I had traveled not only through space, but also through time—from herding water buffalo in the rice paddies, to the streets of Los Angeles? How could I explain how hard I had to study to keep up? Americans look at a hardworking foreign student and see a nerd—I see my past. And after all that hard work, I passed to the next semester, and so one semester passed into another.

In addition to the required courses for an industrial arts major, I had to take some electives from a different discipline, and I wound up taking a ballroom dancing course. My teacher tried to introduce me to the waltz, fox-trot, jitterbug, tango, and samba, but I just sort of walked along with her. It was difficult to concentrate because in addition to the language barrier, I was more than a little distracted by my first experience with a woman in a leotard and tights. My skin became taut, like toad skin, covered with goosebumps, which made it very difficult to dance. Needless to say, I enjoyed this class, but I considered the c I received to be a gift.

During that time, a friend of mine named Sien El, a guy with a proud, haughty air, took offense at something our woodworking instructor said. Maybe it was my friend's attitude, maybe it was the pressure every student from the Third World faces in America, I don't know what was bubbling in his head, but all of a sudden he had his fist cocked, ready for a fight. However, he didn't know that our teacher, Dr. Zart, had once served on the police force. Within seconds Dr. Zart had grabbed Sien El's collar and pulled him up in the air, leaving his feet dangling like a child—he was totally tamed.

I also learned much from Dr. Zart—not about fighting, but about American etiquette and culture. He taught me not to interrupt a conversation, to look people in the eyes when talking to them, and to stand up straight with both my feet on the floor. It's not that Cambodians are impolite, in fact, most people would say the opposite—it's just that we observe a different set of customs than in Western culture.

During the summer of 1963, we had a two-week field trip to Plattsburgh, New York; it was a seminar for Cambodian students who were in the United States under the auspices of the AID program. All of us stayed in a big house on Lake Champlain. I wrote a poem while I was there, describing the city as if it were a sensual woman. Plattsburgh is a beautiful part of this country, but I think I was missing Yan, and like a sailor overseas, I was starting to look at other women—something new for me. I still have the poem—it's clearly the work of a young amateur, but I worked hard on it, and learned a lot from the experience. Apart from whatever function that poem might have served in my literary future, I think it was also a sign that, like Sien El, feelings were bubbling inside me, feelings I didn't understand, and couldn't articulate. But I was surprised when I reacted to those feelings by behaving like a barbarian.

"The AID program," an instructor at the podium told us during the seminar, "demonstrates that the United States cares about you; we want you to be good citizens, to be wise teachers. We want to help Cambodia discover and establish freedom and democracy."

I did not understand exactly what he was saying at the time, but suddenly I was on my feet, pointing my finger at the instructor and saying, "The reason you are telling us what to do is because you want to control the entire world!"

My instructor did not get angry. Instead, he smiled and told us that we had permission to take a break. I was mortified, but too bullheaded to apologize, or to discuss my thoughts with anyone, especially my peers. So I left Plattsburgh in tears, literally, because something happened to me there, something I barely understood. As I look back, I believe my problems with English kept me so isolated that my basically positive, sunny disposition, turned to negativity and skepticism.

Consciously I knew that this experience in America was important to my future, my family, and my country; but unconsciously, I may have resented the AID program for whisking me away from Yan literally right after our "half-wedding." Of course Yan was a source of comfort as well as frustration. I came to dote on every word of her letters, and cherished the way each word was formed on the page. I wish I had even a few of the many letters we wrote to each other, but they were all destroyed when the Khmer Rouge ransacked our house in Chbar Ampeou.

When we returned to California, I registered for classes and tried hard to study again. However, I had fallen in love—not with a woman or a place—but with philosophy. I spent so much of my time reading philosophy books that I couldn't give my full attention to studying general shop and drafting.

I remember one of my schoolmates asking me why I read philosophy instead of economics. Philosophy, he said, makes nothing. You get nothing out of it, not even food—I got so angry with him, largely because I could offer no justification.

But all I knew for certain was that I did not understand life at all; philosophy fulfilled my need to explore the nature of life. I kept thinking about the body, full of life while here on earth; but after death, where does the soul go? That's beyond our human thinking. Such speculation may not be practical, but to a dreamer, it's like a cosmic magnet.

Unfortunately when I tried to get a minor in philosophy, the industrial arts department would not give their consent. I already had a major in general shop, and a minor in drafting. How could I get a second minor in philosophy? My advisor told me that it was the intention of the Agency for International Development to train me to be an industrial arts teacher, not a philosophy teacher. That seemed unfair but I didn't know what I could do about it. Nevertheless, I managed to slip a course in symbolic logic into my schedule. I was diligent in my study, and got a good grade. My logic professor liked me and this encouraged me to continue, but AID insisted that I focus on practical matters. Maybe they were right. Back home, who was going to be interested in symbolic logic?

I was so conflicted, and so alone—I had to do something with those feelings. I began to write poems, as a kind of catharsis, I suppose. Actually I didn't know that they were poems, until one of my classmates read some of them in my notebook and was impressed. Fortunately I had decided to develop my language skills, and had written in English. He asked me if he could print up some of them as a graphic arts project. He chose ten "poems" and printed one hundred copies. Unfortunately I did not keep very many of those pamphlets for myself—what did I know? I had no intention of becoming a poet. Now all I have is a photocopy of the pamphlet, given to me recently by my friend and collaborator, Ken McCullough.

I sent translations of some of these poems to Yan, and I could tell that they worried her a bit, because of their darkness. Although neither of us was comfortable with our forced estrangement, we were coming to accept it. Yan made it clear to me that I should live my life as I saw fit, and that we would pick up where we left off when I returned. In Cambodian culture, as in most Asian cultures, the double standard with regard to fidelity was, and still is, an accepted part of life. It is changing somewhat these days, but Asia changes slowly.

That November, as I was mulling over the future that AID had picked for me, President Kennedy was shot and killed. Everybody cried, the whole campus, and I cried along with the others, because I admired President Kennedy so much. We lost a great man. I was not exactly tuned in to what the press was saying about the ramifications of Kennedy's assassination, but I had a hollow feeling in the pit of my stomach, something like when you are standing in a high place, and are afraid of falling. I learned much later that the day before he had flown to Dallas, Kennedy had spent several hours on the phone with Sihanouk. I am positive that if Kennedy had not been assassinated, Cambodia would probably not have broken off diplomatic ties with the U.S. It was shortly after the assassination that Sihanouk turned sharply in a procommunist direction, and Chinese operatives infiltrated Cambodia, establishing a branch, in every village, of what became the Khmer Rouge.

Kennedy's assassination plunged me deeper in the direction of philosophy, but responding to pressure from my advisor, I used the elective slots on my spring semester schedule for an economics class and a government class. I didn't study those subjects seriously, though. I spent most of my time in the library reading biographies of the great philosophers, and reading poetry. Having been "recognized" as a poet, I started to write poetry for fun, to release my frustrations, to liberate my soul, and as a way to counter the malaise I was feeling. Maybe I was experiencing a combination of angst and ennui—two conditions that were contagious at that time.

During the summer of 1964, before starting my senior year, I met Nellie, a woman from Belgium, who was studying to be a nurse. We lived near each other, and when she moved from one apartment to another nearby, I volunteered to help. That fall I moved to another apartment some distance from her, which I shared with two Cambodian roommates, including a city boy from Phnom Penh who was over six feet tall—unusual for a Cambodian. The apartment was new and clean, unlike most of the other places I had shared.

But during second semester I began spending time at Nellie's apartment because I had to make trips to the art museum to write a term paper, and I needed her help. One weekend we went to downtown Los Angeles, to the museum, and on the way back we stopped at the supermarket and I picked up two bottles of wine. We went to her apartment where she prepared, and we shared, a dinner of steak, salad, and several glasses of wine. Then she told me that she was going to take a bath, which she did—while leaving the bathroom door ajar. I opened the second bottle of wine, and poured some for both of us. I also took a bath, and then she emerged in a sheer pink nightgown. I had never done anything of this sort before, and felt somewhat uneasy about it, but my actions would not have been regarded as inappropriate in Cambodia. Even though men are permitted to stray a bit in our culture, you will hardly find people more devoted to each other than in Cambodia, whether it be husband and wife, or parent and child. These facts may seem contradictory, but as Gandhi once said "I'm interested in the truth, not in being consistent."

In any event, Nellie and I became close; she helped me a lot in my schoolwork, accompanying me on trips to the museum, and typing papers for the class. I don't regret having had an affair with her, but I do regret how self-centered I was at times. Just before spring break I finished a term paper with Nellie's help. We Cambodian AID students were going to leave on a field trip to Canada early the next morning, so I asked Nellie if she would drop off my term paper for the art appreciation class. She said she would, but then she asked me to stay overnight to help her; she said she needed me that night. But I was thinking about the trip, and worrying about getting to the bus on time, so I told her that I had to go. Nellie began to cry inconsolably, "I need you, I need you, I need you." I didn't understand what she meant by "need" —need what? She must have thought I was the most insensitive person she had ever met.

When we arrived in Canada, I met my younger brother Sam Ul, who was studying at the University of Montreal. After being away from each other for so long it seemed at first as if we were strangers from different parts of the galaxy. But we headed over to his apartment and, being thirsty, I went straight to the refrigerator and pulled out a can of concentrated orange juice from the freezer. My brother started acting as if he was convinced that I was such a hick that I would try to drink it right out of the can. I reminded him that in this part of the world, someone living in Montreal doesn't call someone living in L.A. a hick. We had a good laugh, got to know each other again, and had a great time.

AID had sponsored the trip to give us the opportunity to learn about the management and organization of the Canadian government, their university system, and some of their industries. But we were a bunch of young, restless guys looking for a good time. My brother and I were thinking about eating fried rice, and about window-shopping. Sadly the trip was a waste of AID money, and a waste of our potential to learn. As I approach my seventies, I now appreciate the familiar phrase, "Youth is wasted on the young."

Wasting AID money wasn't the end of my foolishness, though. I had saved up $2,500—a lot of money in those days, enough to get set up in business back home. What did I do? I asked my little brother to buy a car—a Volvo for some reason—and we shipped it off to Cambodia. It was a wonderful plan. We shipped it to our brother, Sam Ok, intending that he would drive our parents around the country to see Angkor Wat and the Tonle Sap, and that he would share the car with our other siblings. Well, that dream went sour. When the car reached Cambodia, the wife of my older brother, U An, became jealous of Sam Ok; in fact, everybody became jealous of each other over that car. So my parents never got to travel around Cambodia. Sam Ok's wife became a maniac; she wanted to have the car strictly for her own personal use. This "gift" turned out to be a curse—everybody got angry at me.

Shortly after our return from Canada, I saw a beautiful woman I had never seen before, walking around the industrial arts department, talking with my advisor, Dr. Teague, and some of my other teachers. Occasionally she looked at me following these conversations, but she never spoke. After a few days she left. Although I later learned that she was a Dr. Mary Gray, I didn't have the slightest inkling of what she had in store for me.

In the spring of 1965, I finally graduated, but AID had planned an additional year of independent study and practice teaching for me. That fall, I began teacher observation at Los Angeles High School, in downtown L.A. My only class was drafting, which I observed every day. This may sound like a tedious routine, but I didn't feel that way about it. In my classes at Los Angeles State, of course, I had already learned how to demonstrate the use of the equipment one might find in a machine shop, and how to complete projects of a wide variety; but now I was picking up the nuances and dynamics of managing a classroom from day to day. Then, in spring 1966 I taught at Santa Monica High School, in their industrial arts program. I participated in general shop classes but concentrated in woodworking, demonstrating to the students how to work the lathe and to mill small projects, and to observe proper safety. This all took place at a relatively easygoing pace for me. I felt very comfortable in this situation—I related to the students well, and they responded to me. I remember that, at the time, I was absolutely sure that I would be an excellent teacher when I returned to Cambodia.

I no longer had to worry about grades any more. Instead I was able to spend most of my spare time with Nellie, who apparently forgave me for abandoning her that evening. The more time we spent together the more she told me about herself. I was shocked to learn that when she was seventeen, a French bicyclist had raped her. Since then, she hated the color red because the rapist was wearing a red turtleneck. I happened to be wearing a red tee-shirt when this came up, and she said she hated me because it reminded her of the rapist.

All of this was taking place in California in the mid-1960s, and we were influenced by the spirit of the time. We walked around the apartment naked, even while we were getting dinner ready. The neighbors used to sneak peeks at us out their window. We could see them, but we were shameless! Luckily they did not call the police.

And when my stay in California came to a surprise end, I actually thought it was because of this free-spirited affair of the moment. I was staying overnight at Nellie's apartment, one evening, as I often did, when, close to midnight, there was a knock at the door. A severe man in a uniform asked me if I was U Sam Oeur (he couldn't pronounce it). At the time, I thought he was a policeman, but as I look back, he was probably from a messenger service of some sort—I know he was wearing a uniform. I was actually shaking as I stood there, wondering if I was going to be arrested. When I nodded my head, he handed me a receipt to sign, and presented me with an airline ticket from L.A. to Iowa— that very morning at 9:00 a.m. I was absolutely bewildered. How would I get to the airport? I called my friend Po Lim, who said he would take me. I scarcely had time to pack a few things. My books and other personal items were still strewn around the apartment I shared with my Cambodian roommates. Nellie agreed to ask them to pack my books and send them to Cambodia for me. I really didn't have time for good-byes—I just disappeared like the wind. No one knew where I went.

I boarded the plane, and wow! Where did the tears come from? They just rolled and rolled from my eyes, wetting my handkerchief right through. Where was I being sent? What had I done wrong? I thought I had gotten in trouble because I had a girlfriend. I was sure that that was why the police were sending me away—as punishment. The plane landed in San Francisco, and I was transferred to a flight bound for Cedar Rapids, Iowa. A few hours later the plane landed in the middle of cornfields, a vista that seemed bleak to me then, but which has since become a kind of second home.

An attractive woman, a poet from Belgium, coincidentally, was waiting for me at the airport. She wore jeans, but not the zip-up or button kind—these had leather laces down the front, which crisscrossed in a provocative manner. She drove me to Iowa City and dropped me off at an apartment that had been reserved for me at 303 South Capitol Street. I still had absolutely no idea why I was there.

IOWA CITY—ATHENS OF THE MIDWEST

It was beastly hot on the August afternoon that I was dropped off in Iowa City. But it felt good to me—after four years in California, this weather reminded me of home. The Belgian poet who had picked me up at the airport gave me the key to my apartment and mysteriously disappeared. I was left standing there in a bedroom, noting the small, attached kitchen, and the bathroom. A desk was at the foot of my bed, and against one of the walls was a bookcase with two shelves. I looked in the refrigerator—there was a loaf of bread, three cokes, some cheese, and some carrots and celery. In the kitchen cabinets I found soy sauce, and a few spices, a jar of Skippy peanut butter, a few battered pots, and an ancient cast-iron frying pan. Miscellaneous mismatched implements and utensils were in the kitchen drawers. I sat there and nibbled on a piece of stale white bread, feeling as if I were in some kind of physical and emotional limbo.

The next day, a big man with a shock of white hair and an engaging but brusque manner, pounded on my door at 8:00 a.m. As he walked in, his presence immediately filled the room. He introduced himself as Paul Engle, and proceeded to explain why I was in Iowa City. He told me that the Asia Foundation had funds to provide scholarships for two Asian students to further their studies in the arts, and that Dr. Mary Gray had been acting as a kind of talent scout. She had contacted my sponsor, the AID program, and after reading my little poetry pamphlet, she had called him at the University of Iowa Writers' Workshop, knowing that he was actively recruiting Asian writers in particular. Apparently she read my poems to Paul Engle over the phone, and on the spot they had enrolled me in the creative writing program. I was shocked by this news. Paul Engle sat there, looking at me expectantly. I was going to get a master's degree in writing poetry? It seemed preposterous, when they wouldn't even allow me to have a second minor in philosophy at Cal State. Yan and I were anticipating my return in a matter of months. Now this—another two years? Mr. Engle put some money in my hand and told me to take it easy for a few days—just walk around and "get my bearings."

Other occupants of the building, most of them participants in the program from Asia, stopped by and introduced themselves, one by one. I met Wong May, a beautiful but moody poet from Singapore, who had the apartment right above mine. Across from her was Willy Nolledo, a short-story writer and novelist from Manila. Willy wore a black leather jacket, had a Camel pasted to his lip, and a Belmondo poster on the wall above his desk. He sported a thin mustache and had a threatening demeanor, but it was really just an image he had cultivated from the movies. Willy had been a movie reviewer in Manila, so he was quite hip, having already gotten a very accurate read on American society through movies. In the attic apartment was another poet, Wang Ching-Lin, a former officer in the Taiwanese Navy. He had the bearing of a career military man. His roommate was an engineer, also from Taiwan. Two apartments were still open.

That weekend the Engles threw a party for all the international writers. It was a hot day, and we gathered under a pavilion along the Iowa River. The pavilion had a metal roof, so we were roasting, but it reminded me of home. There were writers from at least twelve other countries. I remember meeting Indira Bhai in particular, a beautiful fiction writer from India, and of course my housemates were there—Willy, Wong May, and Wang Ching-Lin; but I also remember meeting writers from Iran, Uganda, Japan, and Ethiopia. I was fond of Jim Beam at the time, and began swilling it down, but it didn't loosen my tongue or make me more outgoing—I could not find the words to engage in conversation. My recitation teacher from Georgetown would not have been impressed. I sat alone, with tears rolling down my face. Wong May teased me, saying that I was a shy guy, and that she would "look out for me." I told her that I was homesick, but in reality I was feeling sorry for myself. I was still bewildered by my situation—I was surrounded by a plethora of writers, some quite accomplished, who had traveled great distances to sharpen their skills here, and I felt that I didn't even know what poetry was! I did not feel like an imposter, because I wasn't even at the point at which I knew what it was I was pretending to be. I just felt so sad that it made me cry.

But it was just too fantastic an opportunity—and I didn't want to disappoint Paul Engle or Dr. Gray. So suddenly I was a creative writing student at the University of Iowa. That first semester I took poetry writing, and poetry seminar, both with George Starbuck who was the head of the Writers' Workshop. A tall man with a big forehead, he was extremely kind and insightful. Even though he himself wrote very clever formal poetry, and was particularly fond of Auden, he always seemed to suggest new writers to each student in order to take them in new stylistic directions. I also took a philosophy class (aesthetics), and fiction writing from Ben Santos, who was from the Philippines—Willy suggested I take this class so he could shepherd me through.

When the semester started, Paul Carroll, a poet from Chicago who was teaching one day a week, moved into the basement apartment of our building. He was a big man with big glasses, who always wore yellow corduroy pants. He had a kind of leering grin that reminded me of the Cheshire Cat in *Alice in Wonderland* —could he have been related to Lewis Carroll? Mr. Carroll had frequent visitors to his apartment, both male and female, during the one night each week he was there, and I could always hear a lot of laughter and giggling coming up through the floorboards late into the night.

A week later a young man named Ken McCullough moved in to the vacant apartment next to mine. He was a poet who, like me, admitted that he didn't know a whole lot about poetry, and was humbled at being in the company of so many "stars." We became friends, and Ken would often invite me along to parties, or, with Willy, to Kenney's, the poet's bar, on Clinton Street. Willy and I ordered champale, which we didn't know was a ladies' drink. On Willy's birthday, he played "Guantanamera" over and over on the jukebox, and when Irene, the owner, found out it was his birthday, we got free pitchers for the rest of the evening.

Donnelly's, another bar just around the corner from Kenney's, had a long history as a literary hangout. Dylan Thomas once spent several days holding forth in the back booth when he came to Iowa City to give a reading in the early 1950s. Anybody who was anybody, or aspiring to be someone (including undergraduate writers), could be found at Donnelly's. I went along on these forays, but I rarely said much. Of course each person who was there was so taken with his or her own wit and brilliance, that no one noticed my silence.

One of the regulars was a man named "Big John" Birkbeck, who adopted a different persona every evening—once he was a British explorer, another time he was a senator from the Deep South. He was a great raconteur, and his stories were quite outrageous, although he made them sound plausible. I could listen to him for hours, and did, on several occasions. Although he could be a bit over-the-top at times, he was actually the draftsman and personal assistant to Dr. James Van Allen, the star of the University of Iowa physics department, and the namesake of the Van Allen belt.

That fall I remember going with Ken to a Halloween party in an abandoned boarded-up mansion on the south edge of town. I had gone to a Fellini movie the weekend before, and thought the great Italian director would have been quite comfortable using this party as one of his sets. In addition to the blue cloud of marijuana smoke, there was a sense of conspiracy and forbiddenness in the air. As usual, I just tagged along, smiling every now and then when Ken tried to introduce me to someone or attempted to bring me into the conversation. The house was huge and we found our way to the basement, with numerous coal bins and other small rooms where people were paired up, or in some instances experimenting with larger groups; the Sexual Revolution was, after all, in full swing. I tried marijuana that night, but I didn't know what I was supposed to do. And so, like former president Clinton, "I didn't inhale." The last time I was in Iowa City, that very mansion was still there, still boarded up.

When winter arrived, I was not prepared for the snow and the plummeting temperatures. During the second semester, I often cut classes because I just couldn't face the walk of even a few blocks. But on days when the weather was more forgiving, Iowa City was an exciting and very friendly town to explore—at any given moment you might be invited up by someone hanging out a window. And between the hippies and the antiwar demonstrations, the campus felt like a carnival. Feelings about Vietnam ran high, and every day, protesters found new ways to express their anger about the war, such as wearing shrouds, holding silent vigils, exploding several cherry bombs in a trash can, or throwing a rat at the policemen brought onto the campus to restore order. Two years after I left, students actually burned down the Rhetoric Building to protest the bombing of Cambodia. The building had been built early in the century, and was supposedly insulated with corncobs; you can imagine how quickly it went up in smoke.

In the fall of 1966, though, my first semester, things were just starting to accelerate. As you can imagine, I was getting nervous. Vietnam was just next door to Cambodia; in fact, my home town was within walking distance of the border. Nothing in Yan's letters had caused me to worry at that point, but the constant barrage of conflicting information in the media and on campus often caused me to retreat to my room and read Aristotle.

Now and then Wong May asked me up for tea, then showed me her love poems, which she said were written for me. Then she would sulk, and strike provocative poses, and ask me whether I found her attractive. I guess I enjoyed this attention, but nothing ever came of it. She eventually gave up, but we remained friends and continued flirting, though not as intensely.

The letters that passed between Yan and me continued to be intimate, but I expressed to her my uneasiness about being in this new and sometimes baffling environment, and especially about this added period of separation between us. She assured me that she had total faith in my devotion to her. I continued to wonder if staying in Iowa City had been the right decision.

In Janaury 1967, Ken moved out of his apartment to a ramshackle house on the Iowa River that cost all of four dollars a month in rent. It was a large place, but had no running water and only a potbelly stove for heat. There was a breezy outhouse, and if I recall correctly, he did have rudimentary electricity. The back porch, which ran the length of the house, looked out on the river. Ken had grown a beard and was starting to assume a mountain man persona. He used to walk from his place into town until he "inherited" a car from someone who had become a Buddhist and given away all his worldly possessions. I should note that Cambodian Buddhists rarely gave away items of this magnitude.

A wraith-like young fellow named William Golightly, nephew to Holly Golightly, of *Breakfast at Tiffany's* fame, took over Ken's apartment. William began working with Wang Ching-Lin on translating his poems into English. William was only nineteen, but quite well-read. He, like many students, was living on a very tight budget, and the rent for these apartments was steep. Consequently, when Wang Ching-Lin's roommate married and moved out, William moved in. You could hear them droning on late into the night, as they worked on translations—they were quite diligent.

Ken had a number of parties at his house, but the first, celebrating a visit from Allen Ginsberg, became legendary. The party was held at Ken's house because none of the Workshop faculty wanted to take the risk of getting "busted," knowing Ginsberg's reputation for illicit drugs. Ken was living on sixty dollars a month at the time, but people donated a total of five kegs of beer, and some construction workers Ken knew donated a pig, which they butchered. Then a group of volunteers dug a pit and roasted the pig for fourteen hours.

Over two hundred people showed up for the party, some falling through the porch in the darkness, others claiming, weeks later, that they had gotten trichinosis (although I heard that there hadn't been any documented cases of trichinosis in Iowa in many years). A band called Mother Blues played, and as people danced on the road in front of the house to the strobe light the band had brought along, Ken's two dogs fled into the woods. Ginsberg seemed to enjoy the party, and several young people took off their clothes and danced—Ginsberg stayed clothed, however. There was a bit of a stir when Kurt Vonnegut showed up. He appeared to me to be a wrinkled fourteen-year-old boy, with a kind of innocence, enthusiasm, and curiosity. His wife was with him, and I could tell, from the expression on her face, that she was there to make sure he behaved. It was quite a scene, and Ken, who had been something of a recluse, was now an instant and well-known party-giver.

During the next semester I studied with a British poet on the faculty, Michael Dennis Browne. Michael had been a Shakespearean actor, and conducted his classes in an almost swashbuckling manner. It was as if he were conducting, literally—he knew when to bring us up, and when to calm us down. It was refreshing and usually entertaining, and in addition to learning a few things about poetry, I learned a lot about how to present a poem aloud.

Nellie, my girlfriend from Los Angeles, certainly surprised me when she transferred to the University of Iowa College of Nursing. I had no idea that she was going to do this. She just showed up at my room unannounced one evening and stayed until the next morning. Around ten that morning I told her that I was going to return to Cambodia when I finished my degree and that I was going to get married. She left almost immediately and I never saw her again. I found out that she moved back to L.A. two months later. I was so naive that I didn't understand that she had moved to Iowa just to be near me.

At that time I also had another girlfriend, a pleasant woman who was a graduate student in English. During semester break, she drove me to her brother's farm, for a weekend in the heart of Iowa. I remember that their hogs ate all night long. I kept waking up and looking out the window, thinking that burglars were breaking in, but it was just the hogs. In the morning, I went out to observe their feeding mechanism and saw them pushing a board to release more food. In Cambodia, we fed the hogs just once a day. I watched her brother put on rubber boots to tend the hogs. While slogging through manure almost up to his knees, he rounded up about fifteen of the biggest hogs to bring to market to sell. I went along to observe the trade. It was effortless—he just filled out a paper, was handed a receipt, and we returned home. This amazed me, because in Cambodia this whole process would have taken hours of bargaining and strategy.

I enjoyed my trip to the countryside to see an Iowa farm, but I cut short this new relationship. She invited me to go horseback riding and I said I was too busy. She was insistent, I held my ground, and she finally hung up. That was our last conversation. I had also become infatuated with Indira Bhai, and even though she was receptive to me, I held back, and ultimately let the embers fade.

I was becoming disenchanted with some aspects of the lifestyle I was living, a lifestyle emblematic of the rest of the country. It wasn't my style—the drugs and revolving sexual partners. I saw many confused and unhappy people, and I didn't want to be drawn in. Despite these good intentions, I wasn't blind to the beautiful young women in the scanty garb of the day. Part of me was still the gawking farm boy; I wasn't ready to become a Buddhist monk, yet.

I continued to write poetry, but I didn't understand much of what was being discussed in class. I would look at a poem by someone like Robert Creeley, and just not get it; and Frank O'Hara's work sounded as if it was just talk. I didn't take poetry too seriously (fake "gurus" abounded in those days, and I still thought of myself as a "pretender" in the poetry game), but I kept cranking out poems. One, entitled "La Nuit Blanche," got published in the *Daily Iowan*. I think the fellow who moved into the apartment next to mine when William Golightly moved out may have submitted it for me. And eventually I got up the nerve to send a poem entitled "May Peace Prevail in Cambodia" to Prince Sihanouk, and much to my surprise, it was published in his magazine *Kampujea*, the Cambodian equivalent of *Life* magazine.

Lots of important poets passed through Iowa City in those days, such as Lawrence Ferlinghetti, John Berryman, Robert Creeley, Robert Bly, Denise Levertov, and Galway Kinnell. I went to many of the readings and was impressed by the ambience, and the fact that a number of people showed up with copies of books and read along silently. The literary parties were always full of energy, mostly sexual, as many people were trying to "score," particularly with the visiting writer, in the game of musical beds. There were visits from others, such as Jorge Luis Borges, who commanded almost universal awe and respect, even in those times of revolution and pseudorevolution.

But my favorite times were get-togethers at Ken's house. We were joined by a rotating cast of writers including Willy, Andy (Fernando) Afable (a poet born in the Philippines, but raised in the U.S.), sometimes Wang Ching-Lin and sometimes Dai Tien, a well-to-do poet from Hong Kong. Other visitors included Bill Bode, a fiction writer, "T" Wilson, a poet who was also printing hand-set books, and Peter Klappert, poet, who was Andy's roommate. When Wong May came, all of us preened for her. There were lazy afternoons in the spring, when everything was incredibly green, and later on, Saturdays in fall, when the corn husks were starting to turn to parchment and you could hear the roar of the football stadium in the distance. The river flowed by at a leisurely pace, with occasional pontoon party boats drifting by, and everyone would smile and wave to us. Part of me wondered, though, whether some of them thought that we were an enclave of Viet Cong, training on the outskirts of Iowa City. Incidentally, I understand that Andy has gone through several career changes, but is now the vice abbot of a Rinzai Zen monastery in New York. But aside from these gatherings, I spent most of my time reading, and missing Yan. And when I dreamed at night, I was always at home in Cambodia, most often in my village.

Then Dr. Mary Gray came to Iowa City in the spring of 1967, and I stopped in to visit with her at the Student Union hotel. She was a very striking person. She wasn't exactly beautiful, physically, but her soul was so radiant that I fell in love with her—on a platonic level, of course. Many years later, in 1999, I wrote her a poem expressing my gratitude and love for her. She died shortly after I sent her this poem, and I take some satisfaction that I had let her know that she was my mentor, the person responsible for my entire writing career.

Even though I now regard myself as a poet, at that time I continued to believe that my vocation was really in the realm of light industry. But my visit with Dr. Gray was inspiring, and my studies in Iowa were not particularly taxing, compared to my schoolwork in Los Angeles. I suppose that in the fellowship of writers that Paul Engle created, and the fellowship I had formed on my own with Ken and other American writers, I was learning more than I knew. In any event, I decided to stick it out, continue another year, and complete the MFA program.

Classes resumed in fall 1967, and the sleepy aspect that Iowa City took on in the summer was replaced by an electric charge from the presence of so many students engaged in high-powered intellectual exploration. Not the least of which were my classmates in the Writers' Workshop—several had returned from exotic places and their egos had grown commensurately.

There were many more parties that year that I remember in vivid detail. Some were entertaining, others I found quite baffling. I was truly a duck out of water much of the time. Thinking back, I remember so many of the people I met in Iowa City—their names and faces are still as clear now as they were then. Many of these people, fellow students and otherwise, were real characters, almost legendary—Dick Tibbets, Sid Cothren, Gerald Stevenson,

Sad Spoonth, Sharat Chandra, Jim Casteel, Fred Woodard, George Lonseome, Ray DiPalma (a magnificent actor), Ralph Dickey (who was a great pianist), Large Marge, Henry Hanson, David Sundance, Stephen Gray, Bill Joyce, Richard Gehman, Harry and Glen Epstein, Paris Mentis, Bob Slater—I could go on. Each one of them deserves a full-fledged profile. They were what made Iowa City such a glowing memory.

I formed a particular bond with Mike Lally, who was very "hip." Norman Mailer wrote a pamphlet entitled *The White Negro*, and Michael fit that mold. He had a quick mind, was a good poet, knew his music, but more than anything else, he could run circles around anyone when it came to talking politics. He didn't have much use for white people, though he was one of them. Whenever there was a panel discussion with senators and other big shots, Michael would usually be called upon to represent the far left, and he was always the most articulate person on the panel. I recall in a discussion about Ho Chi Minh, Michael made Uncle Ho seem like Mother Theresa. I'm not sure why we became friends—on the surface we were exact opposites, but on the inside we were brothers.

News from home was starting to scare me. It was clear that events in Vietnam would spill over into our country. There was a mournful note in Yan's letters now. I, too, missed her and my homeland, and was ready to return, no matter what cataclysms might await me. I had been gone for six years. Events in the United States were becoming ominous, too—as winter turned into spring, Martin Luther King was assassinated, followed shortly by Bobby Kennedy. And of course the Tet Offensive loomed large.

Actually I had my own encounter with the local constabulary. Keep in mind that police officers were not popular at that time; their role was to preserve order in an era of rapid change. Between drugs, political rallies, and general bizarre behavior, they had come, I imagine, to expect the worst of everyone. On this particular evening, while preparing to attend an international dinner on campus, I decided to dress in a traditional

Cambodian wraparound garment similar to a sarong. I'd walked about two blocks from my apartment when a squad car pulled up, and the officer got out and said to me, "Look, you can't walk around here dressed like that. You'd better put some pants on." Given the level of political turmoil and drug-related incidents at the time, you'd think they would have had more serious things to worry about. But I returned to my apartment and changed, not knowing how else to respond. I hoped no men from Scotland were on their way to that dinner.

Of course that police response symbolized their futile attempt to hold back changes that were sweeping the nation. One last memory of those days, a memory that symbolized those very changes, began at Ken's house, one afternoon, watching the crayfish along the banks of the Iowa River, and the carp feeding lazily near the surface. That evening, Hans Breder, a German painter in the art department, happened out with several art students—including some good-looking young women—and after a few beers, we all went skinny-dipping together. This was a typical Iowa City evening for the late sixties. And although I am a modest person, it was a dark night and nobody was paying attention to me anyway, so I joined in.

Near the end of the spring semester I hired a lady to type my thesis—*The Hunting World*. The typist and her husband—both writers —told me that I should continue writing poetry, that I was a real poet. As I said before, I didn't consider myself a poet. I just wrote poetry to get the certificate, so that I could go home, having "completed my mission." But I was starting to wonder if my life had changed in ways I hadn't recognized yet. Anyway, I submitted my thesis to the committee, and after review by the other committee members, Michael Dennis Browne, who had been my advisor, told me that they had accepted my thesis and that I had passed the exam. But they didn't have the certificate ready. Given the way bureaucracies worked, I wondered if it would ever reach me in Cambodia. Perhaps one sign that I was unconsciously open to a future different than the one I had planned was that I asked Michael Dennis Browne to write me a letter of recommendation for literary teaching jobs.

I had been in Iowa City for two years, and they had been full years. We refer to our college as our *alma mater,* our *foster mother,* but I did not know then that the University of Iowa would indeed become my foster mother at a time in the distant future.

MY RETURN & PERIOD OF ADJUSTMENT

After having gotten word that I passed my comprehensive exam, I called the State Department to arrange for my return to Cambodia. The official asked me whether I wished to travel by way of Paris or not. She suggested that I should travel to Europe before returning to Cambodia, but I didn't want to hear what she was telling me; I was oblivious to anything but my ultimate goal: to go home! I got a bit brusque, and asked her to please send me a ticket for an overnight flight to Cambodia as soon as one could be arranged. Then she asked me if I was sure I didn't want to stay several more months in America. It didn't seem as if she had heard me, but I must have gotten through, because the ticket arrived the next day.

With my ticket finally in my eager hands, I packed my books and clothes and shipped them home. Then I asked Ken whether I could throw a party at his place. He loved the idea. I prepared chicken wings, chicken thighs, and chicken drumsticks, marinating them in ginger, red wine, soy sauce, and black pepper. The following evening we gathered at his house, a small group of my closest friends. It was a wonderful, balmy evening, full of nostalgia, but I felt neither remorse at leaving Iowa City nor fear about what I would find when I got back to Cambodia.

The next day, in the afternoon, Indira Bhai came by and we sat together in my room and chatted. She was beautiful in her pale blue sari, with her long black hair framing her penetrating eyes. Indira told me that she would go to Canada, and she looked around and asked me where my books were. I told her that I had sent everything home already. This surprised her. We parted warmly. I often wonder about her—about her life and whether she continued as a writer.

It was early July when Paul Engle drove me to the Cedar Rapids airport and I boarded the plane. I had an overnight layover at San Francisco, so I paid a visit to Dr. Mary Gray. I don't remember many of the details of that visit—it's almost as if it happened in a dream. I recall sitting in the reception area for half an hour until she came out to greet me. We shook hands, and I handed her a copy of my master's thesis. She looked it over, looked at me, and said, "You are a real human being." To this day I have no idea what she meant exactly. We had a brief conversation, shook hands, then I returned to the hotel.

I passed an uneventful night. All I could think about was getting home, and seeing Yan. I was actually calm; I didn't have any misgivings about my return. I was somewhat worried about what was going on politically in Cambodia. This was before the internet and other forms of instant news—we had to rely on what we read in newspapers, and by experience I had learned that there was always some measure of distortion in the news. I would read about an event, particularly in Southeast Asia, then would get the real story some weeks later from a friend. Spiro Agnew, Nixon's vice president, was always complaining about the media misrepresenting events, and he was right—but I don't think he would have complained as often if the media had praised, rather than criticized, their administration.

Speaking of American politics, I should say something about my feelings toward America in 1968. I came to the United States in 1961 believing in the idea of democracy, but really I had only the vaguest of notions of what the word meant. When I left Cambodia, our nation—in the middle of the twentieth century— was being ruled by Norodom Sihanouk, a man chosen by a colonial power to be our *king*. Then Sihanouk turned the throne over to his father, so that as "Crown Prince," he could also serve as prime minister. But in fact he ruled as a clown prince, making and breaking agreements with other nations on a whim, and imprisoning people if he even thought they were plotting against him (legal proof wasn't required). He ruled as if he believed in the Middle Ages doctrine of the Divine Right of Kings.

I came to America very aware of my inadequacies. I was a farm boy who had spent a few years in Phnom Penh, and suddenly I was in the United States, barely able to speak English, unacquainted with even the most ordinary of customs. At first I was so intent on my studies, the turbulent times I was living through in the 1960s barely registered. But by the time I returned home, I had learned about the Civil Rights Movement, and coming from Southeast Asia I was very aware of the antiwar movement. As I mentioned earlier, Martin Luther King and Robert Kennedy had both been shot and killed that very spring. Many Americans had begun to lose faith in their country. But from my perspective, I saw America in a different way. All the tumult that seemed to be tearing America apart looked like real democracy in action to me. America's "Silent Majority" and the hippies and antiwar protesters were arguing out in public. There were a few ugly moments in those years, and a number of deaths; but there were no mass arrests or mass murders. Political parties weren't dissolved. When the Democrats lost to the Republicans later that fall, not even the most paranoid person fantasized that the Democrats would somehow try to retain power by force and eliminate their enemies. I knew that democracy in Cambodia would look different than in the United States, but my years in America had given me more than modern technical skills. Unfortunately my hopes for my country, inspired in so many ways by Walt Whitman, would soon be dashed.

Enough about politics. The next morning I boarded a Pan Am flight to Hong Kong. I arrived on Thursday, July 7th. I was supposed to land in Pochentong Airport, in Phnom Penh, later that afternoon, but when I reached Hong Kong, they told me that the Royal Air Cambodge aircraft was out of commission, and I would have to stay in Hong Kong overnight. It was afternoon when I grabbed a taxi to the hotel, and along the way, I asked the taxi driver to recommend a place where I could enjoy the evening. The driver told me that he could take me anywhere I wished. I decided to take him up on his offer. After I unloaded my baggage at the hotel, I set out with him to the border of Red China to look at the mainland, and then he drove me to a restaurant for dinner. On the way back to the hotel, I asked him to help me buy wristwatches for gifts, and a wedding ring, so he took me to a few stores. I didn't have the slightest notion about how to evaluate the quality of diamonds—I just bought one, whatever they had there in the store. Then I loaded up on trinkets for gifts, and rode back to the hotel. Thinking back to that moment, I wonder if I had been courageous, naive, or just flat out stupid. He could have taken me anywhere, dumped me off, or killed me.

But the next morning at ten o'clock, the same driver knocked on my door to take me to the airport. He said he was still hungover, but because I had become his friend, he felt he had to come and pick me up. He was so kind.

It took only about an hour-and-a-half to reach Pochentong Airport. I got off the plane and went through the customs office, but when I reached the lobby of the airport, not a soul was there to welcome me. I felt lost—I wasn't sure what to do next. All I could think of was Chbar Ampeou, my father-in-law's house, where I hoped to find Yan. Luckily there was a taxi driver handy, who hustled my luggage into his trunk, and off we went, from the airport, through Phnom Penh, and on to Chbar Ampeou.

When I left Phnom Penh in 1961, much of the city was still a swamp. When I returned in 1968 boulevards and large avenues were everywhere—the swamps had vanished! I started feeling disoriented, but I kept a calm demeanor and made believe that I knew where we were going. It wasn't long before we crossed the bridge and the taxi driver took me to house number 38 on National Highway 1. I got out of the car and approached the house, to make sure that it was the right one but . . . I had never seen this house before! It was new, larger and taller than the old one. It turned out that my father-in-law had rebuilt it completely in 1963, during my absence. Strangely enough, Yan had never mentioned the remodeling.

Suddenly I saw my father-in-law working under the house and I shouted. He rushed forward to greet me with a big smile on his face. I returned to the taxi to gather my luggage, while my father-in-law sprang up the steps into the house to tell my mother-in-law, who was still half-naked from taking a bath. I grabbed my suitcases, paid the driver, climbed the stairs, and entered the living room. Yan seized me and grabbed my neck and we hugged each other, right there, in front of all assembled. This behavior was atypical of Cambodian culture, where couples never hug in public. My mother-in-law and father-in-law were surprised; they stared at us, then looked at each other, speechless.

That was just the first example of how I had changed. I felt comfortable hugging Yan in front of my family, but in other matters I had become used to privacy—such as going to the toilet, bathing, showering, and sleeping in a room behind a closed door. In Cambodia, for example, if you want to take a nap, you just stop and curl up anywhere. This is perfectly acceptable—no one will wake you or shoo you away, even if you are sleeping in front of a fancy restaurant or club. So not long after unpacking, I planned and built a bathroom for the house, with a door that not only closed, it could be locked. Everyone looked at me very strangely. No one could understand why a student who had just returned from abroad would be occupied in such a pursuit. They regarded me as a real intellectual—I just felt like someone who had come home, but didn't *feel* at home.

And then there were the flies, all over everything. I hadn't noticed them before I left for America. I could not even eat for the first few months, thinking about the diseases the flies and mosquitoes carried.

Meanwhile I was wondering what had happened to my own family. Well, I had forgotten that my family thought I was arriving the day before. After the plane I was supposed to have been on never arrived, they assumed *they* were late. And they further assumed that a student returning from the United States would naturally check into a hotel. So for the next two weeks they ran all over the city, searching every hotel in town. As a last resort, they went to Chbar Ampeou, where they finally found me. As it turned out, this delay was fortuitous.

If my plane had arrived on the day it was supposed to, my sister-in-law, Long Van Thet (An's wife), would have tried to marry me off to the daughter of the minister of agriculture, because she had borrowed money from him for gambling. She'd worked out a deal to cancel all her debts this way—without my knowledge or consent, I might add. I've always felt that God prevented this disaster by initiating mechanical problems on that Air Cambodge flight.

Anyway, my heart was still with Yan—that's why the spirits of the land directed me to *her* house, rather than to my family. It may seem preposterous that it took two weeks for them to find me, but keep in mind that not only was this decades before cell phones and e-mail, even telephones were uncommon except for businesses and governmental offices. So we were used to such gaps in communication. For a while, they thought I might have changed my mind about returning, either temporarily or permanently.

Even though I wanted to see my siblings and their families, this time with Yan was the ideal way for me to reenter the world most precious to me. Together we walked up the shaded dirt roads north of the highway, and east, out past Wat Nirodha Temple, soaking up each other's physical presence as if we were sponges. Our reunion was serene and deep, despite the fact that we had not seen each other for seven years. I attribute this to Yan's disposition, which was and is one of charity, patience, receptivity, and affirmation. I, on the other hand, am more of an introvert, and tend to keep my emotions and thoughts bottled for longer than is healthy. Yan, even without trying, has always been able to help me open up.

Now that they had found me, my brothers and other friends showed up several times a week to take me "out on the town." I found this frustrating, but I went along—I guess I thought it was somehow my duty—but all I really wanted to do was stay home.

But then, on August 12th, Yan and I were married and our wedding ceremony took two full days. It was a traditional wedding, with every friend and relative who could possibly be there in attendance. In fact there were many guests I'd never met before—I know I'm not the only one to have had *that* experience.

My mother and father seemed to be particularly happy. While I was gone, my mother had realized that because my father-in-law was such a highly regarded architect, that I was "marrying up," which mothers everywhere think about, I suppose. There was feasting and color galore, traditional Cambodian weddings being excessive and spectacular, but without the exorbitant expense of some of the weddings I've attended in the U.S.

Not long after our wedding, I received my master of fine arts certificate from the University of Iowa in the mail. I must say that I was extremely proud of that diploma. For some time I went around with a slightly swelled head; I was a certified intellectual, available to serve my country in whatever capacity they saw fit for me—the future appeared to be an open road, a wide boulevard lined with waving palm trees, and smiling faces.

But as much as the MFA was starting to mean to me, I believed that practical skills were needed most in my country, and I was really committed to the idea of teaching. I especially hoped to introduce democracy to my students, even while bent over a lathe. I went to the University of Technics and submitted an application. The university had been built by the U.S. while I was away and was on the same campus as the School of Arts and Trade, which supplied most of their students. The director of the university (also dean of the faculty of the School of Arts and Trade), welcomed me right away and I got a job teaching English to the freshman and junior classes. That was exactly the job I had wanted, but because of the political confusion in Cambodia at the time, I became immediately aware that I had to be careful about what I said in the classroom. The government had adopted a hard anti-American line; consequently, the secret police were always harassing students who had returned from the United States. The dean warned me, as a friend, not to be too engaged in my teaching—that the higher priority was to keep our students on an even keel so that they wouldn't riot. If they rioted we would be accused of being communist agitators.

What vexing and perplexing words for me to hear! I had just returned and hadn't had time to fully comprehend the political climate. What I learned, after meeting with people I could trust, was hard to believe. When I left Cambodia in 1961, Prince Sihanouk had been governing the country like a whimsical French king from the Middle Ages. When I returned I discovered that he had become a complete egomaniac, and had turned paranoid distrust into a national policy. From 1967 through 1970, one could be accused of being a communist, of being a nationalist, of promoting democracy, or simply of trying to be an honest bureaucrat. Many advocates of democracy fled the city and joined the Khmer Rouge hoping to find common cause against the corrupt administration. Most of these people were later slaughtered by those same Khmer Rouge troops.

Cambodian students, like most students of college age, were hungry to discuss lofty philosophical concepts, and to question their own cultural underpinnings and values; hence, it was hard to restrain their enthusiasm and curiosity. My goal as a teacher was to give my students demonstrable skills as thinkers and problem solvers. If I discovered that my students were only capable of learning by rote memory—then I wasn't going to waste my time. And I'll admit that I was scared by what the dean had told me—even when I think back now to those moments, I get a hollow feeling in the pit of my stomach.

After just a few frustrating months at the University of Technics, I submitted my resignation. It had become clear to me that eventually I was bound to say or do "the wrong thing" in the classroom. If I worked at an industrial job, however, I wouldn't be tempted to put my family or myself in danger by talking about ideas—I would be working with my hands. My salary at the University of Technics was 500 riels an hour—quite a lot at that time, and quite a comfortable living. The salary for a factory worker averaged 3,000 riels a month.

As I reflect on the past, it seems to me that I made many stupid moves in the course of my life. I once asked one of my Spirit Advisors why I had frequently been such a fool, but she disagreed. "You were not stupid," she told me. *"I sent you to work in a factory, because if you had stayed at the University of Technics, you'd have been killed. You were a bit stupid in one respect—you didn't know a thing about politics."*

KOH KONG

Koh Kong. Koh Kong. It felt as if the wind blew my soul to Koh Kong. When I was growing up it always seemed exotically far away. Actually, Svay Rieng, the province where I grew up, is in the extreme southeast corner of Cambodia, and the province of Koh Kong is on the extreme western edge, bordering Thailand. Koh Kong consists of myriad sea marshes, several small mountain ranges, and forests, unlike Svay Rieng, which is very flat and dry. American readers might wonder why two cities that are only 450 miles apart could seem so far away from each other. Although Koh Kong and Svay Rieng might be "only" 450 miles apart on a map, those miles include many river crossings, a major mountain range, and some rugged territory that is literally a jungle. The elephant, rhinoceros, and many species of monkeys are native to the region. In a nation that still moves mostly by bicycle and oxcart, 450 miles is far away indeed.

THE CANNERY & THE PRINCE

After I quit my teaching position I began looking for factory jobs. One day, as I was walking west of the Grand New Market, I spotted a "help wanted" poster for a government-operated fish cannery in Koh Kong, on the window of an employment administration office. By now, Sihanouk had nationalized all the factories and banks, and implemented what he called "Buddhist socialism." The poster said they were looking for an engineer. I entered, introduced myself, and told the general director, Sao Leang, that I had a bachelor's degree in industrial arts from the United States and also a master's degree. He hired me on the spot. I had begun teaching in September, had quit in January; and gotten the job in Koh Kong in February. I had also applied for and been accepted for a position at a refinery in Kompong Som, close to the beer brewery where my younger brother U Sam Ul worked. Though also remote, it is a metropolis compared to Koh Kong, and being near my brother would have made me feel more at home in my new life. But the director of the refinery was a good friend of Long Van Thet, my brother An's wife. The director of the refinery gave An's wife a letter accepting me for the refinery position, but she neglected to deliver it. I didn't discover this until I had been in Koh Kong for some months.

Everyone in Yan's family discouraged me from taking this plunge, but I was under the spell of democracy and blindly directed toward whatever I thought was going to be best for the welfare of our country. Yan too was upset, but she never expressed this directly to me, which was in keeping with traditional Cambodian

culture. In our culture, we had an open and expressive relationship, but all is relative—Westerners might not see it that
way.

As I think back, I believe most of my colleagues who were at
the University of Technics when the Khmer Rouge took over, are
now dead. They agreed to sign on with the Khmer Rouge, and
cooperated by showing them how to run various machines. But
as soon as the Khmer Rouge soldiers thought they had learned
the ropes, the teachers were executed. It was fate that took us to
Koh Kong—the spirits directed us there.

I packed my belongings, and said my good-byes. A driver in a
company car drove me partway, along National Highway 4, which
had been built by the United States. We took a small motorboat
for the last leg of the trip. The countryside along the way was new
to me—it seemed wilder and more dramatic than anything I had
ever seen. There was the sea, the jungles, and from Sre Ambil
onward, aquatic forests. *Kong kang* trees (used for making cooking charcoal) grew densely along the shallow saltwaterways. I
was in another realm, like heaven—more lush than anything I
had imagined. Despite the remoteness of the area, I was
enchanted. But who, in his right mind, would accept a job in the
middle of the jungle?

We passed the town of Dang Tuorng and approached the cannery a mile south, on the east bank of an estuary that stretched
back inland to the north, toward the mountains in the distance.
We docked at a cement pier in front of the cannery at 8:30 a.m.

The cannery was surrounded by a forest of *prey smach* trees, a
soft wood covered with thin layers of bark. One can produce
torches by soaking this bark in resin. The cannery was not an
impressive structure. You might call the style Red Chinese industrial architecture. There was no shade, and the smell of rotting
fish was overwhelming; I almost retched, but stifled it, knowing
I was being scrutinized. I gathered my gear and moved into a villa
of two bedrooms on the beach of the estuary north of the cannery,
and settled into my new life.

First off I discovered that their lathe was broken. A young worker named Sar Thorn told me that Sok Lay, my predecessor, had thrown all the gears away so that no one could use it. When Sok Lay needed bolts and nuts, or tubes for propeller shafts, it gave him a reason to go to Phnom Penh for parts, where he could run up a big bill for travel expenses. Even then he came back without the gears needed to get the lathe running. My first job was to repair the lathe and keep it running. I ordered gears and other parts, trained other workers to operate and repair it, so we weren't relying on one person to keep this vital machine going. I also introduced the workers to the terminology of a machine shop, trained workers in welding and a variety of other skills, and instituted a safety program. We had four sections to our operation: the cannery, the fishery, fish meal production, and ice production.

I worked in my assigned capacity for three months, when out of the blue they promoted me to technical director of the entire cannery. When I heard that my salary had jumped to 18,000 riels a month, I immediately sent for Yan.

She, too, made the long journey by Land Rover, with the cannery driver. He made runs back and forth from Phnom Penh with raw materials. This time he was carrying a ton of tomatoes, from which we would make tomato paste. By then they had completed a road through the jungle, so her trip was entirely overland. She had never read Conrad's *Heart of Darkness*, but I'm sure she experienced some of the same feeling of dread Conrad describes, as if she were being exiled from civilization. It was a bit of a strain for Yan at first, as this was, in effect, her first time away from home, and the first time she had ever lived anywhere other than the outskirts of Phnom Penh. But she was (and is) an outgoing person, and made friends quickly.

Chao Koy, the director of administration, spent all his time in Phnom Penh. Sao Leang, the general director, had a villa near ours, but he split his time between the cannery and Phnom Penh. When he wasn't in Koh Kong, his home was usually occupied by guests.

But our living situation was not isolated—a complex of 150 very basic housing units had been built behind the factory for the workers and their families. Even though she socialized with the other women at the cannery, Yan was desperately homesick, and felt somewhat helpless in her new environment. I was too driven to notice it, and am not sure I would have known what to do if I had.

This was my first position of significant responsibility, and I embraced the challenge with confidence and enthusiasm. I was in charge of improvements to the factory, which entailed supervising renovation and new construction, and acquiring and assembling new machinery. I implemented what I had learned from my encounter with democracy, including a system whereby housing, clothing, food, health care, and even a trade union, were available to the workers. I discovered that I had a natural ability to manage people and to organize the activities of a factory. Production increased almost immediately. I earned the respect of the workers, and I even won over my white-collar subordinates, most of whom had never put in a day of physical work in their lives.

Probably my most ambitious initiative was the construction of a reservoir to insure an ample supply of fresh water needed for ice production. First I hired a bulldozer to dig the reservoir, and then I entreated an army engineer to build a road from the cannery to the town.

At this time we were producing only ice and fish meal—we could catch barely enough sardines to keep the cannery running for one month out of the year. The ice was used in Koh Kong and the surrounding district, while the fish meal was picked up by a Japanese ship and transported to Kompong Som and Phnom Penh.

In June, we received a letter from my mother-in-law back in Chbar Ampeou. She told us that in a dream, she had observed herself going to visit me at my cannery. On the way, she saw a young boy sitting in a flying armchair decorated with gold. The boy asked, "Where is Grandma Yoeun? Where is Grandma Yoeun?"

My mother-in-law quickly replied "I'm here! I'm here!"

"Grandma Yoeun! Will you let me stay with you? God ordered me to come live with you. If you don't need me, I must return to where I came from."

My mother-in-law was so eager to have a grandson that she replied aloud, "Yes, of course I need you, I need you—come down here, come down," and as she was saying this in her dream, she suddenly sat up in bed and woke up. Sure enough, next month my wife Yan got pregnant. It was the Year of the Rooster. I learned later that my mother-in-law traveled to Wat Khnong, in Kien Svay, twelve-and-a-half miles from Chbar Ampeou, to pray for a grandson. Now, when my son travels back to Cambodia, he goes first to that temple to pray to his spirit grandfather and grandmother and to have musicians play pin peat for them. He goes there even before returning home.

My mother-in-law came to visit many times during the pregnancy and doted on Yan. But she also brought word from everyone in Chbar Ampeou, encouraging Yan to return to the city for the birth. Eventually she would acquiesce. When her mother wasn't there, Yan relied heavily on her mother's prayers to get her through the days. As was our way, we never discussed the possibility of her returning to the city—when the time came, with a month to go, her mother packed her up and told me they were going, so that Yan could be in a safer environment. The Americans had already bombed Neak Luong by then. You may recognize the name of that city from the movie, *The Killing Fields*.

I have mentioned that Prince Sihanouk ruled like a medieval king in the middle of the twentieth century, but when he decided he wanted to be a film star, he unwittingly stepped into the realm of self-parody. Sihanouk made nine feature-length films from 1966 to 1969—most of them directed, produced by, and often starring, himself. As one might imagine, the films were amateurish beyond belief, and of course they were fully funded by the national budget, which was, for the most part, borrowed money. One wonders who was running the country while he was off feeding his ego. The most absurd aspect of his career in the cinema was when he held a "Phnom Penh International Film Festival" in 1968 and 1969. To no one's surprise, Prince Sihanouk's entry won the grand prize (and the solid gold award statuette based on the Oscar) on both occasions. It appeared that no one in Cambodia could tell the emperor that he was not wearing any clothes.

That year, Prince Sihanouk came to Koh Kong to film a few scenes of one of his productions, a film called *Crepuscule (Twilight)*. Many troops preceded his arrival to establish tight security. Even though our cannery was not used as a location, the soldiers flattened the bushes for about a mile around our premises, just in case. Sihanouk did, however, use the boats from our cannery fleet to go out to sea and back to film romantic footage with his costar, his wife Monique. For some unfathomable reason, the film, when I eventually saw it, gave me an eerie premonition that Cambodia was headed for a rapid and devastating decline. It was clear to me that he knew that he was going to be deposed, and was willing to let that happen. Sihanouk was very clever—he often pretended that he wasn't aware of what was going on, but actually he was always trying to manipulate events to his advantage.

An old friend from home was a commander of Sihanouk's bodyguards, and he invited me to meet Sihanouk when the prince was in town for his movie shoot. Without connections, I would never have had such an opportunity. Only the governor and other top officials were allowed to get near him. But one of my relatives told me that the prince was not only corrupt, he liked to be constantly flattered. Since I was in the habit of always being honest, I thought I would probably wind up doing or saying something that would offend him, so I begged off. I really had no desire to meet him.

I was actually very busy at the time—our Czech-made electric generator was old and unreliable and I spent quite a bit of time tending to it. And I had some political situations of my own to deal with. Some of our mechanics—ethnic Thais—objected to my attempt to create a democratic atmosphere in the workplace. Previously, as mechanics, they had had more status than some of the other workers. They were vocal enough to make me suspect that they might try to sabotage the generator; hence, I often took shifts at night so I could watch over it. Many years later, in 1983, three of these ethnic Thais came to Phnom Penh, found me, and invited me to have dinner with them. They told me about the ethnic Thai Vietminh that had been operating in the cannery. One of these men, Say Phaov, had been a captain of my fishing fleet, and I had trusted him implicitly. In 1983, he served as a colonel in the Kampuchea Revolutionary Marines. In the 1940s, his grandfather, Say Phu Thang, had been second-in-command to Ho Chi Minh, and in Cambodia he was regarded as the highest ranking Indochinese communist.

But the mechanics weren't the worst of my problems—I also had to contend with the spirit world. After Prince Sihanouk had left my factory, the wife of one of my close subordinates dreamed that my wife was riding in a richly decorated chariot, like a queen. In the dream, people paraded Yan around the walls of my factory seven times. To a Cambodian, such a dream would be immediately recognized as a sign of divine recognition. In the morning, the woman rushed to our house to tell Yan (who hadn't left yet for Chbar Ampeou) about her dream. "Lady," she said, "you are going to have a son—Neak Meanbon, of course." In folk tradition, the Neak Meanbon is an individual who has gotten the absolute support of a being from one of the Heavenly Realms that manifests itself in his abilities as a powerful and decisive leader. This was almost like predicting that our son would be the Messiah.

In the West, my wife and my assistant's wife might have discussed this whimsically over cups of tea. But in our part of the world, such a story spreads quickly, and often becomes cause for jealousy. As a result of that dream, my working relationship with my staff went sour. Sok Lay, the foreman of the canning section, began reporting my activities in the factory on a day-to-day basis, to the secret police. Then he told the general manager that I was a communist. Finally, one rainy night, he connected an electrical wire to the north gate of the cannery, where I used to go on my rounds to check the night shift—his intention was to electrocute me.

But my guardian spirit Yeay Mao slapped Sok Lay hard in the face, and began strangling him in an excruciating manner. Sok Lay offered Yeay Mao a boiled chicken, a bunch of bananas, and a liter of rice wine, but the spirit would not let go until Sok Lay swore that he would not kill me. Then the spirit eased its grip and let him go free. I had no more trouble from Sok Lay after that. I learned of this incident through another man who happened to be walking by and saw the entire interaction.

In spite of the problems I had recounted above, our cannery operation was doing well. When I arrived, we had a fleet of thirty fishing boats at the factory; during my tenure there, the size of the fleet continued to expand to keep pace with the growing capacity of the canning operation, but these additional boats were privately owned, as the local people were keen to become involved in a joint venture.

But again our schedule was disrupted for political purposes. In March 1969, Premier Lon Nol and his minister of agriculture visited our cannery. After their tour of the facilities, I walked them to General Manager Sao Leang's residence, but did not stay for lunch. I later learned that following this visit, Lon Nol sent a colonel in civilian dress to work at the cannery and to send him reports.

Then, late in 1969, fishermen in boats equipped with weapons joined the fleet at my factory. This squad of twenty men came from South Vietnam. They were good fighters—they gave me a demonstration of their equipment and their skills. In hindsight, I should have thought more about the political implications of these weapons appearing at our peaceful port. But between Yan's pregnancy and my work at the factory, I had enough to keep me occupied.

And then the political situation in Cambodia caught everybody's attention, when on March 18, 1970, a radio broadcast from Phnom Penh declared a coup d'état. Cambodia had had a king since 600 A.D. and possibly earlier, and had regarded the king as either a god or as someone who had been appointed and was being guided by the gods. Most Cambodians had long ceased to believe that Prince Sihanouk was a god, but he had negotiated our independence from France, and had thus far kept us out of the war in Vietnam. Like many Cambodians, I was shocked.

POETS & PROPHETS

Grandpa Intda and Grandpa Pout were itinerant poets who traveled the countryside chanting verse, accompanying themselves on long-stringed guitar. Sometimes they performed together, sometimes not. They were prominent in the 1930s. It is said that they both had very sweet voices and that their songs seemed to have been channeled directly from heaven. In truth, they had memorized material passed down from the Angkor era. In 1935, King Monivong (who ruled from 1928-1941) invited them to perform for him at the Royal Palace. Shortly after that, the king of Siam invited them to Bangkok to perform at court. They were both probably in their fifties in the 1930s. No one is sure when they died.

From 1968 to 1970, Grandpa Intda's and Grandpa Pout's messages, from the Angkor era, were chanted and passed from person to person, but we regarded them only as myths, not as prophecies of what would befall our beloved homeland. These are ancient prophecies, using allegory to predict the future. Many of us, particularly intellectuals trained in the West, looked on those who paid any attention to these messages as being hopelessly superstitious. The West is hardly immune from apocalyptic thinking—witness the Y2K brouhaha. I contend that if one were to read Grandpa Intda's and Grandpa Pout's prophecies, detail by detail, analogy by analogy, allegory by allegory, one would see a blueprint for the Pol Pot phenomenon, and the years that followed under the Vietnamese regime. I remember hearing seers on the street in Phnom Penh reciting these messages, and warning us. I would always stop to listen, and mull over what they had said, and I began to write them down. The short meditative pieces I'd written in graduate school at Iowa no longer fit what I was experiencing. The line from Hamlet seemed appropriate: "Something is rotten in the state of Denmark." I was feeling the same way about the Kingdom of Angkor. I began thinking about writing a long poem titled "This Cursed Land," based loosely on Eliot's "The Waste Land." But the power and relevance of these prophecies didn't sink in until many years later, after the citizens of our country, myself included, had suffered untold agonies.

THE COUP D'ÉTAT & ARMY SERVICE

The first reports claimed that Lon Nol, who had previously commanded the country's armed forces and was now serving as prime minister, would continue as prime minister of the new government, but with far greater "emergency" powers; they announced that Prince Sirik Matak would be deputy prime minister, and they gave Chen Heng the title of chef d'état par interim. At the time, he was chairman of the National Assembly. I never had any real contact with him and never heard that much scuttlebutt about him either. I know that he eventually fled to France and wound up in the United States. He became an interpreter for the Cambodian community in Houston, Texas.

Sirik Matak was chosen to mollify the people by keeping the royal family involved in the new government. Matak was Sihanouk's cousin; his great-grandfather was King Sisowath. When King Monivong died in 1941, Sirik Matak's father should have assumed the throne, but he was an intellectual and the French considered him a potential problem. They didn't want a king who might ask questions. Sihanouk was only eighteen years old at the time, and he was something of a playboy. The French enthroned him as king, assuming that he would be malleable if they kept him entertained. His great-grandfather had been King Sisowath's brother. The quarrel between the two branches of the family had been going on for a long time, and seemed to have culminated in the coup d'état, which promised a return of the throne to the Sisowath line. But it wasn't a feud in the royal family, or Sihanouk's film fantasy that led to the coup. His national and international policy blunders caused his downfall.

Sihanouk's international mistakes grew out of a good idea—that small nations should stay neutral in the struggle between the superpowers. If he had done it right, the United States, China, and the Soviet Union would have all given Cambodia foreign aid, believing that we might secretly be their friend. Instead, each of the superpowers distrusted Sihanouk. Even as they gave him assistance, each plotted to undermine him.

Within Cambodia, he made the same mistake. Instead of making allies, Sihanouk made enemies. Cambodian military leaders didn't trust him because Thai and South Vietnamese troops were receiving money and equipment from the United States, while North Vietnamese and Viet Cong troops were receiving money and equipment from China, and they weren't getting anything. Cambodian businessmen and bankers didn't trust him at first because he couldn't procure foreign aid to stimulate economic growth; when he nationalized all the banks and the few industries that were thriving, they decided he had to go. Of course he alienated other members of the royal family with his ego and his wild antics. And he drove the communists into the jungle, where they quietly continued to grow stronger and stronger with assistance from China and Vietnam.

In January 1970, Sihanouk and his wife went to the French Riviera for a "rest cure." In his absence all the players began to make their moves. Sihanouk's troops downed a U.S. helicopter; U.S. planes attacked communist gun positions inside Cambodia in response to the downing of the helicopter; Lon Nol organized a number of anti-Vietnamese demonstrations including one in my home province, Svay Rieng. While the cat was away, all the mice were trying to get the cheese—control of the government.

Finally on March 13, Prince Sihanouk left the Riviera for a trip that would take him first to Moscow and then to Beijing, to shore up his support from both of these two communist rivals. While he was en route, a small CIA contingent in Saigon decided the time was ripe. They sent a signal, and the National Assembly promptly voted to remove Sihanouk from office. This may be an unsubstantiated rumor, but I believe that that was the sequence of events. In Cambodia at that time, people didn't hesitate where the CIA was concerned—they just carried out the command without question.

I had been in the process of preparing the reviewing stand for the inauguration of our remodeled cannery when I learned of the coup. I was landscaping the grounds to make them look beautiful, planting and transplanting flowers. Sihanouk was supposed to be the guest of honor. And then we heard, over the radio, that Sihanouk was a traitor. Although many of us were quite aware of faults as a person and as an administrator, this was nonetheless quite upsetting.

The governor of the province at that time, Young York Hang, convened a meeting, inviting all the head officials in the province—from the departments of forestry, education, and public works—including me, in my capacity as supervisor of the cannery. Before the meeting, I did my best to find out what was going on and who was involved. It was a full crowd, hundreds of people sitting there in the room. Once everyone came to order, the governor pointed at me first, because I was the only person with a master's degree in the province—apparently they thought that I was an authority, that I knew everything. He asked me "Monsieur Master (everyone in the province called me Monsieur Master in accordance with my degree), what do you think about the coup d'état? And now we're going to declare a republic. What is your opinion?"

I had no latitude to take sides—secret police were everywhere. I thought a moment, then said, "I've had lunch with representatives of the coup d'état since I was a youngster, but my hope for a republic has always remained up there in the clouds (I pointed up). Now if it becomes a reality here on earth, that will bring me great pleasure; my dream is becoming a reality!" Everybody clapped and shouted "Bravo! Bravo!"

And that was that—the meeting adjourned. The governor had asked for my opinion, and mine alone. When I spoke, they all agreed. This pleased me, of course, though I did find it somewhat puzzling. It seemed like an incident from one of those dreams you have just before waking, when you can influence the outcome in your favor.

Then, from Beijing, Sihanouk made a radio address that was heard by most of Cambodia. He claimed that the leaders of the coup were the traitors, and announced that he was joining a new "front" that would bring him back to power. And with that, he believed that he had joined the Khmer Rouge, and that upon victory, they would restore his power. He didn't realize that they were just using his popularity to gain power for themselves. In any event, war had been declared.

Two weeks later, flocks of young students, 2,000 of them, arrived by boat at my factory. Some shouted "Military Police? Bullshit!" Some wept, lamenting their impending plight. They had been recruited in Phnom Penh to be military policemen.

My factory became a military training site, and for a while, work came to a standstill. When the war broke they mobilized everybody, including the 250 workers in the factory, most of whom were eligible for the draft. Everyone had to join a unit called the "Commandos." They were supposed to receive military training in hand-to-hand combat and soldiering in general. They trained every morning and every afternoon to prepare for war, but it was not intensive—just a few hours. Everyone still received the same wages. Actually I just offered a job to anyone in the area who wanted to work. I could afford to be generous—it was the state's money. I let them work so that they could live. Without those wages, they would have had to become bandits or thieves.

As director of the cannery, I was considered an officer, and participated in the training when I could. I took target practice, and went on maneuvers, even at night in the swamps. Although there was no pressure to do so, I decided to submit an application for a commission. But before I actually signed up, a number of people tried to talk me out of my resolve to serve in the Army. The deputy governor said, "Little Brother, you are not a soldier. You are a professor, a philosopher—you are not a soldier! You cannot fight. Go to Phnom Penh and teach. Teach English. They need English teachers." I don't know why I didn't listen to him, but I didn't see any other honorable options. Another captain I knew said, "Monsieur Master, don't join the Army! Do you know what the Army means? You are not the type. You are a professor, you are a teacher, a mentor." He talked this way, every day, but his chatter did not deter me. So I filled out the application and waited.

Meanwhile, with the economy at a standstill, our factory had to become self-supporting. When the men weren't training, they fished, sold the catch, and divvied up the profits—without government control. We sold fish and shrimp to Thai merchants who bought everything we had, including snails. Even though we were right on the Thai border, we didn't need to bother with customs—our ships met theirs at sea, we made our deal, and transferred the fish from our ships to theirs.

In the middle of all this preparation for war, our son was born on April 21, 1970. It was during the day of the full moon, the Year of the Dog. I have already told you that everything of significance in my life always occurs on the day of the full moon. I was not present at his birth—Yan had gone to Chbar Ampeou to have the support of her mother, and to have access to the hospital facilities in Phnom Penh, should they be needed. I did not see our son until a month later. Yan reprimanded me for not being there, but her anger was short-lived; she forgave me immediately because, as she put it, "she understood my destiny." Naturally, we were both pleased with our son. We named him Bun Nol. He was strong, healthy, good-looking, and had a calm disposition.

But it seemed as if the destiny of the country would not let us celebrate. On June 13th, North Vietnamese troops invaded Kompong Speu Province, thirty miles west of Phnom Penh along u.s.-built

National Highway 4. A regiment of fresh troops that had trained at the fish cannery was sent, under the command of Major Heng Phon, to reinforce our troops at Kompong Speu. I was dismayed to hear that they became cannon fodder—the North Vietnamese massacred most of them. They had received only rudimentary training: close order drill, marching in formation, one-two, one-two, for a couple of mornings. That's hardly training for combat. Some of them didn't even know where the trigger was on a rifle, or where to load the cartridges. They just threw down their guns and ran. The majority of them were mowed down in one day. But when battle-hardened South Vietnamese troops joined in, we somehow recaptured the city.

There were many killers at large in our country at that time—South Vietnamese troops, North Vietnamese, B-52s, Viet Cong, Lon Nol's troops, Khmer Rouge, the United Front of the Cambodian Liberation, troops from the United States—and all their victims were innocent peasants. I felt terrible, devastated.

After that battle, I was eager to join the fight. Of course I didn't know how to fight—but I hadn't mentioned that in my letter of application. I also didn't know that a system for assigning rank was in place, along with a way to get around it. If you had medical training or a bachelor's degree, you automatically became a lieutenant. If you had a master's degree, as I did, you were assigned the rank of captain. But if you had any ambition, all you had to do was embellish whatever credentials you had, and ask for the rank of major or colonel—but no one tipped me off about this. I had simply filled out an application form and given it to the governor of the province, who in turn gave it to Lon Nol himself. And on my application letter he personally wrote *Oui—D'Accord*. And so I became a captain. As you will see, I later served in the National Assembly, and elected officials who were in the Army were supposed to get promoted to major automatically; if you served in Parliament for two years you were supposed to be promoted to lieutenant colonel. But alas, I "slipped through the cracks"—I never made it beyond captain, which, as it turned out, was actually fortuitous.

In late June, my commission as a captain in the Army came through; in the same mail packet was an announcement that they were transferring the governor, Young York Hang, to Phnom Penh to be the commander of a brigade. They replaced him with a colonel named Sei Ung, who was eventually promoted to general.

I was assigned to work with Sei Ung. Because I was the only one around who spoke English, he valued my services. He wanted me to stay at his side at all times. I was flattered. He designated me as the ground-to-air contact for our Air Force. I called for the reconnaissance airplane to fly over and locate the position of the Viet Cong, and then ordered air strikes. As it turned out, there were no Viet Cong—they were all ethnic Thais, and Cambodians, but we didn't know this. We were told we were fighting against the Viet Cong—that was the order from the top. In the Army you listen to your orders, you don't listen to anybody else. And our orders were to fight against Vietnamese communists.

Lon Nol's chief of staff sent most of the professors, and those with bachelor's and master's degrees—all political officers, like myself—off to Taiwan to be indoctrinated about the communist invasion all over the world. I was not sent, however—I got lost in the shuffle because I was based in Koh Kong. By this time Yan had returned with our son. While I tried to balance fatherhood with my new responsibilities, she started to work as a volunteer in the hospital, helping with the many casualties from combat. She regarded her work as important, and rightly so. She was doing the same work that Walt Whitman did. The rest of her time and energy went into mothering. Like most new parents, we were both a little confused at times—Yan must have wished we were still living in Chbar Ampeou, but she never said anything.

In August, the Khmer Vietminh launched an offensive on the Khmer Republic fortress around the nearby town of Dang Tuorng. The rainstorms were constant, night and day. My son was very little, so we carried him to bomb shelters in the rain—not a restful existence for an infant! Fortunately the attacks were brief, and Koh Kong returned to a semblance of normality.

Then general headquarters recruited me as a political officer. They sent me to the political school in Phnom Penh for six weeks. Yan could have accompanied me to Phnom Penh, but she didn't say anything, wouldn't talk about it—it was as if she had been captured by unknown forces, and could not leave Koh Kong. I fantasized about returning to the United States to study again. But I only fantasized, and could not step outside my life as it was, nor could Yan. We accepted things as they were.

In Phnom Penh, I was trained to visit troops around the country, giving speeches about the Indochinese communists. I still have the manual we used. It was accurate stuff, written by political scientists in Taiwan. Even though it was technically propaganda, it wasn't too distorted, especially the material dealing with the Vietnamese in Cambodia. I continue to believe that it was Ho Chi Minh's intention to eventually take over all of Indochina.

After the course was over, I went back to Koh Kong, for a brief visit with Yan, before they sent me out to barnstorm. I probably gave at least one speech to every battalion in the province—sometimes two a day, in different locations. If it were a long trip, by boat, then I'd wind up giving just one speech. When I was in Phnom Penh I'd go to my in-laws' house and just kill time between assignments. The speeches were about two hours long, with questions and answers afterwards. From late 1970 through most of 1971, my life consisted of these barnstorming trips, with occasional lulls either in Phnom Penh or in Koh Kong. Although it was not my intention, giving these speeches must have whetted my appetite for the political arena.

This is an abbreviated approximation of one of the barnstorming speeches I gave in those days:

Dear Fellow Combatants:

I wish to convey some important messages to all of you. Regarding the strategies of the war, this is going to be a long war—in essence, it is a war between the upholders of the universal laws, the Dhamma, and outlaws, who, you might say, follow the Non-Dhamma. To be direct about it, this is a war between capitalism and communism.

Remember that Cambodia is not a poor country—we have fertile soil, forests, the Mekong River, and the Great Lake, which offers us a plentiful supply of fish to feed our people. From the sea, we can harvest larger fish, shrimp, crabs, and other kinds of seafood. And we have an abundance of natural resources.

Do you have any idea how many mouths there are in Red China and how many mouths there are in *Yuon* Country? (*Yuon* is a derogatory Khmer word for Vietnam or Vietnamese.)

(Here I would pause significantly, and look from face to face in my audience). Do you? Too many for us to begin sharing our food with them. So we do not need to join the communist movement. If we join the communists, we will feed the Yuon and communist Red China, while our own children will go hungry. Ultimately, they will starve. Do you think that Red China and the Yuon care about the well-being of our children? No! They will milk our country dry while the lifeblood of our young turns to powder and is swept away by winds from the east and north.

So we have to defend our ideology. Let's fight for our independence. For freedom! For democracy! (Here, I would try to work them up, and maybe pace in front of them pensively.)

We should discuss the essence of this war. Yuon Ho Chi Minh persuaded Sihanouk to support his war against the United States. It is common knowledge that after breaking off relations with the United States, Sihanouk allowed Red China to supply weapons and military equipment through the seaport of Kompong Som, otherwise known as Sihanoukville. Sihanouk also allowed North Vietnamese troops and the Viet Cong to use our territory as sanctuaries. Cambodia belongs to Cambodians, my friends . . . to you, every one of you. Sihanouk should seek the approval of the National Assembly, your representatives, before granting the right of any foreign troops to use our territory! Do you agree with me?

Furthermore, Sihanouk ran away, abandoned us, his countrymen and women, on January 5, 1970. And in April of 1970 Sihanouk joined the North Vietnamese in massacring his own people! He may not have pulled the trigger or thrown a grenade, but he was instrumental in the planning and execution of this slaughter.

Everyone knows that Cambodians have never had the guts to kill their own flesh and blood. Very few Cambodians own guns. Cambodians do not know how to fight, and almost no Cambodians have had any military training. We were led like dumb beasts to the abattoir, and Sihanouk knew full well that this would happen! He used his own people as expendable pawns in his political machinations.

If you let the Yuon stay in Cambodia, they will never go away! All you have to do is look at Lower Cambodia—first the Yuon came there to make a living, and we welcomed them, but now they have proclaimed that this land is theirs, not ours! Do you understand what I am saying, my dear combatants? (Here, I would lean toward them and try to look intimidating and authoritative, which is not my true nature.)

Regarding the tactics of war, first, let us consider political warfare. We have the superpower, the United States of America, on our side. We will have access to any weapons and supplies we might need in defending our country and our nation, as long as we stick to the rules of war.

Psychological warfare is always an important aspect of a campaign, my dear combatants. Now we need the people more than ever to stand with us. We should be kind to our fellow citizens, take care of them when they need our help. Do not take anything that belongs to noncombatants. Even if it is a matter of one single chili, you must still ask for it. And if your request is denied, bow, and walk away.

Do not touch a daughter of a fellow citizen, without the consent of that daughter. Remember, we fight against the Yuon invaders not against our own people. Do not turn your neighbor into your enemy by taking advantage of him or her. This is only common sense, common decency. War brings out both the best and the worst in people—do not compromise your standards, do not give in to shoddy behavior—your actions will influence everyone around you.

And then there is popular warfare, my dear combatants. If we walk on high moral ground and our fellow citizens recognize this, then they will join the fight. They will trust us. They will give us information as to the whereabouts of the Yuon. Together, we will stand! If we go it alone, we die!

Thank you for your time! Good Luck! Buddham, Dhammam, Sangham bless you all!

Fortunately, for me, and probably for the troops, the Army never assigned me to combat, because during this period war raged throughout our country. North Vietnamese and South Vietnamese forces attacked each other. American B-52s dropped hundreds of thousands of tons of bombs that turned farmers into refugees in their own country. With no one to plant rice, famine followed. Through it all, Cambodian forces kept losing provinces, regaining them, and losing them again. And Lon Nol, Sirik Matak, Cheng Heng, and Son Ngoc Thanh continued to elbow each other, as they queued up for American money and political power.

Meanwhile I was either barnstorming as a political officer, or using my technical skills to take care of the generators for transmissions, or serving as an administrator, preparing logistics, and working out the budget for salaries and supplies.

During my military service I wrote many poems, but few survived the Khmer Rouge. Here is one of the few I have found from that period. My poem confirms a sad truth: each time the details are different, and yet each war brings the same pain.

Only Mothers Will Ever Embrace Sorrow

I wade through solitude
to the cottage where we used to
gather to drink rice wine,
enjoying false peace.

I sit under the same palm leaf roof,
gaze at your chairs
but see no one,
hear only your laughs.

Here, it's like everywhere else—
deserted,
villages of black roofless houses;
I don't see even one dog.

The explosions of mines,
the roaring of heavy artillery
from frontier to frontier, shake every
grain of pollen from the champa flowers.

No places to hide, no skies under which to rest;
and the moaning of children,
and the cries of mothers
out of the blazing fire across the land.

And your bodies, brothers, shielding us
from the bullets, and your blood
splashing over our Mother, inducing my soul
to ever worship jasmine and lotus blossoms.

MY INVISIBLE SISTER

Many of us in Cambodia have personal guardian spirits. I discovered mine in 1972. The Vietnam War had found its way into our country, and the Khmer Republic was proving a disappointment, making me agitated and restless. One day in late November I decided to visit Auntie Yen's house, a trusted friend and medium, whom I mentioned earlier. Once we were seated in front of her, she became possessed by a spirit who introduced herself to me as Bido Mean Roeuddhi, my Invisible Sister from Indtanimit Borei, the Magic City, which is an invisible island here on earth, possibly in the Indian Ocean, although no one is exactly sure of its whereabouts.

Bido explained that I was her older brother and that we had another sibling, a sister who was the youngest of the three. She told me that one day I was walking with her in the garden, and I told her that I was going to pick a flower, a forbidden action. Just as I was reaching for the stem of the flower, I disappeared, instantly dismissed from the Second Realm for my sin. Since she had been looking for me, she said, I had gone through several incarnations, but she did not know exactly how many.

"For forty years I have been looking for you, my big brother," she explained. "I searched in the eternal fires of the underworld. I looked in Kirivonghat in the Himalayas (a mythical area from which no one has ever returned), and in the Sacred Naga (Cobra) Kingdom, but I could not find you. One night I fell asleep, exhausted, in a cave, or so I thought. But when I woke, I discovered that I was really in the Sacred Naga's mouth. He is our spirit father. He gave me a pearl to protect you from the fire to come." Tears rolled down her soft cheeks. She dabbed at them with a white handkerchief, and there was a pearl between her thumb and index finger, small, but brilliant. She presented it to me, and I have kept it with me ever since.

Bido has great power—she is capable of sneaking anywhere to spy on or to communicate with other realms, such as Heaven, the Naga Realm, the realm of the deities in Cambodia or the United States or in Spain to gather information concerning my safety. Since Bido met me that first time she has been taking care of me, helping me acquire, at various times, wealth, security, healing, and even arranging for other lives to be exchanged for my own. But she has not been able to bring freedom and democracy to Cambodia.

CHAPTER THIRTEEN: 1972-1973

I BECOME A POLITICIAN

War continued to rage in Vietnam and in Cambodia, but we pinned our hopes on the newly declared Khmer Republic. After more than fifteen hundred years of being ruled by kings and princes and foreign countries, it felt as if we were finally becoming a modern nation. In April 1972, a constitution was approved by a popular referendum, and in May, elections for president were announced for the following month. Even the possibility that we might finally have an elected president "of the people, by the people, for the people," filled me with pride.

On election day, I asked every motorcycle taxi driver I saw to drive through the streets encouraging people to vote for Lon Nol. When my commander, General Sei Ung, found out what I was up to, he was concerned. "What are you doing, Captain?" he warned, "Don't you know that's wrong?"

I said, "No, it's politics, isn't it?"

"You shouldn't do it," he replied.

It was, of course, a fixed election, although I didn't realize it until later. The candidates were Lon Nol, prime minister and previously head of the armed forces, In Tam, chairman of the National Assembly, and Keo An, dean of the Phnom Penh University law school. Keo An's campaign promise was that if he were elected he would invite Samdech Sihanouk home from exile, and the two of them, in collaboration with the Khmer communists, would solve all the problems besetting the country.

But it was the soldiers who made the difference; they overwhelmingly supported Lon Nol, who had won their loyalty over many years. In Tam won at the civilian polls, but because the soldiers actually counted the votes, Lon Nol won the election. Accusations of impropriety flew thick and fast. In Tam was so furious with Lon Nol that the new U.S. ambassador to Cambodia, Emory Swank, had to set up a meeting to reconcile the two of them or the entire government, such as it was, might have toppled.

After the presidential election we prepared for the Parliamentary election. Son Ngoc Thanh reentered the picture around that time, when Lon Nol appointed him prime minister. Son Ngoc Thanh had been one of the founders of the first Khmer language newspaper, and one of the grand old men of the independence movement going back to the mid-1930s. But a long feud with Sihanouk led him to become allied with the CIA and the U.S.-backed South Vietnamese government. Son Ngoc Thanh had built a small army of his own in South Vietnam, trained by the CIA. They were called Mag Force, and as a unit they were very impressive. When Lon Nol appointed him prime minister, Son Ngoc Thanh brought his troops from Vietnam to fight in Cambodia, but Sirik Matak shrewdly broke the Mag Force into small units that were dispersed into the Army of the Khmer Republic. Before long, Son Ngoc Thanh lost the muscle he needed to legitimize his power as prime minister, leaving Lon Nol to run the show. As for the ultimate fate of Mag Force—they were very good soldiers, but eventually the Khmer Rouge killed them all, down to the last man.

Prior to the election, a committee went to Koh Kong to search for candidates. They didn't have to search far. Everybody and his uncle submitted applications for the National Assembly. And after reviewing the qualifications of the proposed candidates, I decided to throw *my* hat into the ring.

At first, General Sei Ung, my commander, rejected my application. He told me he thought I could best serve the province by continuing as his second-in-command, but I wasn't convinced. I went to Phnom Penh to consult my brother, An, who was a member of the democracy movement. He pled my case to Son Ngoc Thanh, who told the election committee to put my name on the list as a candidate for the National Assembly.

It's one thing to get on the ballot, and another thing to win, and I had no idea how it would turn out. The word on the street had it that whoever wound up listed first on the ballot, got voted in. Three parties—the Social-Republicans, the Democrats, and the Republicans—were announced. The candidates were In Tam, president of the Democratic Party, Prince Sisowath Sirik Matak, president of the Republican Party, and Lon Non, Lon Nol's little brother, who was secretary general of the Social-Republican Party. At that time I still believed in Lon Nol, and ran as a Social-Republican. My opponent turned out to be Chhay Neth, my classmate in California. Once he heard I was running, he dropped out; hence "Monsieur Master" ran uncontested.

Our constitution guaranteed that soldiers had the right to vote, so the results of the election were a foregone conclusion; accordingly, In Tam and Sisowath Sirik Matak withdrew from the race for prime minister, and their parties followed suit. Powerful forces that were still nebulous to me at the time pushed me to represent Koh Kong in the Assembly.

The election was held on September 3rd and 17th, 1972, and all candidates ran uncontested; we all "won" seats in the National Assembly. The Assembly opened at the end of September 1972. General Thappana Nginn called the names of the elected assemblymen in alphabetical order. Mine was the last to be called. The ceremony of the opening of the National Assembly was presided over by the president of the Khmer Republic. I was one of 126 members, and like a swarm of flies, we did nothing, just buzzed around. Oh, we had many debates about finances, but most of the young intellectuals were naive. A number of them listened to me, but I myself didn't really understand the machinations of politics. Lon Nol, on the other hand, took to it instinctively. He broke us up into three or four factions, to keep any one group from gaining too much momentum—one group in the National

Assembly might be pro-Lon Nol, another might be pro-Hang Thun Hack (who had been a professional playwright), and so on.

Immediately after the election we hurriedly moved back in with Yan's parents in Chbar Ampeou—they were quite pleased at this turn of events, especially that their grandson would be a daily part of their lives. I set up a "field office" in Koh Kong, which consisted of little more than a shack. A soldier and his family lived there as caretakers. It is where I stayed and conducted business whenever I made my sporadic visits back to look in on my constituency.

It was clear to me that I did not understand politics, but I did understand numbers. Soon, spotting and speaking out against corruption became my forte, and the more I saw, the more disillusioned I became. On one occasion, Lon Nol submitted a 121-million-riel budget to build a series of protective fences around the Presidential Palace. Several of us in the Assembly who had backgrounds in engineering calculated that a mere six million would accomplish the job more than adequately. But the majority of the committee figured that Lon Nol might take an appropriation of only six million riels as an insult, and would lobby against it, so they bumped it up to twenty million to get it through. Then it went up to the National Assembly for discussion and adoption, and even though I had been on the committee that sent the bill to the floor for a vote, I argued against it. I thought we needed to reserve our limited resources for education and health. But I didn't know about the power of the presidency—that you could do anything you wanted once you got in. Inevitably, Lon Nol somehow wound up getting the 121 million riels, despite the fact that the Assembly killed the appropriation. This bit of chicanery took place in December 1972.

The only result of my opposition to the bill was that I was observed with increased scrutiny. To give you an idea of the absurdity of the times, Lon Nol started to suspect that I was one of the communists in the National Assembly because *I didn't have a car*. But the Great Spirit was protecting me and nothing came of it.

Of course while all this was going on, the civil war was driving farmers out of their fields, until our nation—which once not only fed itself, but was able to *export* rice—now had to ask the U.S. for food. In October, Henry Kissinger visited, and before he left, Lon Nol agreed to let U.S. advisors into Cambodia to fight the Viet Cong. And somehow, whenever Americans came to a Southeast Asian country, corruption followed, despite their best intentions. They sent us rice, medicine, and weapons, but most of it found its way to the communist forces who were using Sihanouk as a front. The government troops had no guns and no rice. Ambassador Swank was aware of all this, but unable to stop it. The press in the U.S. didn't learn of such shenanigans until after the fall of Pol Pot.

Unfortunately graft didn't end with the armed forces. Most of the legislators were more interested in using their influence to make themselves rich than in assisting their constituents. Once they became assemblymen they established a business, or more likely several businesses that "somehow" wound up with very favorable government contracts. They'd just go back and forth from their offices at the Assembly, to their businesses, and back again, and from what I've heard, it continues to this day. They had the usual list of excuses—their salaries weren't enough to live on, or everyone did it—but corruption is corruption. Even today in Cambodia, you may find that your taxi driver is a major in the Army—everyone moonlights, just to make enough to get by.

But the most egregious example of corruption was the "ghost soldier" scandal. When it came to Cambodia's treasury, the cupboard was pretty much bare, so the United States offered to subsidize salaries for the armed forces. Each general sent paperwork to headquarters with a list of soldiers under his command, and headquarters sent the money back to the generals to disperse to the troops. But for every flesh-and-blood soldier in the field, the generals made up at least ten additional "ghost soldiers" and pocketed their salaries, along with half the money that was supposed to have gone to the real soldiers. When the National

Assembly held hearings to get to the bottom of this, the generals were fairly brazen. One general actually had the nerve to say, "If you'd like to have real soldiers, why don't you go ahead and join up?" What could we do? In theory, the civilian government supervised the Army, but in fact, they had the men and arms, and our power wasn't worth anymore than the signs on our doors. One should not get the impression that this "ghost soldier" phenomenon was limited to just that particular moment in time; in fact, it had been going on for aeons. This practice was symptomatic of Cambodian society and was one of the reasons we had always suffered military catastrophes.

As 1973 began, the United States signed the Paris Accord, which called for them to withdraw from Cambodia along with Vietnamese troops. Lon Nol declared a cease-fire, and in a radio address, offered amnesty to any Viet Cong, North Vietnamese, or Khmer communists who were willing to surrender, but civil war continued to ravage our country, and foreign "assistance" assured that both sides would be able to kill each other with increased efficiency.

Lon Nol had good political instincts, but he was not an effective administrator; he not only failed to learn from his mistakes, but compounded them. By the end of January 1973 he actually took over everything, even down to the level of commanding individual battalions. We had the trappings of democracy—a president, a prime minister, a parliament with an upper and lower house, and a judicial branch—but in actual fact we were living under a dictatorship. As they say in human resource manuals today, it was a clear example of "top-down" management.

My impressions of Lon Nol were not particularly positive. I noticed, of course, that his left arm was paralyzed. Whenever I saw him at meetings of the National Assembly I thought that he did not seem to be very intelligent and that he appeared to be indifferent to everything. I heard from my colleagues that he never paid attention to the opinions of "outsiders." In fact, he wouldn't take advice in general. I was told that he believed only in superstitions and that his medium was the only advisor he trusted. I recently heard, on a Free Asia broadcast, that he spent the equivalent of $25,000 a month on fortune-tellers. Around March 1973, Captain So Photra, Sihanouk's son-in-law, dropped two bombs intended for the Presidential Palace, killing more than a hundred people. Accordingly, Hang Thun Hak resigned as prime minister on April 17, 1973. Hang Thun Hak had been prime minister since the National Assembly was sworn in on October 17, 1972. He was a member of the Dang Rek Mountain contingent, second to Son Ngoc Thanh, who had been prime minister from March 20 to October 14, 1972. The people in most of the key posts had remained the same after Son Ngoc Thanh's resignation.

Then, on April 24, 1973, President Lon Nol suspended the two houses for six months, based on Article 39 of the Constitution of the Khmer Republic and set up a High Political Council. In Tam proposed himself as prime minister, with Lon Nol as chairman, Sirik Matak as vice chairman, and Cheng Heng as member-at-large.

Once In Tam became prime minister he announced that in order to bring about peace more efficiently, he was sending the members of Parliament on vacation. Parliament was not formally dissolved—but no more meetings were held. The members still drew their salaries, but they couldn't convene a General Assembly for six months.

Next, In Tam attempted to settle peace with the Khmer Rouge —"the other side." But in six months he didn't accomplish a thing in that direction. He was not very shrewd, and had no idea how to approach Sihanouk, who was living the life of a "leader-in-exile" in Beijing. He might have sought out Kissinger—not that that would have helped. Kissinger was basking in praise over the Paris Accord and didn't want to take responsibility for the devastation in Cambodia. In Tam tried to persuade the Khmer Rouge to desist, but he could never find anyone who would speak for them. Officially there *was* no Khmer Rouge, which made any attempt to negotiate peace with them a protean prospect. So the

U.S. Air Force continued to drop bombs, the Khmer Rouge continued to control more and more of the country, and more and more Cambodians died from gunfire, disease, and famine.

While all this was going on, an unexpected honor came my way. In early March of 1973 some of the original members of the independence movement were organizing a Cambodian branch of the Asian Parliamentarian Union (APU). To my surprise I was elected secretary general of the APU, and invited to Taipei to participate in their general meeting on culture. Dr. Ku Cheng Kang, the honorary chairman of the World League for Freedom and Democracy, was in attendance. After the APU meeting, Dr. Kang invited me to stay on in Taipei for another two weeks to participate in the Asian Peoples Anti-Communist League. This might lead you to assume that I had done something to create a favorable impression. Actually, the situation was more a case of the League wanting to have faces sitting behind their respective flags. Their goal was to indoctrinate us—to actually saturate us with information about freedom and democracy from as wide a variety of top-notch sources as possible. And this they did.

Upon my return from Taipei, on March 25th, President Lon Nol appointed me as secretary general of the Khmer Anti-Communist League. (Every country in Asia had a chapter with slight variations in its name. In Indonesia it's called the Anti-Communist Front, for instance.) Dr. Duan Chuong, my fellow assemblyman, and consultant to Lon Nol, proposed me for this position. He was president of the League, and also a professor of the school of medicine. He favored me because he knew my brother, An, and also because I spoke English fluently; he knew that I would be an effective go-between. Duan Chuong was *Khmer Krom* (a Cambodian from South Vietnam), and sympathetic, philosophically, with Son Ngoc Thanh. I agreed to accept the appointment under one condition: I wanted the name changed to the Khmer League for Freedom; my condition was accepted.

In July 1973, I once again found myself in Washington, DC, but this time I wasn't a timid student eating dog food because I didn't know any better; I was representing my country at the General Assembly of the World Anti-Communist League. The keynote speaker was retired Admiral John S. McCain, Jr., former commander in chief of the U.S. Pacific Command (and the father of the well-known Republican Senator John McCain). I remember that Admiral McCain spoke to us about Soviet submarines.

Admiral McCain was a close associate of Lon Nol. In fact, Lon Nol asked me to present a copy of his book, *Samgrama*, to Admiral McCain at his residence. I remember this clearly. I was starting to become impressed with myself. I was one of three delegates representing Cambodia, each with a different portfolio—one attended sessions on the subject of mass organization; one attended sessions regarding youth-related organizational opportunities; and I was selected as the "generalist," and attended meetings on a broad range of issues. I would be hard pressed to tell you what we discussed. In truth, I think my primary function in being there was to raise my hand in support of whatever Taiwan proposed. Whether or not the meeting was successful, again, I am not sure, but I remember feeling proud of myself.

Before we left, several members of Congress took me aside and said, "You can't return to your country . . . stay here . . . you cannot win." I listened politely, but nonetheless returned home, totally obsessed with the dream of a working democracy in my homeland.

Democracy looked so good in America, but America wasn't looking good in Cambodia. In August 1973, shortly after I returned, a U.S. B-52 dropped all its bombs on Neak Luong, a bustling river town thirty miles east of Phnom Penh, an area that later became known infamously as the Killing Fields (more about this phrase later). One of my uncles, a lieutenant, was one of more than a hundred people killed that day, and of course hundreds more were wounded. In the chaos of the moment, he was decapitated by a helicopter to which he was returning.

The movie *The Killing Fields* chronicles American journalist Sydney Schanberg's efforts at revealing this scandal. I heard personally that the bombing was the result of a spy among Lon Nol's troops, who told the air-ground support, the B-52s of the Seventh Fleet, that the Viet Cong had built a gigantic fortress in Neak Luong. Actually, the Viet Cong were five miles away from that area, but immediately after the bombing they recognized their opportunity, swarmed in, and took over. One blunder led to another; the war was like a train wreck in slow motion.

U Sam Oeur and Dy Yan during their engagement.

U Sam Oeur in Mike Lally's
apartment, Iowa City, 1967.

Photo by Mike Lally

"May Peace Prevail in Cambodia,"
as it appeared in Prince Sihanouk's
magazine *Kampujea,* April 1967.

U Sam Oeur in Khmer Republic Army uniform, 1973.

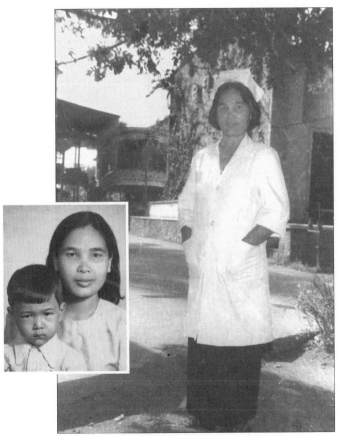

Sim Syna (Dy Yan), 1990.
Inset: Dy Yan and son Bun Nol, 1974.

East bank of the Mekong, near Pre Ta Am,
where author buried his twin daughters in 1975.

Photo by Ken McCullough, 2000

Ken McCullough and U Sam Oeur
upon his return to Iowa in 1992.

Photo by Ed Trebes, courtesy of *Iowa Alumni Review.*

Author's house in Chbar Ampeou.

Photo by Ken McCullough, 2000.

Sim Syna, with author's sister U Touch, in the village of Thlok at a Sen ceremony (offering food to ancestors by way of asking them for permission to leave the country).

Photo by Ken McCullough, 2000.

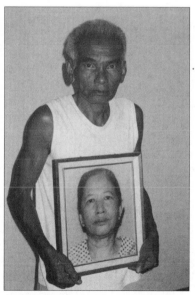

Prum Choeun with photo of Auntie Yen.

Photo by Ken McCullough, 2000.

U Sam Oeur and Sim Syna, on a visit to Minnesota in 2004.

Photo by Ken McCullough.

The grandchildren, John, Daniel, and Edward.

Photo by U Sam Oeur, 2005.

OVR DOWNFALL FORESEEN

In 1973, Bido Mean Roeuddhi, my Invisible Sister, had foreseen the downfall of the Khmer Republic. She went to Spain to beg for mercy from the deity of that land to accept me as ambassador of Cambodia to Spain. But I didn't believe that the United States would abandon Cambodia, which they did in 1975. So I was noncommittal to her proposition. I just wanted to restore peace to my motherland. Bido had told me repeatedly that I could not carry the country by myself. She invited the Princess of Spain to possess Auntie Yen, the medium, in an attempt to persuade me. We didn't actually talk to each other directly, for she was prohibited from speaking English and I could not understand Spanish.

The Princess of Spain was slender, and beautiful like an angel. She wore a white dress. She was sixteen years old at the time, and has remained that age to the present. I adored her immediately. We looked at each other for a long time; then I spoke to her in English. "How are you, my pretty princess?" I greeted her. She nodded her head, indicating, to my reckoning, that she was fine. "Does my pretty princess think that I should become the ambassador from Cambodia to the princess's land?" She nodded her head again. "Why don't you speak English for a few words?" I asked. She shook her head. Then the Princess of Spain left Auntie Yen, but Auntie was immediately possessed by Bido again. Bido explained to me that the Princess of Spain had accepted me as ambassador, but I wasn't convinced. "How can I go if the government doesn't nominate me?" I asked.

"If you say yes, then I will persuade Lon Nol to nominate you this very moment."

But I balked at this chance—I didn't have the courage to say yes.

FROM HIGH HONOR, TO UNHOLY HELL

The occupants of the government offices changed as if they were going around and around in a revolving door, but from the moment the National Assembly gave power to Lon Nol, he never relinquished it until shortly before the fall of Phnom Penh. In December 1973, Lon Nol asked Long Boret to serve as his new prime minister. Long Boret reconvened Parliament, and announced that considering the volatile times, the selection of Cambodia's United Nations delegation was the next order of business. Lon Nol selected the minister of foreign affairs, the chief of staff of the military, General Sak Sutsakhan, and General Les Ko Sem as members of the delegation, but two National Assemblymen and one senator were also to serve in the delegation, and they were to be elected by Congress.

Bido, my Invisible Sister, pushed me to put my name on the ballot, but I didn't believe anything would come of it. Who would elect me to the United Nations? In the past, the wealthy members of Parliament had always been selected. It was a plum assignment—everyone wanted to go. But Bido said to me, "just put your name on the ballot. Little Sister is going to take care of everything for Big Brother. Don't worry about it." So I did.

Of course I was on a long list of candidates, and didn't know anything about campaigning. But my sister-in-law, Long Van Thet, my brother An's wife, was a member of Parliament, and she lobbied on my behalf. (In Cambodian culture, the spouse does not take her husband's family name, but their children do.) One-third of Parliament was Son Ngoc Thanh's party, and they helped me. I spoke to one, and he bent the ear of another, and when the votes were counted, I was one of the two National Assemblymen selected to join the Cambodian delegation to the United Nations to negotiate for peace. The election took place in June 1974. It was the highest honor I could imagine. Of course it was an honor that involved considerable risk, but I was not aware of that at the time. As I now recall the other delegates who joined me on that important mission, I believe they are almost all dead, killed during the Pol Pot years.

But even though, in hindsight, it seems clear now that the days of the Khmer Republic were coming perilously close to the end, I still had hope, like a flame that can't be extinguished no matter how much water is poured over it. The fighting back in Cambodia was very fierce at the time. The American presence in Vietnam was waning, and the Khmer Rouge leaders were coming out in the open, now that their army was taking territory all over the country.

In early August 1974 I left Phnom Penh for the Los Angeles area, where I still had friends from my college days. I traveled with Assemblyman Lu Lay Sreng, another delegate, and his family. His plan was to leave them in L.A. where they owned a house, then travel with me to New York.

I spent a few weeks in Long Beach, before heading to New York. I stayed with an old friend, Smith Leng. He had been my roommate and classmate in 1958 when we studied at the School of Arts and Trade in Phnom Penh, and we wound up together again in Washington, DC in the fall of 1961. In the spring of 1962 I was transferred to California State–Los Angeles, and Leng went to Long Beach State University. I also visited with Ell Sean, who had been my roommate when we'd studied industrial arts together in L.A. He had stayed on in the States, finding work in the L.A. area. After I told him my war stories, he told me how much he hated Sihanouk, even though he was Sihanouk's cousin. He said that if he had to choose between going to Africa or Cambodia he'd choose Africa, where he could hunt big game animals, because if he went to Cambodia he might hunt Sihanouk. I had no idea what

had happened between Sean and Sihanouk. Actually I wasn't convinced that they were cousins, since their family names were
different, but I humored him anyway. While I was visiting, many
friends came to see me. They threw a big party in my honor, and
after dinner they showed pornographic films. I wound up getting
very drunk.

The next day, on August 17th, we left Long Beach for New York
City, to attend the 27th General Assembly. When we arrived at JFK
International Airport I thought of its namesake, and my mind
went back to November 1963. Tears rolled down my cheeks just as
they had at my own father's cremation ceremony.

We took a Yellow Cab to the Newton Hotel, two blocks from
U.N. Headquarters, to settle into our rooms, but the manager of
the hotel told us that we were two weeks early. So we had to go
to see Ambassador Chhut Chhoeur to arrange for our rooms.
That was a fifteen-block walk each way, in mid-August heat—this
cleared my head pretty well. Then I walked over by myself, to see
the U.N. Building.

I had been to New York twice—in the fall of 1961, when Prince
Sihanouk had come to participate in the U.N. General Assembly
all Cambodian students in the U.S. had been invited to have
lunch with him at his hotel (that was during my stay in
Georgetown). Then, in 1963, during my second year as a student
in L.A., we took a field trip to New York and visited the Statue of
Liberty and the U.N. But I was still walking around like a water
buffalo in those days—I certainly had no notion that I would be
returning as a diplomat.

This time was different. There it was, all thirty-nine stories!
The shining aluminum and the green-tinted glass were dazzling
in the midafternoon sunlight. Across from the U.N. Building was
a large, concave cement wall with this inscription etched into it:
AND THEY SHALL BEAT THEIR SWORDS INTO PLOW-
SHARES, AND THEIR SPEARS INTO PRUNING HOOKS:
NATION SHALL NOT LIFT UP SWORD AGAINST NATION,
NEITHER SHALL THEY LEARN WAR ANY MORE. I confess that

tears again came to my eyes—this was the vortex of political action for the entire world, and I was here, on the verge of taking my place within it. I went to my hotel in a daze and slept a deep dreamless sleep.

My room had a kitchenette, so I spent some time, during the next few days, buying cheap cooking items and basic groceries, like rice. As I walked around New York, I thought of Whitman: "the blab of the pave, tires of carts, sluff of boot-soles, talk of the promenaders." This is what I was hearing. I absorbed the images of the city. Though I had seen New York before, I still felt my body floating in the air. Everything amazed me—the buildings invading the sky, the perfect streets. Most of all I wondered who was going to buy the merchandise in all those big department stores. How were the owners going to pay the rent? How could they possibly make a profit? In Cambodia, a prosperous Chinese merchant would open a store, but not to sell what they displayed. They didn't make their profit off that merchandise—it was just a front for what they were really selling, sometimes legal, sometimes not.

As I walked, I studied faces, and I recalled the ease with which, they say, Whitman could converse with ordinary people. And here they were, around me everywhere: "The carpenter singing as he measures his plank . . . The mason singing as he makes ready for work . . . The boatman singing what belongs to him in his boat . . . the shoemaker . . . the hatter . . ." All laughing and talking away in loud, happy voices, some of them with accents, some of them with features similar to mine.

Another day I went down to Battery Park and took the Staten Island Ferry, and Whitman's lines played through my head: "Others will enter the gates of the ferry and cross from shore to shore. . . . Others will see the shipping of Manhattan north and west, and the heights of Brooklyn to the south and east . . . A hundred years hence . . . others will see them. . . . It avails not time nor place . . . just as you feel when you look at the river and sky, so I felt. . . . Just as you stand and lean on the rail . . . I stood." A peace settled over me unlike anything I had ever felt before. I actually felt as if Whitman were standing there at my elbow.

Two weeks later, Senator Hem Chamroeun, Ith Sareth (director of the Khmer Press Agency), Ambassador to South Korea Pok
Thoeun, and General Les Ko Sem showed up at the Newton,
while Prime Minister Long Boret, Foreign Minister Keuk-Ky Lim,
and General Sak Sutsakhan took rooms at another hotel. For
some reason, after all these years, I still remember my room number—405.

The main objective of our delegation was to secure a peaceful
settlement to our deteriorating situation at home. But all my fellow members seemed to be busy with extracurricular matters, so
they assigned *me* to attend the General Assembly. Prime Minister
Long Boret and Foreign Minister Keuk-Ky Lim spent most of
their time lobbying other nations. I rarely saw Lu Lay Sreng and
never did find out what his assignment was.

Each day I put on my ID, which allowed me entrance to the
General Assembly. The assembly room was huge, lit in an almost
celestial way, the tables arranged like water buffalo horns. There
were 190 tables, one per country, each with five seats. Observer
seats were positioned to the right and left of the delegate tables,
on a plank about eighteen inches higher than the delegates.

I went into the situation with high aspirations, thinking that I
would be given opportunities to step forward and offer my opinions, but in reality my opportunities were far more limited.
Ambassador Chhut Chhoeur instructed me to pay close attention—my primary function was to press the red button for *no*, or
the yellow for *abstention* whenever the African countries and the
communist countries presented a proposal. I basically had my
orders, with no other options. Whenever our delegation made a
proposal, second-rank diplomats from those other countries
were assigned to give us the red or yellow response. This system
was disappointing, but I did not become cynical.

If a resolution of real importance to Cambodia were scheduled,
Ambassador Chhut Chhoeur would show up to press the green
button for *yes*. And whenever a VIP of Kissinger status was on the
agenda, Ambassador Chhut Chhoeur, Ambassador Pok Thoeun,

General Sak Sutsakhan, Ith Sareth, and other dignitaries from our delegation came, and I wound up in one of the observer seats.

Kurt Waldheim was serving as secretary general at the time, and actually presided over many of the meetings—a tall, slim, remote presence. Once, after he returned from a World Food Conference in Rome, I listened to one of his speeches. He spoke clearly, but he wasn't particularly inspiring. Nonetheless I decided that this would be my moment to shake his hand and introduce myself. But when I met his eye, I felt that his look showed disdain. I walked away, and that was that.

Between sessions, members would congregate in the lounge for drinks. On two occasions I entered the lounge to see if I could strike up conversations with some of the African diplomats. Several were well-spoken in both English and French, as was I, so I thought I'd make an attempt at bypassing the red-yellow protocol. I consider myself dark brown, even for a Cambodian, but the African diplomats were almost blue-black—quite striking. Whenever I approached, their reaction to me was the same—they regarded me as if I were a white man, not as an Asian. I can't define the distinction, but it was something I sensed on a biochemical level. In any event, my overtures did not bear fruit.

I didn't frequent the lounge, but it was a good place to track down SEATO delegates (South East Asian Treaty Organization—from the Philippines, Singapore, Malaysia, Thailand, or Indonesia), introduce myself, and lobby their support for the Khmer Republic. Every evening I returned to the hotel loaded down with documents: transcripts of speeches, declarations of universal human rights, international laws, resolutions, etc. After each session, members would often leave papers and notes on their desks. I collected those left by groups or individuals who had just stated something that interested me, and pored over them to see if I could glean any kernels of wisdom. My hunger was insatiable. During four months I accumulated more papers than I was allowed to ship home.

My life was fairly solitary, in part because I was trying to save money. I missed Yan and Bun Nol and wondered how they were doing, but our letters back and forth on this trip were rare. Yan's were chattier than mine, reporting neighborhood gossip, while mine were laced with platitudes related to our mission.

Occasionally I ate at the U.N., but more often than not, I ate by myself in my room. I'd cook up some rice in my rice cooker, and add vegetables out of a can. Only twice did I actually order a sit-down meal. I got in the habit, which persists to this day, of ordering a steak and a glass of red wine, not to be Frenchified, but to fortify my blood. During my entire stay, no one invited me to a famous restaurant, and I regarded it as somewhat sinful to eat an expensive meal by myself, so I never did experience the haute cuisine of New York.

On my weekend outings, I'd buy whatever was handy from a street vendor. I remember buying one of those huge hot pretzels and dabbing mustard on it as I had seen others do—not bad, but too big and too much dough for my palate—I left half of it near a trash barrel so that the squirrels might feast on it.

On several weekends I went to the Statue of Liberty. The statue really stirred my emotions—I wondered what it would be like for Cambodia to have a statue of this magnitude symbolizing human freedom. I climbed up to The Lady's eyes to contemplate the beautiful panorama of New York City.

New York used to be referred to as the Melting Pot of the World. I got a glimmer of this whenever I rode the subway and had the opportunity to observe the incredible gallery of faces. Had Leonardo da Vinci grown up in New York, his sketchbooks would have been overflowing. In the subways I saw faces in repose; in the streets, they burst into flower. Walking in New York was like watching an endless living, breathing, kinetic tableau of humanity.

But I took no notes. I was not there to be a poet. I was there to be a diplomat, to represent my country, to study the world situation and apply what I could at home. I am a bit of a dreamer, I admit, but have never really been a stroller and idler in the way of Whitman. Then, I had neither the time nor the focus. I was looking at the "big picture" and often missing out on the magnificence of the details. But one day I happened to notice the smell of the autumn air—a mixture of sunlight, decay, sweat, cooking food, standing water, diesel exhaust, and the odor of verticality, if such a thing exists. A volatile but heady mix. I would be able to identify that odor to this day.

One afternoon, as I was leaving the U.N., a ragged woman waved her arm at me, asking for a handout while cradling her child in a makeshift sling. I thought of Yan and Bun Nol in Cambodia, and how tenuous all our situations were. I worried about them, and hoped that they were protected.

On November 30, 1974, the last session of the year, the "Resolution of Peaceful Settlement by Negotiation in Cambodia" was adopted, recognizing the Khmer Republic as the legitimate government of Cambodia, authorizing our delegation to maintain our seat at the U.N., and asking the various parties in the war to enter into peace talks. Ambassador Chhut Chhoeur celebrated the victory with a reception for the Khmer delegates. You might think that we would have celebrated wildly, but it was just that— a reception, and fairly sedate. But you could recognize unmitigated satisfaction in the faces of our entire delegation. Recognition by the United Nations was a major achievement for us. It turned out to be a meaningless victory, of course, but I didn't realize that at the time.

After the resolution was adopted, my friend Kylin Chhor invited me to attend a dinner. Kylin had been a Fulbright exchange student at Bucknell University in Pennsylvania and American University in DC, and went on to earn a PhD in political science. He began working at the United Nations in 1967 and climbed up the ladder. In 1974 he was appointed to direct the United Nations Technical Cooperation and Development Program (African Project). Three years later, he became the first Cambodian to compile a Khmer-English dictionary. Over our meal, he told me not to return home. He told me that the Khmer Rouge would soon take

over, and that soon, the u.s. State Department would discontinue
aid to Cambodia. But before I had left Cambodia, I had vowed to
offer alms to the monks. I was not about to break such a vow. And
of course Yan and little Nol were waiting for me back home.

The next morning I went to the Pan Am office to arrange my
travel plans. A hostess named Patricia welcomed me and paid me
an unusual degree of attention. We chatted about New York and
Cambodia and Buddhism. She suddenly mentioned that her apartment was within walking distance from my hotel, and invited me
to her apartment for dinner. I was surprised, but I accepted.

A few hours later, when she got off work, Patricia called for me
at my hotel, and walked me over to her apartment. She had so many
cats that I couldn't begin to count them. One was a calico—I mentioned to her that, in Cambodia, it would bring good luck. In a corner of the room, I saw a very fat man lying in a bed so high it was
almost to the ceiling. On the other side of the room, a table had
been set and the food was all ready. It was a very strange evening.

Patricia and I continued to spend time together in my few
remaining days in New York. She brought me to her friend's
house by subway, an hour's ride—I had no idea where we were
or what we talked about on the way. At our destination, she
introduced me to other airline hostesses and we had coffee until
two in the morning. An eager young woman named Rose, an
American Airlines hostess, seemed very interested in Cambodia,
and asked me one question after another.

On another evening, Patricia took me to the cathedral to light
candles for her and pray on her behalf for world peace. Her voice
had an instantly calming effect on me; I did whatever good deeds
she asked me to do. She was one of the most peaceful, attractive
persons I have ever met on this earth. In addition to her job with
the airline, she was also involved in volunteer work. She showed
me a warehouse full of medical equipment to be donated to
underdeveloped countries around the world. The last evening we
spent together, Patricia came to my hotel room and helped me
box up the u.n. documents I was mailing to Cambodia. Then we

walked in the snow. To keep each other warm, we walked with our arms around each other, but this was only a Platonic friendship. It was such a relief, after all those months, to have a casual meandering conversation with someone. In any event, when we parted, I thought it was the last we would see of each other.

I had arranged my flight home with a stop in Iowa City, so I could visit Paul and Hua-Ling Engle. Paul welcomed me at the Cedar Rapids airport and put me up in a dormitory with a Malaysian poet. The Malaysian poet and I joined the Engles for dinner at their residence on top of a nearby hill, overlooking the Iowa River. At the dinner table, Paul said that he had been disappointed that I hadn't kept in better touch. I told him that I'd been in the battlefields far away from town—that seemed to placate him. We talked about the political situation in Cambodia and Malaysia, and Paul held forth a bit, as he was wont to do. It was a short evening. Paul asked to be excused as he had work to do in his study. After dinner, Hua-Ling wrote me a check for $200.

The next morning I bought a travel suitcase and clothes for Yan and Nol. It was Christmastime, 1974—the campus was empty because it was semester break, and there was snow on the ground. I looked at the yard and house decorations around Iowa City, and one in particular stood out—the lights on a modest single-family dwelling spelled out PEACE ON EARTH. Tears came to my eyes—maybe this would actually come to pass. I believed I had done my best.

In the afternoon, Paul drove me to the airport and we hugged each other farewell. Thus I began my return journey. I spent the night in Bangkok and reached Phnom Penh the following day.

It was comforting to see my family again, but once the excitement of returning home wore off, I was still a National Assemblyman in recess, with nothing to do, nothing at all. We had no power, no forum. During our "recess" many of my fellow assemblymen went about their respective businesses. My optimism was fading fast.

On February 5th, shortly after I returned home with the delegation, the communists closed the Mekong River, preventing any convoys of food, fuel, or ammunition from reaching besieged Phnom Penh. That same morning, our family went to Wat Nirodha Rangsei, the temple just east of our home, and joined others from the U.N. delegation, offering alms (rice, cakes, money, and medicine) to 125 monks (always an odd number, according to custom), to celebrate our victory. Bodhivang So Hay, the abbot, presided over the ceremony. Second in rank among Cambodian Buddhist monks, he disappeared along with the monks, during the Pol Pot years. In 1983, when I was working at the Ministry of Industry, someone whispered to our minister, Nuon Sareth, that there was gold buried on the grounds south of his office building. In a war-torn country, a rumor like that soon sounds like a fact worth acting on. They dug up the grounds, but they found no gold—only the remains of a monk who had been killed by the Khmer Rouge. The robe was still bright yellow, though his body had decomposed. When we opened his identification, we saw his name: Bodhivang So Hay.

But to get back to the ceremony—in the middle of the service, a long black limousine rolled up to the temple where the 125 monks were seated in rows. To my surprise, out stepped Patricia. She walked straight up to me and abruptly announced, "The cat is at your home."

I welcomed Patricia and showed her around the temple, which had, in fact, been designed by my father-in-law and built by hand over a twenty-year period. Patricia seemed somehow indifferent and bid me good-bye. Meanwhile the ceremony concluded, and I talked a bit with some of the guests, including other assemblymen, several Canadians, generals of the Army, and a number of my relatives.

When I came home I discovered that Patricia had, in fact, left a cat for us—the calico. When I put water in front of her, she just stared at me; she was obviously in shock. I felt sorry for her. We gave her cooked beef and fish but she was not used to Asian food. Even the very air seemed to irritate her.

That evening the moon was huge and round and shone brightly. Machah Bong Catu Muk, the deity of the Four Affluents of the

Mekong River, who resided in front of the Royal Palace in Phnom
Penh, urged me to go to Auntie Yen's house. After the deity possessed her, he said he had prepared a lottery for me. "Little
Brother," he said, dressed in a beautiful silk garment, "it's time
to test you now. Here are five lotus buds (the buds were in a crystal vase, pointing straight up). Now, if you pick the right bud, you
will find a small Buddha image within. If you find the Buddha on
the first try, you will be a warlord. If on the second try, a bringer
of peace. If on the third try, a healer."

I closed my eyes and prayed to Father Indrakosei, the King of
Angels: "Please let me draw the lotus bud that will make me a
bringer of peace!"

I snatched up a lotus bud, the smallest one, opened it, and
found it empty.

"Make your second pick!" said the Deity.

After reciting the prayer *Namo Tassa Bhagavato Arahato Samma
Sambuddhassa* (Praise be to Him, the Blessed One, the Fully
Enlightened One) three times, I picked the second lotus bud from
the left. I broke the stem from its bud, then opened it—Yes! There
was a small Buddha image, *Preah Kwom* (Buddha with hands covering its eyes, in the traditional see-no-evil pose), which settled
into the palm of my hand. I have been carrying that Buddha in my
pocket ever since that day. It was especially important to me during the years when the Khmer Rouge held sway.

Just as the dream of the Khmer Republic was about to crash and
burn, Rose, the American Airline hostess I met in New York in
December, arrived in Cambodia. By some Dickensian coincidence, I had business that took me to the lobby of the Phnom
Hotel, where she was staying, and we bumped into each other. It
was not clear to me what she was doing in Cambodia. I think she
had quit her job with American Airlines and was working for one
of the American peace organizations that was trying to help out.
But she claimed she had come to visit me, although she didn't
even know my address. I hailed a cyclotaxi and took her to my

house in Chbar Ampeou for lunch. It was around 10:30 a.m.—
normally we have lunch just after noon, but this was a special
occasion. I introduced Rose to Yan, who brought out a large bowl
of Cambodian noodles with chicken curry, but Rose just picked
at her food. After lunch, I took her on a tour of the museums. This
must have been April 4th, because that afternoon the U.S.
Embassy told all Americans to evacuate as quickly as possible.

As soon as I heard the news, I took Rose to Pochentong Airport.
The airport was closed, except for her flight—she got on the last
commercial flight to leave Cambodia. Even though I was a
National Assemblyman, I was not allowed to go beyond the gate.
She gave me a Kennedy dollar pendant, then ran alone to the
plane. Poor, sweet, naive Rose!

When Lon Nol left Phnom Penh for Honolulu on April 1st, 1975,
General So Kham Khoy became president, since the chairman of
the senate was next in line under the constitution. But the chief
of staff of the military, General Sak Sutsakhan, with whom I had
served at the U.N., also coveted the role of president. In a ploy
typical of the period, he accused General So of being a traitor,
claiming that he had invited Sihanouk back, to take over.
Personally, I don't think this was true. In any event, Beijing wasn't
going to let Sihanouk bring back the monarchy, although they
might have promised to do so to get his temporary support. I
don't know if he realized that Beijing was really allied with the
Khmer Rouge and its leader, Pol Pot.

But General So knew that innocence means nothing when a
country is falling apart. He fled to the U.S. Embassy and stayed
with Ambassador Dean in his residence until the last moment,
then flew with the ambassador to the United States. A "Supreme
Committee" was then formed, consisting of Long Boret, Hang
Thun Hak, Op Kim Ang, General Thong Van Phan Moeung,
General Ear Chhong, and Admiral Vong Sarindy, with General
Sak as President. This Supreme Committee lasted from April 12th
to the 17th.

Of these men, only General Sak escaped. He got on a helicopter to Thailand during the morning of April 17th, even as the
Khmer Rouge were evacuating Phnom Penh. All the other members of the Supreme Committee were killed by the Khmer Rouge
that day, along with Samdech Sangha Huot Tat, the highest-ranking Buddhist monk in Cambodia. Lon Non and Sisowath Sirik
Matak were hacked into bloody scraps by the Khmer Rouge and
spread as fertilizer for newly planted coconut palms around the
Grand New Market in Phnom Penh. But I believe the spirit of the
violence of that era lingers, because those coconut trees have
never borne fruit.

A REFUGEE IN MY OWN COUNTRY

And now we return to the New Year's feast at my father-in-law's home on April 15th, and to the fall and subsequent evacuation of Phnom Penh, and to the beginning of our long trek on the road, with the few possessions we could carry in a hand-drawn cart.

I have noted the many times, when I was in the United States, that people warned me not to return to Cambodia, and the many people who urged me to escape, just before the Khmer Rouge takeover. But I took my vows to restore peace, freedom, and democracy to Cambodia very seriously. Nevertheless, on occasion, I had tried to initiate conversations around our dinner table about escaping Cambodia. I had friends in Thailand who knew that I had a master's degree in poetry, and they were positive that I could secure a university position in Bangkok teaching poetry. But I was good friends with a military attaché from Bangkok who would have felt betrayed if we had escaped to Thailand. Furthermore, my father-in-law said that he could not leave—that he was too old, too crippled. He said he didn't know anything about politics, but that this was his home, and this was where he should be. And my mother-in-law would nod in assent. At night, Yan and I would talk before sleep. She expressed misgivings about the world that Nol was going to grow up in. Whenever we had these discussions, Nol would get up from his pallet and climb in between us to snuggle.

There was an eerie atmosphere everywhere I walked. On April 14th I noticed that thousands of monks had disappeared from four monasteries (Wat Bo Preah Baat, Wat Sampong Andet, Wat

Roeussei Sros, and Wat Nirodha Rangsei) in Chbar Ampeou. Many people have remarked that wild animals know when a disaster is imminent and exhibit peculiar behavior; this was a permutation of that phenomenon, with our most spiritually advanced beings disappearing from our midst.

What led the Khmer Rouge to evacuate the cities, to kill anyone with an education, to turn Cambodia into a synonym for insanity? Two old ideas that the Khmer Rouge recycled. The first idea was that farmers were the only pure people. It's an idea that has been shared by Thomas Jefferson, French philosophers, and the back-to-the-land American hippies of the 1960s. The second idea was the old myth of national/racial superiority. The Khmer Rouge recalled the era when Cambodia controlled most of Indochina, between 900–1100 A.D., and believed that if they could purge the country of all outside influences, of all traces of education, all traces of modern industry, that a perfectly balanced society would come into being. When those two ideas were combined with a smattering of modern weapons and mass paranoia, the result was a catastrophe that killed millions and destroyed my country. Of course we knew none of that back then; all we knew was that madmen seemed to be in charge, and when madmen are carrying guns the best course is to do what they say.

*   *   *

Phnom Penh had fallen on April 17th. We arrived in Prek Eng, six miles southeast of Chbar Ampeou on the north shoulder of National Highway 1. It was May 1975, only a few weeks later, but it felt as if years had gone by since our New Year's feast. After we erected a tent from a two-yard-square plastic tarp beside Auntie Yen's tent, I began to quietly ask around to find out where I might find a safe refuge for my family, but every possibility turned out to be a dead end.

One day, during our stay in this tent city, I ate three jackfruit seeds, and immediately got diarrhea. In America, you take a pill when you have diarrhea, and by the next day you're better. But almost as many Cambodians died from diarrhea during the Pol Pot years, as from a bullet to the head. I took sulfite guanidine, but it had no effect. I swallowed six pills, but they passed right through me unchanged. Soon I couldn't walk. I was rapidly approaching the threshold of death, when Princess Lotus Bud, my guardian from the Heavenly Realm, possessed Auntie Yen, and ordered Yan to pick thirty-one young guava leaves, without breathing on them. Yan ran out to pick them, and brought them back to Auntie Yen, who was still possessed by the princess. She held the leaves close to her lips, blew on them several times, and handed them to me. I chewed the young guava leaves and even before I swallowed the juice, the diarrhea stopped. We stayed at this place for three more days, so that I could gather my strength.

Rumors about refuge continued to abound. As soon as we decided to go to Kompot Province, we heard that the Southwest Zone was very "hot." In fact that rumor turned out to be true—that area was overseen by Ta Mok, "The Butcher," who came to be regarded as the most brutal enforcer of Khmer Rouge policies.

Every day I walked to the river port on the Chroy Ampil Peninsula to inquire about some way out to South Vietnam, to no avail. Everyone I met had conflicting advice. Chum, a colleague from the assembly, told me to go to the Chup rubber plantation, about 100 miles northeast and inland some distance from the river, in Kompong Cham Province, and not to say a thing about my previous position in the government. Some old schoolmates counseled going to our native villages, others to go northwest even further, to Battambang Province, while others recommended escaping to Thailand.

On one thing everyone agreed—the old form of currency wouldn't be in use much longer. I remember that while looking for a safe way to get my family out of the country, an opportunity presented itself, and I bought a lot of lighter flints, thinking I could barter them for food sometime in the future.

One day my youngest brother, Sa Lorn (who is now called Un Buntha), and two of my nieces (my sister Touch's children) showed up with my mother. My mother had been visiting Phnom Penh from our home village. Like my father-in-law, she could no longer walk. They had to tow her in a handcart. By coincidence, U Leakena, a daughter of my oldest brother, Sa Em, also appeared that same day. We were so proud that Sa Em had become deputy governor of Svay Rieng during the Khmer Republic days. When Leakena broke the news that he had been executed, we howled with grief. They spent the night camped next to our tent at Prek Eng.

I remembered that during Sa Lorn's senior year in the School of Commerce at the University of Phnom Penh, I had been concerned about his safety. Now we were all in danger, and we were all floundering, pinning our hopes on unconfirmed information. I asked him what his plans were. He said he was planning to go to Klar Lot back in Svay Rieng Province, where our sister, Touch, still lived. Yorn, one of my nieces, asked if I'd join them. I thought about it. Keeping the family together is a strong instinct in times of trouble.

But Yorn warned me that it might be wise not to join them. Everyone in our home province knew I'd studied in America. She told me that if I started for home, Khmer Rouge cadres would be waiting for me as I stepped off the ferry at Neak Luong, and would be looking for me anywhere in Svay Rieng Province.

I thanked her for the advice, and decided to stay put for the moment. Touch's husband, my brother-in-law Ou Yim, was very smart in negotiating with those devils in his area. In the old days, Yim told me that he could talk his way around ferocious gangs by deceiving them: "One day, as I was walking home at night, I spotted three thugs getting ready to ambush me. Knowing that, I rubbed both my arms against a sugar palm trunk to lacerate them. When the thugs accosted me, I told them that four other guys down the road had just tried to rob me, but that I had fought them off, and I showed them my bloody arms. They took one look, and left me alone." He was quite a character. Yim and Touch had been living at Klar Lot since 1965, so there was a good chance that they'd be regarded as base people. It made sense for them to return, especially with Yim to protect them.

It was comforting to see family, but we were all so traumatized, that after eating and agreeing on our plans, we hardly spoke. My mother didn't even make much of a fuss about seeing her grandson. And then the next day they set off, Sa Lorn towing our mother in a cart. I prostrated myself, touching my head to the ground as they left, all of us weeping. I stood, watching them until they disappeared from sight. For some reason that I no longer remember, Sa Em's daughter took off in another direction.

But later that same day, I found Sa Em's wife, Mey Thol, camped at the Prek Eng marketplace with their nine other children. Though Sa Em had been working in Svey Rieng City, Thol and their children had been living in Phnom Penh, because Svay Rieng was surrounded by Khmer Rouge. Their oldest son, U Phal Kun, a successful pharmacist in Paris, had been visiting for the New Year, and was now traveling with them. Thol told me, tearfully yet matter-of-factly, of my brother's execution. She also told me that she had been assured that Angkar was going to accept all of them back into Phnom Penh if they returned immediately. Although I wanted to tell her not to believe this, for some reason I kept my mouth shut. Two months later, on the road to a forced labor camp, an old schoolmate told me that all returnees to the city had wound up in mass graves. If I had had a pistol at that moment, I would have put it to my head and blown out my brains. I felt so guilty then and still do to the present day. As it turned out, Kratie Province in the Northeast Zone *was* relatively safe at that time. If I had been given instructions from my guardian spirit, I would have urged them to go there. But my sister-in-law had grown up in Phnom Penh, and would probably not have been easily persuaded to go off on a journey into the jungle.

All who survived the Pol Pot years have some residue of guilt about surviving, as do the survivors of any holocaust. Why was I allowed to survive, when so many others, possibly more deserving, were not? God's plan is obviously beyond the understanding of any of us.

A few days later, following Auntie Yen, her lover Choeun, and their oxen, we crossed the Mekong north of Prek Eng and stayed, for three days, at Areya Khsat, on the east bank of the Mekong River across from the Royal Palace.

One morning while I was scavenging vegetables, I saw a procession of half-naked people, about fifty of them, with an armed teenaged boy leading them, and another following. I nudged a man I knew to be a policeman and asked him where they were taking these people. He said: "To be reeducated." When I returned to my tent I asked the local people what was meant by "reeducation." They told me, bluntly, that it usually meant either execution or imprisonment.

Although I had been a National Assemblyman and a delegate to the United Nations, I had given Auntie Yen veto power over all important decisions. This may seem strange to American readers, but any Cambodian would have recognized her spiritual authority, and done the same. Thus, when I heard about the "reeducation" of that sad line of walking skeletons, I implored Auntie Yen to authorize another move, and she agreed. I had finally picked a destination that I thought might be safe—the mountains in Kompong Chhnang, about one hundred miles northwest, where Prince Yukanthor (Ta Phnom) had established a kind of stronghold. I had become friends with him during my days in politics. I heard that he was looked upon favorably by the Khmer Rouge, but that he had not been taken over by their madness. I was certain that if we could reach his district and I could get back in touch with him, we would be safe, but the trip involved crossing the Mekong, then the Tonle Sap, and then heading west into the mountains.

It was June, but the rains had not started yet, so we were able to cross over to the west bank of the Mekong at Chroy Roeussei, six miles north of Phnom Penh. Our party included Auntie Yen and Choeun, my mother-in-law, Yan, and Nol. I found a canoe that we could use for free, but we had too much gear for one trip—actually we had too much gear for three trips. I can't remember how many times I went back and forth, loading and unloading that canoe. Finally, we positioned the cart across the canoe, got it across, and repacked all our possessions once again. I remember feeling utterly exhausted after the last trip. Of course the oxen just swam across and waited on the other side, swishing their tails.

After crossing the river, we tried to head northwest toward Kompong Chhnang. We traveled through Rokar Kong, a temple town and small commercial port, where I saw six Buddhist monks destroying an American-built bridge. The bridge was solid concrete, and each monk was chipping away at it with a hammer. When I asked them why they were destroying the bridge, one monk told me that Angkar did not need capitalist bridges. This monk had been at the Wat Unalom and was a Pali scholar. (Pali is the sacred language used for writing most Cambodian scriptures. It is derived from Sanskrit and was brought in via Sri Lanka through Thailand in the thirteenth century, although Hinduism had been a factor in Cambodia since probably some time in the fifth century.)

Shortly after this, I saw Yang Lor, an ex-assemblyman like myself, hands tied behind his back, and almost a hundred other men, all high-ranking officers, all wearing nothing but shorts. They were led along the road by armed men. I asked somebody what was happening. In a loud voice he said the group was being escorted to a school, a new school where they would learn to be patient. Then he whispered to me, "This kind of school means death. They're going to kill them all. Don't go along with them." It was now apparent that the Khmer Rouge were indeed purging all intellectuals.

The next morning, when Yan woke, she had a strange look on her face, between a smile and something else. I asked her if she was O.K. She said she had a strong craving for tamarind fruit, and then paused as if I should know what that meant. Then she patted her belly. Again, I wasn't sure what to think. Finally, she said "I'm pretty sure I'm pregnant." I rushed to hold her tight. My feelings soared while, at the same time, a great fear rose like a bird of prey from my gut. Traditionally, Cambodian women do not conclude that they are pregnant until they have missed two periods. Yan had probably conceived in late March, and, as with Nol, she had not experienced any morning sickness, so there hadn't been any tell-tale symptoms. I should have known, though, because Yan had been looking very healthy, exhibiting what we call a "saffron-colored complexion." I was elated but even more concerned about the course of our daily lives. Not only did we have Nol, who was vulnerable enough, but now another innocent being in our care.

At Rokar Kong we came across my nephew, my older sister's son, Mam Phan. He, like me, had been a soldier during Lon Nol's Khmer Republic. He told me that we should get out of this area as soon as possible because the Khmer Rouge were purging "new people." So after I consulted with Auntie Yen, we crossed back over to the east bank, and from there we traveled north along the Mekong.

The peasants who lived in rural areas at this time came to be called base people, and were not usually relocated. Many of them were Khmer Rouge supporters or sympathizers. City-dwellers were referred to as new people. They were considered corrupted, and therefore expendable. Throughout the next four years they were shuttled from place to place, depending on workforce demands. Since we had lived on the outskirts of Phnom Penh, we were regarded as new people. As we entered into this itinerant existence, I felt as if I were watching a movie. We passed village after village, each almost interchangeable with the village where I'd grown up. The houses looked the same, as did the people, and their way of life . . . but it was as if we—my family and I—were now in a negative parallel universe, on the outside looking in. And speaking of parallel universes, you can find many of those same base people still there, in those same houses, to this day.

At Prek Ta Meak, about eleven miles upstream from Phnom Penh, we stopped and spent a few days with an acquaintance of Auntie Yen. During the days, I reconnoitered with my wife looking for any way out of our plight. One night, a battalion commander of the Revolutionary Army came to visit his mother in this village and told her that what was going on was not a revolution, but a total usurpation of power, and that Angkar intended to execute all those who were educated. I had been out for a walk, and overheard the entire conversation. (Note: *Angkar* was sometimes used to refer to the entire Khmer Rouge party, sometimes as the title of the head official in a district, or the chief of a forced labor camp.)

The next morning I asked Yan to go find a plot of land on which we could build a shack. At noon, when it was quiet and there was no one around, I burned my bachelor's and master's degree certificates and the eighty-poem manuscript on which I'd been working; I felt as if I were cremating my own body, not unlike those Vietnamese monks who had doused themselves with gasoline then lit a match. My perspective had been pretty warped in the first place to think that having those items along was going to be of some importance. The title of my manuscript was *The Cursed Land*—a conscious nod to Eliot's "The Waste Land." (I have only been able to resurrect a few of those poems from memory.) I had also brought along a copy of Mao's biography, in French, thinking this would put me in good standing with the Khmer Rouge. It dawned on me that it would have been a death sentence if they'd found it on me, so it, too, went into the fire.

From that moment on, I began living as they wanted—as if I were a cipher. This was also the moment when my wife and I agreed to change our names, for the sake of anonymity. She would no longer go by Dy Yan; she would be Sim Syna. (Syna was a pet name her mother called her. Although I now use my original name, my wife continues to use Sim Syna as the name she goes by.)

I called myself *Sowann,* a shortened version of the spiritual name given to me by my guardian spirit. My whole spiritual name was Sowannaroeuddhi Keo—*Sowann* meaning gold, *roeuddhi*, meaning strong, *Keo,* meaning crystal. So I became Ta Sowann, or "Grandpa Gold." We called our son *Proelung* (soul). My mother-in-law used her birth name, Sum Yoeun. The Khmer Rouge did not need the family name. They used *Mit,* short for *Samamit* (Comrade). Gone were courteous greetings, like Big Brother, Elder Brother, Little Sister . . . to be safe, I called *everyone* "comrade."

Auntie Yen and Choeun had their three oxen with them, so they were allowed to stay with the base people at Prek Ta Meak, but I had nothing, so they made us move on. Auntie Yen, however, decided to continue traveling with us, hoping we could cross the Mekong at Prek Dambok to Kompong Chhnang on the other side.

We kept moving to the north. The eight of us traveled all day. I towed the cart along oxcart trails, across paddy fields. We prepared food under the open sky—that's why I had brought along a small metal oven—so I could cook in any condition, even in the rain, in the wind, or in the mud. When night fell, we unrolled a mat, tied a plastic tarp to the cart on one side, and staked it to the base of a tree. If we were in the middle of a paddy field, we staked it to the ground, lean-to fashion. At night, we passed out, as lifeless as stones. At 4:00 a.m. we prepared breakfast, then continued our journey. On the way, we collected dead twigs for firewood. We rarely used the petroleum lamp at night. For quite a while we were on our own. We had some rice with us, and we scavenged. We were scared and desperate, but we didn't know the worst of it. While we were on this meander, the Khmer Rouge were sending thousands of people to mass graves.

One day we arrived on the open plain of Ta Kleang Moeung, three miles farther north from Prek Ta Meak, almost to Wat Prek Po. We spent that day and night in the shade of a mango grove. That night I burned nine sticks of incense and prayed to the spirits of Ta Kleang Moeung to spare our lives.

The next day we continued our journey another three miles to Prek Dambok Pagoda, hoping we could cross there to the west bank. We arrived at Prek Dambok in the late afternoon. The wind was strong and the surface of the Mekong was roiling. The river is very wide at this spot. The clouds were darkening. The locals said it was too dangerous to cross the river in strong winds, so we stayed at Prek Dambok Pagoda overnight. At one point, monks came out and searched our cart, when they saw me standing guard over it alone. One of the monks took a pair of my undershorts. He must have been a real yokel; he put the underwear on his head and said "Aren't you a goddamned old fool, Grandpa—I can't wear this tee-shirt!" He wasn't trying to be funny—he had actually never seen underwear.

Once, Buddhist monks in Cambodia had been great scholars and an important political force, providing a check on the power of the king. But since the 1950s, corruption and complacency had crept into the orders. While I have the utmost respect for traditional Buddhism and continue to practice it, the monks of that day were often little more than village bullies.

Later that night a Khmer Rouge cadre with an AK-47 approached me and started talking about how glorious Angkar was: "With bare hands, Angkar struggled to annihilate American imperialism and capitalism. Now Angkar needs to reconstruct the country. If Nhom (Father) used to work as a civil servant or as a captain in Lon Nol's army, Nhom may confess without fear of reprisal. Just tell Angkar the truth. Angkar will tolerate Nhom and let Nhom maintain whatever position you had before. Angkar will not punish anyone who was mistaken in their choices." The devil talked on and on.

"No, I'm just a farmer. We are going back to our native village." I responded.

"Where is Nhom's village" he asked.

"Phnom Neang Kangrei." I answered.

"Where is that?"

"In Kompong Chhnang Province."

"Well, just tell Angkar the truth about what Nhom was doing during the Lon Nol regime, and Angkar will let Nhom stay here."

I kept saying that I was a farmer on my way back to my native village, and eventually he left me in order to go torture others.

The next morning we backtracked to Areya Khsat, east of Phnom Penh, because we couldn't cross the river. This was a distance of about twelve miles, one way. It took us two days to make this trip. Everything—pots, pans, and such, was hanging off the upper beam of our cart. We reached Areya Khsat in the evening and settled in for the night. Deep into the night, maybe 4:00 a.m., I heard voices in the dome of the sky: "To be safe, proceed northward! To be safe, proceed northward!" When I woke up, I tried to get my bearings—which way was north? I was lost. For some reason, the psychological disorientation of those days had spread to my sense of direction, and, to tell you the truth, I have never gotten it back completely.

Our supply of rice was almost gone. I towed our cart toward some villages to the east, hoping to exchange a wristwatch that I had kept hidden for more rice, but my watch, purchased at the United Nations gift shop, turned out to be of no exchange value. The base people wanted only Orient wristwatches, a brand name more highly prized by Cambodians than Rolex.

My mother-in-law insisted that we go to her native village at Phum Svay, twenty-five miles directly south of Phnom Penh, in Takeo Province. She assured me that her relatives would welcome us, but I was not convinced. Instead we walked southward along the Mekong. Along the way we met a young man whose father had been an American, his mother, Vietnamese. His name was Touch, and he appeared to be in his late teens. My wife and I both liked him exceedingly, and invited him to join our household. He agreed that this would please him, too.

Around ten in the morning we stopped at Wat Khpok (a half-mile from Areya Khsat, on the north bank of the Mekong) to cook yams for lunch. I built trivets and my wife fetched water from the river. While we were boiling our yams, a Khmer Rouge soldier came up to me and pointed his AK-47 at my chest and ordered us to board a motorboat that came our way from the other bank, from Chroy Ampil. You have heard how strong you can be when you are afraid? Well, single-handedly, I moved fifty kilos of rice from the cart to the boat, no problem. Then I hoisted the cart onto the roof of the boat. Then we got in, and the Khmer Rouge took off upriver. It was just us—me, Syna, my mother-in-law, our son, and Touch—Auntie Yen and Choeun could only stand by mutely as we were loaded aboard. It would be the last we would see of them until 1979.

The sky darkened and it began drizzling as we crossed the confluence of the Mekong and the Tonle Sap, in front of the Royal Palace. Then it began pouring. We cruised along for three hours, then the devil pulled in to Rokar Kong (on the west bank of the Mekong, maybe twelve miles upriver) for half an hour before continuing to Prek Po. It was dark when we got there, around midnight. I had stayed at the temple in Prek Po twice before, so I knew my way around pretty well. I towed our cart under the brick stairs of the ashram. That evening, Angkar welcomed us with a meal of rice and pork.

The next morning while I was walking around, I met Sar Kapon, a political colleague who had been working at the Ministry of Refugees (he survived, and is now vice minister of education). He whispered that we should flee the area immediately before Angkar purged newcomers. "Whatever you do," he said, "don't wear new clothes—leave now—go north." It turned out that the central recruiting office of the district was located in Prek Po. They were concentrating their "recruiting" efforts on high-ranking officers of the Lon Nol regime, and passing over civilians who had been professors, teachers, or civil servants.

That night I quietly reloaded everything on the cart, and we left the temple. I towed the cart northward without any idea of our destination. I no longer counted the days. We walked from daybreak to dusk. Along the way, we asked several village Angkars if we could stay there, but they turned us down. We crossed woods, rivers, creeks. We walked through rubber plantations. We had to cover ourselves from head to toe, because the mosquitoes were swarming around us like angry bees. Whenever we stopped, base people searched our cart for weapons, but when we gave them aspirin or vitamins, they left us alone. It was the season for transplanting rice. We had no idea where we were going. The base people cried out: "They must be CIA! If not, they wouldn't be out walking around like that—they'd be transplanting rice like the rest of us." I started trembling when I heard those words. Nevertheless, my wife, son, and mother-in-law were each in a good frame of mind, and since my bout with diarrhea, none of us had been threatened by sickness.

As we traveled, we saw thousands of Vietnamese being evacuated back to Vietnam, along the road to Kandol Chrum—Angkar headquarters. Hundreds of trucks transported rice via Kandol Chrum, day and night. From the trucks, we heard their voices crying about the way they had been beaten by the Khmer Rouge. My wife had dreamed that someone was waiting for us in South Vietnam at Prey Nokor, the Khmer name for Saigon, or what is known today as Ho Chi Minh City. I couldn't speak Vietnamese, so going there hadn't really entered my mind as a reasonable possibility, although from time to time I had made inquiries. I sometimes wonder how things would have turned out if we had actually fled to South Vietnam. (A year before I finally left Cambodia, in 1991, my relative Soeung came to visit me in Chbar Ampeou. I had lived with him in the 1950s while attending high school. He told me that he had been waiting for me and my family at that time in Smach, the border village through which the Vietnamese were being deported. Syna's dream had been a reality. If only we could have blended in with the Vietnamese, and slipped onto one of those evacuation trucks.)

But the Khmer Rouge were evacuating Vietnamese, and Vietnamese Cambodians, and Yan and I were Khmer—we knew Angkar would notice. Sure enough, when our party—Syna, Proelung, Touch, and my mother-in-law—arrived at Kandol Chrum, about fifteen miles east, on what is now Highway 7, we mingled among the Vietnamese, but Angkar knew that I was Khmer.

"You are dark, old man—you are not Yuon, are you?" I knew I had better not lie—after all, I couldn't speak Vietnamese. I admitted that I was Cambodian. Angkar asked me where I would like to go. I said that we'd like to go to Stung Treng, in the Northeast Zone. If you were to follow our route, it would make no sense—there was no logic, no plan—we were in the Death Kingdom, and our only guiding principle was to go in whatever direction seemed to be a safe haven at the time. The Angkar said he understood my reasons for wanting to go to Stung Treng, but that we ran a great risk of being killed en route. He asked us to stay there to help produce rice for one season, before we left for any other destination. It was early July.

The previous night, a spirit told my mother-in-law, in a dream, that when Angkar invited us to stay anywhere, we should agree to stay. We stayed the night in the space right under Angkar headquarters, according to the spirit's instructions.

The next morning I urged Touch to leave for Vietnam with the Vietnamese. I explained to him that in a very short time I had come to feel like he was part of our family, but that he was too light for the Khmer Rouge to believe that he was our son. We wept bitterly, my wife and I, as Touch took off with the Vietnamese.

Within minutes, a Khmer Rouge cadre ordered me to his office upstairs. He started to interrogate me to find out what I had been doing during the Lon Nol regime.

"What is your name, Nhom?"

"Sowann," I answered.

"What was your profession in Phnom Penh?"

I told him that I was a laborer, carrying water for the Chinese. He said that my head was not a coolie's head. He tried to persuade me to tell him the truth so that he could offer me a good job commensurate with my knowledge and rank.

While the cadre was questioning me, the Angkar arrived and shouted, "We don't need his autobiography. Let him go. The buffalo cart is waiting for him in front of the office."

So I was released. We loaded our belongings on the buffalo cart, topped off with my mother-in-law and my son. I towed our hand cart along behind the buffalo cart. The paddy fields we passed had already been plowed. Through the palm tree groves, lush rice shoots were already visible. After two hours, we arrived at the oxcart driver's cottage. As he climbed up into his house for lunch, he asked me where Angkar had told me to stay. I told him that we hadn't been told anything.

After he ate, he drove our gear to an abandoned two-room school pavilion and we unloaded. This was in the subdistrict of Doan (Grandma) Tei, a two-hour walk southeast of Kandol Chrum, in Prey Veng Province. It was the night of the full moon, so I took the opportunity to pray to Preah Intda Kosei, the King of Angels, and to the spirit of the Khmer Empire, and the spirit of Doan Tei, for safety during our journeys across the three wildernesses. I had no idea who "Grandma Tei" was, but I had gotten into the habit by now of praying to the local spirits wherever we happened to be—it couldn't hurt.

It seemed clear that in order to survive, we needed to eliminate all vestiges of our life in Phnom Penh. So during our stay at the abandoned school pavilion, Syna and I cut off trademarks from our shirts, and saturated all our garments with cattle dung mud to make them look old and dirty, like the clothes of farmers. My wife stripped off her city *sampuot* and made pants and a vest out of it, in preparation for the hard work facing us.

During our third day at the pavilion, a Khmer Rouge militiaman with a French 36 mm rifle on his shoulder ordered us to gather our belongings, then escorted us to what turned out to be the first of the forced labor camps we would endure during the next three-and-a-half long years. I towed the cart behind him, and my wife, son, and mother-in-law followed. A base person hollered to the militiaman: "Where are you going, Comrade Meang?"

"I'm escorting the enemies to East Bodhibreuk!"

I felt sorry for my son who had been born just after the civil war had broken out and now, already, had become an enemy of the people. Tears rolled down my cheeks. I could only look up at the sun and plead "Oh, Preah Indta Kosei (Celestial Father), please spare my son's life! And the life of this new one yet to be born!"

SUGAR PALM CAKES

Sugar palm cakes, a Cambodian favorite, are enjoyed by children and adults alike. To make them, the ripe sugar palm fruit is rubbed back and forth against a woven basket, using it like a sieve, to separate the yellow pulp from its skin and nut. The yellow pulp is then mixed with rice flour and wrapped in a large leaf, like a banana leaf. As they are steamed, the air is filled with the promise of pleasure.

CHAPTER SIXTEEN: JULY - NOVEMBER 1975

TWO CRIES, THEN SILENCE

East Bodhibreuk, Doan Tei District, Prey Veng Province, Eastern Zone: Our First Forced Labor Camp. East Bodhibreuk was only a half-hour walk from where we had been staying. Comrade Meang, our "guide," was the chieftain of the militia at East Bodhibreuk. He took us to his small cabin that, like most Cambodian dwellings, was built on stilts. The floor was made of shredded bamboo stalks. If we were not careful where we stepped, we might fall through to the ground below. My wife and I stayed on the front veranda, and my mother-in-law and son stayed below. That evening, Comrade Meang began a litany in praise of Karl Marx. He warned me that even if I disagreed, to keep my mouth shut. I didn't say a word.

The morning after our arrival, Comrade Meang called five base people to help me build a leaf hut. The *khanma* leaves were eight inches long and four inches at their widest section. I had never seen this kind of leaf before—in my native village we used only sugar palm thatch to roof our houses or huts. We overlapped them and sewed them together to produce a surface a yard wide and two yards long. It became part of the roof and the wall of the hut, which was set up to the southeast, in front of Comrade Meang's lean-to. This area had been the spot where he tethered his water buffalo at night. The hut itself was about fifteen by twenty-one feet, with three poles on one end, three on the other, and three taller ones in the middle. We hung a plastic military tarp from the middle poles, dividing the hut in half.

Some of the base people lent me two sleeping platforms made of shredded bamboo, which we placed within the hut. The platforms had four legs, elevating them from the ground. My mother-in-law and Proelung slept on the bigger platform. My wife and I slept on the smaller platform. We stored our clothes and supplies on our side, since there was more room.

I built a miniature altar for the small Buddha statue I had found in the lotus bud, over the head of my son's bed, while I hung my Spinster Prateal in a small bucket in the eaves of the hut. (A prateal is a bulbed herb, similar to an onion, but with smaller, bladed leaves, from the Sharp Mountains, Kompong Speu. They take human form on occasion, as a virgin or spinster, and they serve as guardian spirits.) During the day I carried the small Buddha with me wherever I went, in a hidden pocket. One day during transplanting, a young Khmer Rouge militiaman approached me and asked me what was in my pocket; I quickly drew out some tobacco that had been in contact with the Buddha from the same pocket and gave it to him. The next day he died of a high fever. Was this cause-and-effect, or mere coincidence? I believe the former.

Because the rain did not fall very often over East Bodhibreuk, Comrade Meang and other members of the group trained me to fish and to find firewood and bamboo shoots to store for the coming busy season. My mother-in-law preserved bamboo shoots by pickling them. The woods were not very far from the east of the village. As I was driving an oxcart to the woods, I came across many B-52 bomb craters, five yards in diameter and three yards deep. The people there said that the bombs had blasted the bamboo thickets, and that some trees wound up as far away as two to three hundred yards from where they had been rooted. They told me that little *carros* (spaceships) blew open the thatches of the roofs, and that no one could hide in their dwellings. They claimed some of the spaceships blew off women's skirts, searching for concealed weapons; the women were terrified of these spaceships. One day the wife of Sar Phim, the commander of the Eastern Zone, shot down a carro, and afterwards many people referred to her as Yeay Carro (Old Lady Spaceship). What were these "spaceships?" I never saw one, but from what I have pieced together, I conjecture that they were some kind of surveillance device, made in North Vietnam, and driven by a propeller in the rear. I think it was this propeller that emitted strong blasts of wind, not unlike a large hair dryer. They were not helicopters, because our word for helicopter is *kontom rue,* which means, appropriately, "dragonfly." These people did not use that term to describe them. I have not heard anyone mention these devices since then.

But back to our daily routine. There was a "life meeting" every three days. The base people liked to show off; they talked and talked about how mighty Angkar was. I did not understand the word "collectivism" yet. The only English word the Khmer Rouge used was "meeting." If any of the new people used English or French words other than "meeting," it was as good as a death sentence. Our pledge at each meeting went something like this:

> Respected Angkar,
> Respected collective,
> Respected Comrade Chieftain,
> I am ever-honest, loyal, and love Angkar.
> Angkar is my only benefactor.
> Today I woke up early; I took care of water buffalo;
> I bathed them, kept watch over them while they grazed,
> then brought them into their stalls.
> I always obey Angkar's instructions.
> If I was reckless in any way, may the collective help straighten
>   my mind,
> so that I can be a good member of Angkar.

My first task was to cut little trees, load them on the cart, and return with them to the hut (it was hard for me to choose which ones to cut, because I love trees so much). But by the end of July, I was assigned to plowing the paddy fields. The fields started near the village, and stretched westward as far as the eye could see.

Alone, out in the savanna, stood a tall *bodhi* tree, that the villagers called the *Pokambo*. A man by that name had lived in Kompong Thom, in the area where Pol Pot was born. He was the leader of a resistance group against the French. When the French captured him and subsequently hanged him, he became a legendary martyr. The Khmer Rouge began circulating the rumor that he had been reincarnated as Saloth Sar, the given name of the man known to history as Pol Pot. The Pol Pot legend was starting to take hold. Today a similar story is being told: supposedly Hun Sen is the reincarnation of Lord Korn—who was illegally executed by a king in the sixteenth century—and according to this manufactured legend, he has returned to bring down the monarchy.

Anyway, because I handled the water buffalo just as the base people did, wasn't squeamish about walking in fresh water buffalo dung, knew how to hitch up the water buffalo, and could plow straight, Comrade Meang told the base people that I was truly a farmer. I began to hope that we might find a way to fit in there, and weather the political whirlwind we had been caught up in. But they remained suspicious of Syna, who had grown up in the city and had never really had experience with rice plants before. Since she could not differentiate between tall grasses and rice shoots, she uprooted all of them and transplanted them together. The base people mocked her mercilessly, but she ignored them.

The oldest man in the village, Uncle Dim, befriended us, and visited often. He warned me to be particularly careful about talking at night, because that was when the communist militia eavesdropped. My mother-in-law returned the visit and got to know Uncle Dim's wife, Yen, who gave her sugar palm cakes to give to my boy.

Of course even before Uncle Dim's warning, my strategy was to avoid talking to anyone, to even avoid eye contact. Despite these precautions, a young man approached me one day, and asked, "How could Great Uncle survive and reach this place? Angkar told us that all the people in Phnom Penh had been burned alive." I told him that I was not from Phnom Penh; I was from Chbar Ampeou, four miles east of Phnom Penh. Fortunately he had no idea where Chbar Ampeou was, and eventually left me alone.

By August, the Angkar of the Doan Tei District had thrown the Buddha statues from the temples upside down into the nearby ponds and transformed the temples into prisons. But family life in that district was still intact. We pestled rice and cooked as family units; husbands, wives, and children lived and slept in the same huts. We fished and scavenged vegetables, picked leaves and harvested grasses to add to our food, all on our own.

Wrapped away, far out of sight, I still had a new long-sleeved shirt and blue jeans that I had purchased from JCPenney in Iowa City back in December of 1974. I traded them to one of the base people, Comrade Lorn, for a fish trap. The net he gave me, called a *dhnuok,* was about two yards square, with one-inch square holes, and was hung on a cross frame, with a long handle the size of my wrists made from a bamboo stalk.

After our plowing was done at 1:00 p.m., the Angkar of the village allowed us to go fishing. The Bo Kmpo River ran through the plain. It was actually more of a stream, flowing toward Vietnam. It had a number of deep pools along its course, however. The big fish were in the river, while only small fish, frogs, and crabs could be found in smaller ponds nearby. Naturally I decided to try the river. I threw my dhnuok in the water and pressed it into the mud, then pressed the four rims around into the mud to make sure that fish could not escape. Then I touched the net all over very carefully with my palms. If fish were caught in it, they'd try to struggle out. If I caught a catfish, I planned to use my checkered scarf to hold it and break its horns; if I caught a *trei ross* (a mudfish— a big round river fish, like a bass), I planned to break its neck. But as it turned out, I didn't catch any fish. Lorn, on the other hand, caught many, as did the other base people. They gave me the small, bony fish, which they weren't planning to eat. Obviously the base people knew where to find the big fish and what their habits were, and like fishermen the world over, they weren't telling. From then on, I fished in small ponds to catch little catfish, mudfish, frogs, and crabs.

By mid-August, the "new people" had been moved in. New leaf huts were built. But these new people were depositees; they belonged to other groups. More about this later. Because of my farming skills and because we worked hard to blend in, our family had almost come to be considered base people. This meant that we could stay at East Bodhibreuk as if we were natives of the village. Nonetheless, I trusted no one.

Rain fell in abundance. In the morning I plowed the fields and in the afternoon I was assigned to transport bundles of rice seedlings by oxcart to scatter in the harrowed paddy fields for the next day's transplantation. Please note that this was not the usual time of year for growing rice. The Khmer Rouge had already set in motion their plan to grow rice on a year-round basis, or as close to it as possible, regardless of conditions.

One morning, I hitched up my water buffalo to the plow and drove them across the paddy fields through water up to my knees. When I started to plow, the blade didn't cut the ground. I checked the plowshare: it was lost. I traced my way back, looking up at the sun, praying to Preah Intda Kosei for help. I walked for a while with tears pouring from my eyes, thinking that my son and wife would be miserable without me, because if I didn't find the plowshare, I would be accused of being a traitor by Angkar, and inevitably I would be executed. While I was thinking about my sacred vows, I stepped on the plowshare. I was so relieved.

Every time I kept watch over my water buffalo, I picked five lotus flowers to offer to Buddham, Dhammam, and Sangham, and for my Prateal Spinster. One night I dreamed of seeing bullets spraying all over the Bodhibreuk area. When I woke up, I assumed that in the near future, Bodhibreuk would be a battlefield. Every day the base people would ask whether I still had my glasses. I always said no, I had never had a pair of glasses.

They discussed the physical traits of intellectuals. One man said that I must be an intellectual because I had a receding hairline, which made it appear as if I had a large forehead. They argued that I was a habitual thinker and that was why my head was bald. But I spotted a nearby farmer who was also bald, and pointed to him. Their laughter meant I was safe—at least for a while longer.

By this time, Syna was six months into her pregnancy. She experienced bleeding on a regular basis because of the hard work she had to do. Angkar sent her to rest in the shade in a hut in the adjacent hamlet of Roeul. It was understood that this was essentially a place where they sent you to die, unnoticed, as there was no one there to attend the afflicted. She was one of two sick women: the other was a Chinese woman who had gobbled a piece of raw beef and gotten diarrhea. She died two days later. Then my wife was alone. Angkar did not allow me to see her at night. In the deepest part of the night, Syna saw an apparition of the Chinese woman who had died. The woman stretched her tongue from the roof above my wife and licked my wife's navel. Syna bled more in the morning. When I went to see her, she told me about the apparition. I asked Angkar to let her come back to her family and they accepted my plea.

One day a blacksmith called me over, and when I approached him, he asked me to heat-treat an ax. So I heated the metal until it was cherry red, then soaked it in water. The blacksmith laughed and said it was not the correct technique; he said you were supposed to plunge the heated metal into mud from a termite mound. I responded that I had learned it the other way when I was young, in my home village, that I did not have the knowledge of a blacksmith. Accordingly, Angkar let me plow the paddy fields, which gave me time for activities such as catching fish, frogs, and crabs, and to scavenge leaves and grasses for my family.

While I was transplanting rice, I once overheard two boys, around seventeen or eighteen years old, talking about their loyalty to Angkar. One boy asked the other: "Would you consider cutting your own mother's throat?" The second boy answered

"Oh, yes! I would slash the throat of anyone who is Angkar's enemy. And that's what she would be—not my mother." I got goose bumps when I heard this. Then one of the boys scolded a Chinese woman who, to his eye, was transplanting rice too slowly: "You lazy Chinese—work faster!"

His harsh language and insulting tone made me lose my instinctive caution for a moment. "In three or four years, you'll be servants of the Chinese again, boys," I told them. As I said this I became light-headed, and could feel myself leaving my body. Fortunately for me, they ignored me, and after about an hour I recovered from my spell of dizziness.

Soon after that, Angkar sought a machine operator. Comrade Meang asked me if I had technical knowledge of this kind. I was suspicious. In any other place and time, I would have said yes, but under the Khmer Rouge, that yes would have led to questions about when and where I had acquired such skills, and those questions would have led to more questions, and one of the answers might have eventually meant death for me and my family. So I said I was only a simple farmer.

Before long I started to fall into a routine. The work was deadening but I was getting used to it. Angkar assigned me to a number of tasks; it wasn't all plowing. One was cutting high grass called *sbauv* to produce thatch for the roofs of shacks. If one did not wear slippers, sbauv shoots punched holes in the soles of one's feet. These slippers were fashioned from two pieces of rubber tire, with a loop for the big toe and two straps across the top.

One night, a young base person asked me to go with him to fish. It was October and getting cold. The rice was ripe, and water was beginning to evaporate, isolating the fish in small ponds, where they were easy to catch. The young man, who told me his name was Sao, built a fire in the rain and roasted what we caught that night. While we were eating, Sao talked about Sihanouk. He said that Angkar would not accept Sihanouk as the head of state, and our country would not have peace. I actually gave him the shorts I was wearing to appease him, because I was scared that he might kill me. When he asked me to go again on another night, I begged off by saying that Angkar had assigned me to keep watch over the water buffalo. I trusted nobody.

Harvest time came. Syna was assigned to work in the fields like all the others even though she was now eight-and-a-half months pregnant, and was still bleeding. We could do nothing except keep quiet. During the harvest, when we were almost finished putting the grain into the granary, Angkar told us we were going to be moved to another camp.

We waited for two weeks. Finally, they loaded us onto a truck and transported us to Chhlong, to the northeast, near a Chinese-built paper factory. We traveled for a day-and-a-half through the jungles and across paddy fields so it was impossible to determine the distance we traversed. We camped there for three days. It was then that Syna's labor pains began. Then her pain was gone. We asked for a midwife to examine her. The midwife explained that my wife was not pregnant, but had a kind of ailment that had caused her belly to swell. She reached up into my wife's womb and ripped out some tissue. My wife, knowing the consequences if she complained, did not even emit a cry, despite intense pain.

On the fourth day, Angkar sailed us across to the other side of the Mekong. When we arrived there, we had to wait while Angkar delivered other families to other camps. It was always my fate never to wind up in a good situation. An old crone and her son had attached themselves to my family. I told her to go ahead, not to follow me, but she paid no attention. We stayed there until deep into the night, with those specters in tow. The moon rose, fully waxed. The sky was cobalt blue. The wind was cold. It was the dry season. Everybody was gone. Only my family and the old woman and her son remained. Then two oxcarts rumbled up to where we were huddled. A driver shouted: "Is this Ta Sowann and family?" I answered as forcefully as I could: "Yes, Comrade." The oxcarts stopped. We loaded our meager gear and they drove us across the night.

Prek Ta Am, Kratie District, Kratie Province, Northeast Zone: Our Second Forced Labor Camp. The bulls loped so fast that I couldn't see anything, until we finally arrived at a big house in a labor camp in a town called Prek Ta Am (Old Man River), to the southeast of Kratie, on the bank of the Mekong. The base people were considerate, and helped us unload. Just as I unrolled a mat, preparing a place for us to sleep, Syna's labor pains began again. The local midwife wasn't very experienced, so a man went to the next village for another midwife. My mother-in-law was sitting beside my wife, when he returned with two more midwives.

I sat at her head while we waited. Syna's cries pierced the silent night of that kingdom of hell. One midwife squatted above Syna's chest and pushed down. Another reached up into her womb and ripped the baby out. I heard two cries, then silence. Then water came out of my wife's womb again. Again, the midwife reached up into my wife's womb and ripped a second baby out. Two cries, then silence. My mother-in-law, who had to watch helplessly, noticed that they were both girls. She communicated this to me with her eyes. Although the action was blocked from my view, it was apparent that this "midwife" had strangled our twin daughters.

Before I knew what had happened, the midwife had wrapped the twins separately in black plastic and ordered me to carry them to the Mekong and throw them in the water. As if in a trance, I staggered in that direction. I could feel the warmth of their bodies but dared not open the plastic to look at them. When I reached the bank of the river, I saw the beautiful sandy shore in the moonlight, and I thought of my Father, Nagaraja. I held my babies in my hands, looking up at the full moon and howled from deep in my soul:

> O, babies, you never had the chance to ripen into life—
> only your souls look down at me now.
> Dad hasn't seen you alive at all, girls . . .
> forgive me, daughters; I have to leave you.

Even though I'll bury your bodies here,
may your souls guide me and watch over your mother.
Lead us across this wilderness
and light our way to the Triple Gem.

Then I dug away the sand with my hands and buried my babies, hoping that their souls would be carried by the Mekong out to the sea, where they would soar to Father Nagaraja and tell Him this horrible story, so that he would help my family to cross the three wildernesses. I prayed to my babies' souls to guide their mother, big brother, grandmother, and me to a safe world.

After Syna gave birth, the owner of the house told us that we couldn't stay *in* their house, but that we *could* stay *under* it. We borrowed a bamboo enclosure and built a fire inside to warm Syna. Traditionally in Cambodia, after delivering a baby, the mother stays in such an enclosure for a month to nurse the baby and recover. We found firewood from a *krasamng* tree to give Syna a pleasant fragrance to breathe. But those Angkar ogres of the forced labor camp at Prek Ta Am told us that Syna had go back to work building a dam only three days after giving birth to her twins.

I have not been back to Cambodia since I left in 1992, but in late December 2000, my good friend Ken McCullough visited, and he and Syna arranged to go to Prek Ta Am together. They took the fast boat to Kratie, then traveled the few miles to Prek Ta Am on rented motorbikes, crossing Prek Ta Am Creek on a rickety ferry. My wife described it as a beautiful day. She recognized the houses and the fields of the area, almost as if she had been there the week before, although she hadn't been there since 1975. Then she saw the house where this atrocity had occurred. She asked the driver to stop, then ascended the steep steps to the door of the house and entered. There, inside, were several people, including one of the midwives who had been responsible for our daughters' deaths. She was a crippled old woman now, with closely cropped gray hair. She couldn't even rise from where she was seated on the floor. My wife, who has an ebullient personality, chatted away with several of the women there, who were happy to see her again. The old midwife stayed at the periphery of the conversation, pestered by her granddaughter. During the conversation, my wife never mentioned the death of the twins, but she said it was obvious, from the expression on the old midwife's face, that she recognized Syna, and remembered what she had done.

Syna continued talking about old times for about twenty minutes, then left with one of the friends, Grandma Tan. They walked, hand in hand, to Tan's house, where they spoke for another half-hour.

While Syna had been visiting with Grandma Tan, Ken had had found the likely spot where I had buried the twins, prayed there, then gathered sand that he placed in a film canister and eventually transferred to a small silver box he bought in Phnom Penh. He gave me the box when he returned. I keep it hidden away in a special place.

Ken met up with Syna, and they began the return trip. She kept her composure until they were at the ferry again, waiting to cross. It was then that she turned to Ken and said, "My daughters would be twenty-four years old now—if they had lived." Suddenly the weight of those memories hit her like a lead fist, and she began to weep uncontrollably.

LET THEM LIVE, NO GAIN; KILL THEM, NO LOSS

Shortly after I buried my twins, the Angkar at Prek Ta Am assigned me to pump water to the paddy fields. It was the dry season. The camp was located along the eastern bank of the Mekong. The paddy fields had been underwater during the monsoon season and, as water receded, Angkar ordered farmers to transplant young rice shoots. Since the water evaporated rapidly from the heat and the temperature of the ground, I had to pedal the watermill all day and half of the night to pump the water to the paddy fields, two miles northeast of where we stayed.

The region was spotted with stands of bamboo. Angkar ordered people to cut it down and burn it to ashes, in order to transform the land for use as cornfields at the beginning of the rainy season, and as paddy fields after the water receded. The yield from such fields was marginal at best for the first two years. This type of corn, incidentally, had been introduced from Hawaii in the 1950s. The kernels were white, and the ears about six inches long.

The water had not dried up yet. In fact, there was a pond behind our house. At night I went fishing with my dhnuok in the one section where the water was still deep. I caught little bony fish and sometimes elephant fish. The elephant fish is poisonous to a woman who has just given birth to a child. My wife, in fact, got sick after eating an elephant fish—she shivered violently, until I gave her the antidote, which was another elephant fish burned to charcoal, then ground into powder and boiled in water. I gave her a portion of this to drink and she recovered instantly. This is a traditional method, used specifically for women who are suffering from ailments after childbirth. These ailments are referred to as *tdorh*. On another occasion, shortly after that, I brought Syna a honeycomb to eat, but the bees growing in the cells stung her tongue and she became feverish. I burned the honeycomb to charcoal, mixed it with water, she drank it, and the fever subsided.

The water was cold at night, but I had to feed my wife, son, and mother-in-law. And I gave some of the fish to the base people who lived around us. Angkar was now classifying people into three groups: in addition to the base people and the new people, a third category had been created: the *depositees*—people like my family—who were known to be city-dwellers. The depositees could be, and often were, executed at any time, for no real reason at all.

The base people let us stay under the house so that they could spy on us at night through the spaces between the floor planking. And, of course, the walls didn't extend to ground level, so we had no privacy. But we unrolled our mats, tied a mosquito net to the four columns, and tried to stay warm, when the cold October wind began to blow in from the north.

As I mentioned, my wife was required to return to work just three days after she'd given birth to our twins. Angkar forced Syna to carry dirt balanced in a shallow basket on her head to help build a small dam. By forcing her back to work this soon, they put her health in serious jeopardy. In a few days, inevitably, she got sick, could not walk, and could not eat. She lay on her back on our mat under the house. And since she wasn't working, she wasn't given the daily ration for someone who was part of the work force—one can of pestled rice a day (half a can for a boy). As it turned out, she couldn't hold down food anyway. Her sickness persisted unabated for almost a year.

While I was pedaling the watermill one late afternoon, Comrade Phuong, Angkar of Prek Ta Am, walked by with a hoe on his shoulder. "Old Man, tonight you should come see me at my office," he ordered.

"Yes, comrade!" I responded without thinking.

I continued pumping water to the paddy, which covered an area of two hectares. The sun was blazing, and the earth in the fields was starting to crack open in places. I pedaled the watermill from dawn to dusk, but still I could not get enough water for the rice plants. That watermill was heavy. It took two people to pedal it, but Angkar assigned me alone to the job, and I was skinny and light. I stood up with my hands grabbing the upper beam and pushed and pulled to add more weight to move the mill.

In the evening when I returned to the shelter, I asked Comrade Phy, whose house we slept under, to lead me to the Angkar office. He asked me why I needed to go there. I told him that Comrade Phuong had asked me to see him. Phy said that that was a bad omen: "No one sees Angkar at night; it usually means . . . but let's go." He escorted me to the Angkar office, but stopped a significant distance from it. The Angkar office was a thatched shack located in the woods some distance to the west of the camp, a sinister and spooky place.

When I entered the office, I saw five Angkar members conducting a secret meeting. Uncertain what to do, I just stepped right in. Comrade Phuong seemed surprised: "What does Old Man come here for?"

"Comrade Angkar asked me to come see him," I answered.

"Oh, right. See those two cows?," he asked. "Take care of them."

I led the two cows back to the shelter.

"You were lucky," Comrade Phy exclaimed, when he saw that I had returned unharmed.

"Usually, when Angkar asks someone to come see him at night, he disappears."

Every morning, I woke early to carry water from the Mekong—enough to fill two four-hundred-liter jars for the base people and my family. I also chopped firewood for them too, then swept the ground around the house before leaving for the paddy field.

From that time forward I had five stomachs to feed, and the hardest to fill were the two old cows. (Actually those cows each had four stomachs, but who's counting.) Drawing water to the paddy fields was my top priority; then I had to find aquatic grasses for the cows. One day while I was wading in water up to my knees, plucking aquatic grasses, I saw a mud fish the size of my forearm. I prayed to the spirits of the swamp to hypnotize the fish so that I could grab it. I moved toward its head very slowly, grabbed it, and pushed its head into the mud while breaking its neck. I was elated—I could stew it for my wife. But I made the mistake of cutting the fish in half and giving the tail end to Comrade Phy's wife. She reported me for not working hard; I had squandered my time fishing instead of doing my assigned work.

Another day, while I led the two cows to the Mekong River to wash them, an old woman yelled, "You're lazy, Old Man—only two cows and you can't fatten them?"

"What about you, *Yeay* (Old Woman)? How come you aren't fat?" I answered, recklessly. I should mention that although several industries are devoted to keeping Americans thin, Cambodians actually aspire to be fat; they believe that when you have become fat, it means you have been blessed by the gods.

The two cows were toothless, as was the old woman, who became furious with me. She reported this back talk to Angkar, and the next day I was sent to the site of a dam being built at Prek Ta Kao (Old Man Kao River), fifty miles northwest of Prek Ta Am. The dam was to cross a dale three miles long, from east to west, in the curved shape of a buffalo horn.

At the site, we had separate sheds for the men, women, young men, young girls, and Angkar. Work began before sunrise and went on until 10:00 a.m.—then we had a fifteen-minute break. We were not given or allowed to have any breakfast.

During this break there was a life meeting. Each member of the group of five, including the chief (Comrade Sock, in this instance—remember, the Khmer Rouge never used last names), had to relate what he had accomplished, and what he had been thinking about. This might go as follows:

Respected Angkar, Respected *Samohabheap* (group)—
Today I woke up early. I prepared my gear, making ready to chop
dirt and carry it to the site of the dam to build it up. I did this without any slack in my pace, and I put all of my strength into my
efforts. But if Samohabheap has seen me either acting recklessly
or dawdling, please point this out, here in front of the group.
Please help me, in this way, to be a good member of Angkar.

After each member had self-criticized, the chieftain of the group
educated us as to how mighty and vigilant Angkar was. Angkar
had eyes as numerous as pineapple eyes; hence, each comrade
must abandon capitalist habits (ideas about eating steamed hard
rice, chicken and fetal duck eggs, cake, or noodles; of owning a
house, or having a modest wardrobe of one's own, etc.). We were
allowed to drink water, and water only, during our break.

After the life meeting, work resumed. During the first month,
each person had to dig a cubic meter a day. The dam was twelve
yards high, twenty-four yards at the base, twelve yards on top,
and three miles long. Thousands of forced laborers carried dirt to
build the dam continuously until noon. Then we took a lunch
break, for gruel.

Work began again promptly half an hour after lunch was over.
The scorching sun came close to the earth. After a day of hard
work, Angkar escorted us to bathe in the river, Prek Ta Kao, half a
mile from the site of the dam. If one reached the river first, he or
she could bathe in clear water; but within a minute, with all the
bathers, the water became muddy. Nevertheless, we had to bathe
anyway—this consisted of a brief soak, before we rushed to the
common kitchen to take gruel (again) for dinner. And after this,
we convened for a meeting of the group in its entirety. Angkar
talked about the wheel of revolution—if anyone was not happy
with the revolution and tried to put out his or her leg to stop the
wheel, his or her leg would get broken. Their attitude was
summed up in this slogan: *tduk min camnenh dawlk cenh min khaat*:
let them live, no gain; kill them, no loss. Over and over again,

Angkar told us to abandon capitalist habits. For instance, don't think about one's family, because Angkar has already taken care of them. I fell asleep many times while the meetings droned on. On one occasion, I fell asleep and dreamed that I was in my shack, and was awakened by the bell after only three hours sleep. In truth, the bell was a bomb dropped by a B-52. It was frightening, and resulted in a preponderance of loose bowels among those of us close to the explosion.

This time of year swarms of flies usually get stirred up. Some dived into my gruel when I was eating. I didn't have time to pick them out so I swallowed them along with the gruel.

April 16, 1976 was Parliamentary Election Day. All forced laborers were herded to the polls. It took half a day to get to Boh Leav Loeu Temple, where the polls were located. At that time I heard that both Syna and Proelung were very sick and Angkar had sent them to the recuperation center at Boh Leav Loeu Temple, forty-five miles southeast of Prek Ta Kao. Actually it would be more accurate to say that this was a place they sent you to die.

My comrades and I were lined up to vote. No one recognized any of the candidates, even after looking at the five stacks of pictures. We were told to take one from each stack and place it in the ballot box. The ballot box was open, so each of us just threw in the five pictures. I "voted," then went to find my wife and son.

When I found them, Syna told me that after I was sent to the dam site, Angkar had confiscated all pestled rice and salt, and consequently my son and mother-in-law had started to starve. Yeay Tanm, a neighbor, took my mother-in-law to wade across the swamp to trade old shirts for a pittance of rice, and my son, who was then six, was sent out to scavenge for wild edible leaves, small frogs, snails, and crabs, and anything else he could find.

Then, she said, one morning an old midwife visited her and heated a large round stone, which may have weighed as much as twenty pounds, and placed it on her abdomen. Afterwards, Syna said she became very ill—it was almost as if her blood stopped circulating from her hips down. So Angkar of Prek Ta Am sent her to a recuperation center. The Angkar in charge of this "facility" asked Syna why she was sick, and my wife told her about the birth of our twins and the fact that they had had no drugs. Angkar asked to see the twins, but Syna told her that they had died. Angkar did not believe her, and called her a liar. Angkar said she was lazy and was faking it, and called her illness a "rabbit ailment."

Eventually, Angkar left Syna and our son alone for a week. Her illness intensified until the night before, she said, when a spirit from the nearby temple where she had been sleeping, visited her. She said the spirit was tall and well-proportioned, with a brown complexion. Suddenly the spirit spit on her, but she somehow knew that it had not been intended as a gesture of defilement, but of healing. Syna had awakened that morning feeling good enough to return to the main shelter at Prek Ta Am, which is where I found her.

We were herded back to the dam site during the afternoon of "Election Day." The dam we were building was made of mud, so, now and then, the dirt we were massing shifted. As the dam got higher, we had to climb a ladder with two shallow baskets of dirt balanced on a pole across our shoulders. In two months, I became desperately weak and hungry. At night I chewed bamboo stalks to appease my hunger. I missed my family terrifically and became depressed. The chieftain of my group asked me why I was not smiling. I told him that even water buffalo missed their offspring. So he called a life meeting and reviled me for mocking Angkar.

After dinner that night I was sent to my family. An old man named Ta Chhem, a base person, was the oxcart driver. When we reached the middle of the jungle, he gave me a coconut shell full of sour palm juice. Then the old man started to wonder out loud why *Samdech Auv* had joined the communists. Samdech Auv means Prince-Father, and was the traditional term by which the king's divine attributes were acknowledged. I told him that Samdech Auv had declared, since the Popular Congress in 1967, that if koan chao liked communism, Auv would get there first, because Auv knew Chairman Mao on a first-name basis. The term *koan chao* was Sihanouk's way of referring to his subjects—all of us were, to him, in essence, his children. Sihanouk was the first one to use this term, but now even Hun Sen uses it.

When I got to my family, another oxcart was waiting for my arrival with our stuff already loaded, and my wife, son, and mother-in-law aboard. The driver, a Comrade Phy, shouted, "Hurry, Old Man, get on the oxcart, quick!" I swung up onto the oxcart. And again, as before, the bulls loped through the dark night. Everyone we passed stood aside and looked at us with expressions of deep pity.

I didn't know what direction the cart was taking us. He stopped in front of a newly built cabin and said: "Uncle, here is your house. I built it myself before you came to our camp. Unload your things and stay here." Comrade Phy helped me to unload, then turned the bulls in the other direction and set off like the wind. I didn't know where we were or what we were doing there, but we were safe, and we had enough milled rice to last us for three months. For the moment, we were the only family at the camp; there were forty cabins in a row and ours was in the middle. It is true that Phy had taken somewhat of a liking to us, but the truth is that he was a bit lazy, and couldn't be bothered with carrying out his "mission"—he just wanted to be left alone. He was, of course, inadvertently risking his own life by saving ours.

The moon rose high, the sky was clear, the wind was fresh. The cabin was about four by four yards, built on stilts of course, with an open kitchen at the rear, and a cornfield in the backyard. While Syna began to prepare a meal, I took a twenty-liter bucket and a big twenty-liter aluminum pot and reconnoitered, looking for water. It turned out that we were staying on the west bank of the Mekong. At this point in the river, the bank was steep, the water deep, and the current too swift for wading or bathing, but I was able to bring back reasonably clean water.

After dinner, we sat in the open kitchen and praised our deities. My mother-in-law told us that while she was alone by herself the day before, she heard young girls laughing in the bucket where I hid the Spinster Prateal. When she looked in the bucket she didn't see anyone. She sat down again, and the voices returned. I didn't say anything, but I knew that it was my Spinster Prateal and her retinue. Three years later, in the days following the "liberation" by Vietnam, in 1979, I happened to cross paths with Sock, chieftain of the group. This was at Wat Boh Leav Loeu. He told me that while I was away working on the dam, a meeting had been called and it had been decided that I, along with my family, of course, should be executed. At that moment I finally understood the situation. It seems that my Spinster Prateal and her retinue were holding a meeting at the same time as Angkar, and the reason they were laughing was that Angkar had the audacity to think that they could actually execute me and my family.

THE PRINCESS & THE CROCODILE

Boh Leav, Kratie District, Kratie Province, Northeast Zone: Our Third Forced Labor Camp. We had the place pretty much to ourselves for almost two weeks, before new people were brought in, mostly Chinese, accompanied by a dark, thin little man who stood outside our shack and yelled, "That Old Man! That Old Man!" I didn't know that he was talking to me, so I walked away. He had come to make up a list of everyone in the camp. I never would have guessed that he was Angkar, he was such an unimposing figure.

Again he yelled, "You! Old Man! Are you deaf?"

I finally realized he was talking to me. "No," I answered.

"Why didn't you answer me?"

I shrugged, but did not look him in the face.

"How many members are there in your family?"

"Four, comrade."

"You are now at the Boh Leav collective. Who let you stay here?"

"Angkar Prek Ta Am brought me here."

"Next time when I call, answer. You hear?"

"Yes, comrade."

"Tomorrow, go get paddy rice at Comrade Tdung's. You hear, Old Man?"

"Yes, comrade."

Now at least I knew where we were. Cambodia was divided into zones, provinces, districts, and subdistricts. Several forced labor camps were in each subdistrict. There were five zones: Southwest, Northwest, Central, East, and Northeast. The

Northeast Zone was sometimes called the Special Zone because it had been Saloth Sar's hideout since 1962. The Boh Leav camp was in the Northeast Zone, forty miles east of Kratie City, on the north bank of the Mekong.

The next morning I went to see Comrade Tdung, who showed me the paddy granary, twenty meters west of the main house. I filled two bushels with paddy rice, then received permission to use Tdung's manual rice mill to unhusk the rice. It was difficult for me to push and pull the rice mill alone, because of its weight. But after unhusking the paddy, I piled it, so that I could clean the bran off the grain. I poured the rice in a mortar, stepped on one end of a long shaft, then released, then repeated this maneuver until all the grain was white.

I learned that Comrade Tdung had been a prosperous rice farmer whose nearby property had been confiscated, but they still put him in charge of our agricultural endeavors. I knew it would be some time before Angkar gave me a specific job to do; as it turned out, I had the opportunity to continue fishing for another three days. The way I did it was to draw water out of small ponds, because it was the dry season; once the fish were exposed you could just lift them out.

Just before I was assigned to a working group, my wife woke me up in the middle of the night. "Auv, I have seen a huge robust man sitting with his knee supporting his chin and his other leg bent flat on the ground. His penis was as huge as a Pepsi bottle. While I was walking in front of him, he said "Grandchild, if you offer me a tamarind fruit, you will be safe wherever you go!"

"Well, tomorrow I'll pick it for him," I whispered under my breath.

I went to the site of the *Neak Ta* (Spirit Cabin) in our village. It was west of my shack in the shade of a bamboo thicket. Every village has such a communal spirit house, but this one had been torn down. All that was left was a bit of the post on which it stood atop a termite mound. But I did what he requested—I left a tamarind fruit. Of course under Pol Pot all organized religion was banned, but in many places the older practices were left alone.

I was finally assigned to a group of ten, under the control of Comrade Tdung. Our job was to gather young *tramng* palm fronds a foot wide. It was hard for me to choose which fronds were the right ones. After cutting them, I had to tie them in bunches, which also proved harder than it looked. The base people laughed at me while I was doing it, rather than showing me how. Base people always tried to find fault in new people. I have to admit they did work fast; in the time that it took me to load an oxcart full of palm fronds, any one of them could load two. But Comrade Tdung tolerated my ineptitude.

One day, the Boh Leav Angkar mobilized all the groups to clear bushes in order to create a field for a new way to grow rice—they called it mountain rice. They burned the forests, then poked the ground with a round sharp pole and deposited four or five grains, then covered it over. They said that when rain fell, the rice shoots would come out and in six weeks we'd have a rice paddy. To my mind, I thought that ants would be the ones to get those seeds. In the period of a month, not a single rice shoot appeared. That was the first defeat that Boh Leav Angkar encountered. In addition to mountain rice, Angkar grew dry season rice. To this end they set up lagoons, and when water receded via evaporation, rice seedlings were transplanted there following the edge of the receding water.

The Angkar assigned me to cook meals at Boeung Krum, one hour northwest of my cabin. Even though I was raised on the farm, and had caught a lot of fish in my time, I was lost when it came to preparing fish soup mixed with edible grasses. But I gutted the fish, then boiled them, adding whatever I could find, then I threw in some salt and some fish paste. The soup turned out black, but everyone said it tasted great. Our crew stayed at Boeung Krum for a month. It was close enough to my cabin that at night, I could sneak out to bring grilled fish to my son.

The paddy fields at Boh Leav were far apart. The camp was in the mountains, the soil was fertile, and had lots of lime trees. One afternoon, while we were keeping watch over our grazing water buffalo, Comrade Tdung picked about twenty small limes, dipped them in red chili pestled with salt, and ate them. He invited me to share them, but I told him that I couldn't eat them because they might bring on another bout with malaria.

He said "Bullshit! Who told you that?"

I replied, "No one told me that, but my system is not in any shape to handle limes." I remembered a party I'd attended in graduate school at the University of Iowa, in 1968. I'd had a gin and tonic with lime, and experienced an instant malaria attack. I had contracted malaria as a child, and it had been dormant for many years up to that point. Anyway, Comrade Tdung enjoyed the limes, all the while chuckling at me and my lime phobia. After he finished eating, he started shivering; his body actually shook, as if five people were shaking a cart, and his temperature soared—the spirits in that place were powerful. He had to be carried to a resting place.

And speaking of chili trees, they were plentiful and quite large in this area. I always climbed one of the trees when Syna or I wanted chilis. The base people, on the other hand, just broke off branches to more easily satisfy their needs—they didn't worry about the trees—it seemed as if there were an unlimited supply. But between the poor agricultural practices of the Pol Pot era, and the deforestation by the Vietnamese that followed, much of that area is now a wasteland.

After Bodhi Camp, we were moved to Sre Loeu, on the other side of Kanhcap Lake. This was a large lake, with no apparent connection to any rivers; we needed boats to cross it. It took a full day to reach Sre Loeu, and when we arrived, nobody was there. As soon as we got to work, the monsoon arrived, so they withdrew our crew. I was lucky that our crew transported the plows by oxcart, so I hitched my two bulls to a cart and we departed. It rained hard.

When I arrived back at Boeung Krum, water rose to my neck. The current was swift. The bulls swam effortlessly; they knew their way to my cabin, but I had to swim for my life. I carried a yoke across my shoulders, and a backpack that contained a checkered scarf, a mosquito net, an aluminum kettle, an ax, a big knife, and a little jar of salted crabs. This stuff weighed me down when I crossed any ditch or canal. I sank and almost drowned several times, but somehow pushed up to breathe and swam forward until I reached shallow water.

The next day, our group went to the glades with Comrade Tdung, who had recovered from his bout with the shakes, after eating too many limes with chili. The paddy fields were in the deep jungles. If I had been alone, there would have been no way I could have found my way back to the shed we had built in the dry season, supposedly for the storage of mountain rice. We plowed the paddy fields from sunup until noon, released our bulls for grazing, then resumed at 3:00 p.m. and worked until dusk.

One day while I was plowing, everybody rushed back to the shelter without telling me. When I released the bulls from the plow yoke to hitch them to an oxcart, they loped off on their own, dragging the chassis, but leaving the wheels behind. The bulls dragged the chassis faster than I could follow them. I just ran along behind them, as best I could. When I reached the shed, everybody was asleep, so I didn't get dinner that evening. I just went to sleep with soaked, wet, ragged clothes.

That night, Bido Mean Roeuddhi, my spirit sister, came to comfort me by putting my head in her lap. She wore a dark green sampuot and carried a syringe, which she used to give me an injection in my left shoulder. She neither talked nor smiled, but maintained an expression of compassion.

When I woke up in the morning, I felt as if I'd had a dinner of roast chicken, but I was worried about the oxcart. I decided to approach Comrade Tdung. I was so relieved when he offered to help. Comrade Tdung put my oxcart chassis on his, and I led the bulls after him. He showed me that someone had sabotaged my cart, and helped me make the necessary repairs. You would think that something as simple as an oxcart wouldn't need explaining, but until then I had never really taken a close look at the way they were designed.

After fixing the cart, we went back to Boh Leav Camp and began plowing the cornfields and yam fields. It took a week to finish this job. Next Comrade Tdung sent me to crush corn, again basically using Stone Age technology. I worked from sunup until noon, then left for lunch.

On the way to lunch one day, I saw my son crying. He was in the children's mess hall, extending a plate high in the air with his right hand, begging gruel from the cook. The base children were going through the line several times, but my son hadn't been served one ladle of gruel. I was afraid that if I spoke up, I might make things worse. Standing there, feeling helpless, and watching my boy crying, just broke my heart. I sobbed silently, unable to contain my tears. I had been beating corn all day, and I hadn't filched a single grain. Meanwhile my son was going to our cabin with an empty stomach.

We finished transplanting rice ahead of schedule, so the Boh Leav District Angkar mobilized all forced labor camps to help transplant rice at the Dambann paddy fields located west of Upper Boh Leav. I was assigned to rake the paddy fields before plowing them, in an attempt to get rid of thorny creepers called *praklob*, which were growing all over the fields, obstructing the plowshares from cutting the ground. It took five of us, raking full-time, to clear the fields of praklobs. My feet were cut all over from thorns, and became infected. Since there were no antibiotics, I applied buffalo dung, freshly excreted, on the infected areas. I know it sounds incredibly primitive and highly unsanitary, but experience has shown it to be effective. Given a choice, I would have preferred antibiotics, but when one is desperate, one uses whatever is available.

We were sheltered in a shed on the highlands in the middle of several glades. The paddy fields were located along the Mekong, so we had plenty of water with which to wash ourselves after work. The south bank of the Mekong formed the border of Kompong Thom Province, in the Northwest Zone. On the north bank of the Mekong were cabins of new people, including a woman who was once an extremely wealthy film producer, and one of her friends from that coterie. They were still quite beautiful, despite the fact that they worked all day in the fields out in the sun and rain. Khmer Rouge cadres often proposed to them, but they always refused. Then, one afternoon while they were transplanting rice, someone burned their cabin.

Next, the Angkar sent me to care for the dry season rice paddy at Khjieap, about an hour and a half walking distance northeast of my cabin. The chief of our group was a high-school student named Nguon who was kind, and one of the brightest, most capable men I'd met for quite a while. But at that time, it may have only made him more vulnerable.

While on that job, I met up with Nuth Dara, who'd been an English teacher at Lycée Sisowath in Phnom Penh. We were responsible for drawing water to the paddy fields at night and clearing the canebrakes during the day. While we were drawing water we quietly chatted in English about how miserable we were. Dara sang that sappy Bobby Vinton song "Roses are red, my love," and I, in turn, recited Whitman's "O Captain, My Captain!" and President Kennedy's inaugural address. But in such times, I continued to be careful, even with a former English teacher. I never divulged any specific details to him about my background. He told me that he had enjoyed life in Phnom Penh without a care in the world. His beautiful wife, Pressarun, had been a head nurse. She and their ten children were all at that particular camp—amazing that they had suffered no casualties.

One day we were working separately. While I was clearing the canebrakes a water buffalo cobra rose up and opened its hood in front of me. I did not draw back. I recalled everything that my guardian spirits, my mother from Heaven Island (Intdanimitta Borei), and Bido Mean Roeuddhi, had told me. My mother and

Bido told me that in my journey across the three wildernesses I would encounter a big naga (the inhabitants of the Invisible World call snakes nagas or crawling beings) and that I should be polite to it and speak to it as if I were speaking to Buddha himself. No killing, no eating its flesh, if I were to survive. So I addressed it as follows:

> O, Naga! Your flesh and blood are truly
> Buddha's flesh and blood.
> I am just a prisoner of war.
> But I am not your food.
>
> You, naga, are free,
> and if my flesh is truly your blood
> plead my case with the spirits of this swamp
> to lead me to Buddham, Dhammam, and Sangham.

After a pause, the snake lowered its head and slithered to the south. I later found out, by reading Buddhist scriptures, that the south is traditionally where the Teacher resides. I continued to clear the canebrake as if nothing had happened. And I never told anyone, figuring that all they would do is mock me anyway. Or chastise me for not killing it and cooking it up for them.

I finished my quota ahead of time, so I got permission to visit my son. I couldn't take a straight path—I had to walk in an arc to avoid water. When I arrived at the cabin, I noticed that all the Chinese neighbors were gone. Once again, our cabin was the only occupied dwelling.

I thought it might be an opportunity to build on a developing friendship, so I went to ask permission from the camp chieftain to move close to Dara's cabin. Then I returned to the work site.

We worked for a few more days, until the night of the full moon, when a cry pierced the silent night: "Ta Sowann! Hurry up! Angkar is already moving your family to another camp!" The moon shone brightly. The fragrance of the rice paddy floated on the wind. I grabbed my *ballot* (French for backpack), looked at the golden paddy and said, "I never had a chance to taste you, my goddess!" Then I ran through the bushes. Fortunately, the oxcart arrived late to pick up my family. When I reached the cabin, Syna and my mother-in-law were loading our belongings. So for two weeks we went off in a northwesterly direction, to Peam Te (the No Tributary), which eventually flows into the Mekong. During this interlude we had a good time together. We cooked, ate, and rested.

While we were there, my mother-in-law saw Bido and Grandpa Suos, our guardian spirits, in a dream, betting each other as to which direction our family would be moved. Bido pointed to the northeast, her right arm raised up high. My mother-in-law was sure that meant our next camp would be far away. On the other hand my wife dreamed about an old man yelling, "Is this Ta Sowann's family? Angkar will move this family forward again! Prepare your belongings!" in her dream the night before.

Actually the Peam Te figures in a legend. In 1495, the King of Cambodia, Preah Srei Dhamma Raja, visited Wat Nokor in Kompong Cham Province, sixty miles north of Phnom Penh, and just west of where we were staying.

One day the King's daughter, Princess Ratana Mealea, wished to bathe in the Mekong River. Her father worried about the dangers of such a big river, but the princess kept after him, and eventually the king gave in to her plea. Both the king and the queen accompanied their daughter to the beautiful river. Sandy beaches sloped gently to the water. Ratana Mealea and her retinue swam joyfully.

There was a rumor that a crocodile had been living in the Chhlong River. This crocodile was reputed to have a head seven-and-a-half-feet in length, he was supposed to be wild and fierce, and it was said that he could transform himself into a handsome lad.

The very day that the princess was bathing, the crocodile left the Chhlong River in Kratie Province swimming west into the Mekong, at the head of his school of crocodiles. As they approached the spot where the princess and her retinue were bathing, he was instantly smitten with her and wanted her for his wife. He exhibited typical crocodile behavior by beating his tail against the water, causing huge waves. The courtesans and the princess were frightened and began wading ashore quickly. The crocodile moved like a flash, snatching the princess in his mouth and swimming back toward his sanctuary.

The courtesans and the troops who witnessed this event were in a panic. The yelling alerted the king and queen, who were devastated at the loss of their daughter. The king commanded his men to go after the crocodile in boats. Some fired guns in hopes that the crocodile would get frightened and release the princess from his jaws. Others carried spears, bows and arrows, and crossbows with the intention of killing the crocodile.

When the crocodile heard the reports of the guns he realized that he would not have time to court the princess, so he swallowed her and swam as fast as he could toward his den in the Chhlong River.

When the Army reached the very spot where we were camped, they asked people who were living there: "Have you seen a crocodile swimming this way?" They were frightened, and answered, *"Te!"* (No!). Since then, people have called this mouth of the river *Peam Te* (the No Tributary).

Finally the king's hunters caught up with the crocodile and captured him. The king ordered that the crocodile's belly be cut open and the princess's corpse removed. The king prepared a cremation ceremony of his beloved daughter on that very spot.

After the cremation ceremony was over, the king ordered craftsmen to shape five Buddha images in gold, five in silver, five in bronze, five in *tongwea* (an alloy of gold, silver, and copper), and five in copper in her honor. A stupa was erected to store her ashes. The king also built a one-hundred-column temple in her memory. This temple has recently been restored, and is located in Sambor, about thirty-five miles upriver from the present-day city of Kratie. The original stupa is still there.

One evening, while we were there, I told the story to my wife and son. They were electrified when I came to part of the story that took place where we were camped. First I spoke in the insistent voice of the king's hunter, then I turned and faced the river and assumed the voice of the people saying "No!" Though he was only six at the time, my son has never forgotten that night.

FIRST QUALITY FERTILIZER

Sre Pring, Snuol District, Kratie Province, Northeast Zone: Our Fourth Forced Labor Camp. At the end of two weeks, two military trucks drove in. They loaded us up and Peam Te became another bad memory. As the trucks rolled along on dirt roads full of potholes, we slaves in the back were rocked back-and-forth and up-and-down as if we were on an amusement ride, although none of us was amused. We tried to talk to pass the time, but to make ourselves heard, we had to bellow at each other like hogs. Then, for half a day we were on asphalt roads. Though the ride was somewhat smoother, our anxiety was compounded by the fact that we had no idea where we were going, or what Angkar's intentions were. A few of us had heard of the White Bone Village or the Plentiful Food Village—our rumored destinations—but most of us assumed that Angkar wanted our labor, which meant they needed us alive. A while back, when I'd been at Bodhibreuk, some base people told me that Angkar would send the new people to clear the mountains and transform them into paddy fields, but I thought that was just to scare me. I couldn't believe Angkar could be that unrealistic.

After many hours on asphalt roads, the driver turned off onto a jungle path, down into a dry creek bed, up and down some hills, and then stopped in the middle of the jungle. We had arrived at the Sre Pring Forced Labor Camp. The familiar sight of a tall mango tree, similar to those in my native village, somehow put me at ease. I noticed that the common kitchen was at the edge of the camp, near two cattle stalls. Angkar's cabin was in front of the common kitchen, which bore the word *Mornty* (Office), painted on a warped board. Three granaries east of the kitchen faced five rows of ten cabins. That first night we camped out in the open, among the sandy glades. Only thorny trees called *dhmea* grew there. My wife had seen this camp in her dreams back at Boh Leav.

The next morning, the Angkar assigned most of the new families to the nearby collection of fifty cabins. The remaining families were moved on to destinations unknown. Our cabin was an old one. Just to the north of us, an old widow and a young spinster lived together in a small shack. Comrade Keng's cabin was south of us—he was our Angkar's spy.

After we had settled into our shelters, we were called in for an orientation session. Everybody assembled at the common kitchen, a long shed with two rows of long rough-plank tables, with an aisle down the middle. Ten people sat on either side of each table, men on the south row, women on the north. Old women and babies sat in the northeast corner, in an enclosed area that took up about three square yards.

The first session was devoted to camp regulations. Angkar Chheang announced that everyone should observe camp regulations in the strictest manner. No one could step beyond the marked boundaries around the camp. After work, everyone was required to bathe in the Chhlong River in groups—no one was permitted to bathe alone. At the end of this exercise in rhetoric, Angkar gave each of us an ax, a hoe, and a big curved cleaver. Then we were herded to the river to bathe. Why didn't we turn these implements into weapons and fight against the Khmer Rouge? Our strength and morale was so low at that point that it never occurred to us.

The riverbed was cluttered with big rocks. The cold water flowed softly. Soan, our group leader, advised us not to bathe facing upstream because we might be attacked by malaria. After bathing, I drew water into two bamboo tubes to use for drinking. I always boiled it with several kinds of bark and roots, making a traditional potion. They fed us porridge (no water), and nothing else for the first week. There was no breakfast.

That tale about clearing the mountains came back to haunt me, because sure enough, they ordered us to cut down trees and vines to transform the jungle into vegetable fields. At the start, the woods were so thick that we couldn't even see any sunlight. This "field" we made extended fifty acres along the bank of the Chhlong River. It took us two weeks to clear the woods. After we'd created the "vegetable fields," they assigned us to claim paddy fields.

Fifty families had been assigned to Sre Pring Camp—forty of new people and ten families left from before, many reduced in number because they had lost members while at the camp. Angkar's plan was to grow two hundred hectares of rice. The existing paddy fields covered seventy hectares, leaving another one hundred thirty hectares to claim. Men, women, and children were put to work from 5:00 a.m. to 5:00 p.m. We had an hour lunch break and an hour dinner break. Then we started again at 6:00 p.m. and worked until 10:00 p.m. We uprooted small trees and bushes, and hacked at big trees leaving the stumps a foot and a half high. Torches made of resin and dry leaves, about two feet long and as big around as one's wrist, were used to light our night work. When the moon was full enough, we worked by moonlight. Because we never knew who might turn informant for a little extra food, we hardly spoke to each other, except to shout warnings when we were felling a tree. One night while I was working on uprooting a tree near a base person, he hacked at another tree, and when it fell, he didn't warn me. Fortunately a strong wind was blowing from my direction and it pushed the tree just a foot away from landing right on top of me. Everyone nearby saw the tree fall in my direction. One young guy, a new person, told me that Angkar wanted to kill me, and this "accident" would have been an easy way to cover it up.

After clearing the woods, we built dikes and dug canals. The dikes were a meter high, and two meters across the top—basically a road for oxcarts transporting paddy rice from the fields where we were harvesting, to the threshing area. The canals were dug two yards wide and a yard deep. The Angkar's plan was to use canoes to transport the rice shoots for transplantation. Each paddy field usually covers an area of one hundred square hectares. Pol Pot wanted to show the world that all of Cambodia was covered with paddy fields, like a chessboard. He called that the "Great Leap Forward." We assumed, of course, that we would eventually be given some of that rice to feed ourselves with, having slaved to clear the jungle, plow the fields, and plant and harvest the crop. We didn't know that the Khmer Rouge were trading the rice for weapons and ammunition. As far as they were concerned, we were expendable.

But believe it or not, on April 13, 1978, the beginning of our annual New Year's celebration, they gave us a day of rest. Of course they used it as an education day. Angkar gave a long lecture about the bare-handed struggle the Khmer Rouge had fought against capitalism and imperialism. "Now," they told us endlessly, "we are the masters of our own fate. We are self-sufficient. In the future, we shall have everything we need and work only when we want to: self-cooked rice, water from a faucet in the wall, feces that disappear by themselves . . ."

In the afternoon, Angkar served the traditional seasonal cakes called *num anggunh andet*—the sticky sweet-rice flour cakes wrapped around a ball of cooked green beans at the core, and boiled. Two guys, one named Hak, the other named Ny, bragged that they could eat forty cakes each. So everyone chipped in one cake to come up with a total of eighty. Both of them finished forty, but afterwards they both rushed to the river for a cool soak. Sticky rice is so high in calories that they felt as if they were going to pass out.

After participating in claiming the paddy fields, I volunteered to produce "first quality" fertilizer (human feces mixed with termite mound dirt). Every morning I went around among the cabins with a large bamboo tube to collect feces that people had excreted during the night. I dried the dirt of a termite mound and pounded it to powder then poured the feces over it and smoothed it by hand to make sure it was evenly mixed. In doing this, naturally I fouled my body. When the Angkar came close to me, I'd actually stick a finger in my mouth to taste the mixture. Whenever I did this, he'd spit and walk away in disgust. And that was my strategy. Stay out of sight and out of mind, and I would be able to live one more day with my family. I deliberately became a pariah, so disgusting that they avoided coming anywhere near me.

In the morning and in the afternoon I drove an oxcart to transport cattle dung to fertilize the paddy fields. The rice shoots, on the other hand, were soaked in my "first quality" fertilizer before transplanting them. The women's Angkar assigned Syna to balance bunches of rice shoots on her head to the paddy fields. These rice shoots were prepared with fertilizer, and since it was raining, it dripped down all over Syna's body. During lunch she washed her hands before she ate her porridge, but naturally it always tasted of excrement.

Whenever it rained, I was assigned to plow the fields. I built the plow I used. At the time I was making the plowshare, three young base people praised Karl Marx. "Do you know, Grandfather Marx is higher than God," quacked a comrade. Forgetting that I was among a pack of jackals, I said, "Oh, Karl Marx? He was a German. And he was just a man." It was noon then. One hour later a meeting was convened.

I was seated in the front row, face to face with Angkar Chheang. He opened the meeting: "Today we have a new lesson to learn. Angkar has liberated all of you from the slavery of capitalism. We have fed, sheltered, and clothed you all, but enemies of Angkar remain among you. Who among you knows who Grandfather Karl Marx was? If you know, stand up and teach us this new lesson."

A Mr. Seng, who had been the treasurer general during the Khmer Republic, stood up and told the meeting that he had been Hou Yorn's student. Hou Yorn was a professor of law in Phnom

Penh, and pro-Marxist. He joined Pol Pot in 1970, but was executed by Pol Pot in 1975. Seng started talking about Marx in detail, though I blinked my eyes at him, trying to signal him to stop. When Seng finished, the Angkar pointed at me. "Now, Old Man Sowann! Tell us what *you* know about Grandfather Marx!"

By then I was no longer speaking in the heat of the moment. After deciding that evasion was the best course, I stood up and said, "The sky is high and the earth is low. When I stretch my hand, I touch nothing. I like everyone, young and old, but I cannot help anyone."

"You're crazy, Old Man—sit down," Angkar Chheang sneered.

When the Angkar realized that he was not going to get anything out of me, he told us the work plan for the next day. And the next day Mr. Seng was nowhere to be seen. I asked his relatives where he was, and they told me that the Sre Pring Angkar had sent him to help the High Angkar. He was never heard from again, of course.

One dark evening, while sitting with my back against the wall near my door, I became aware of a female hand coming through a crack in the wall, and seductively stroking my behind. I was reasonably certain that it was a tactic to find an excuse to execute me. Sexual dalliance was considered as heinous as being a traitor. Adultery, at this time, was nonexistent—in part because people who are being worked to death don't have the time or energy to fool around. In any event, I sat still and pretended to be unaware of what was going on. But the next day, we learned that the family in the cabin north of ours had disappeared—maybe the woman had found a taker, and the entire family had been removed for execution, to pay for the one sin.

Every morning I got up to boil water between 3:00 and 4:00 a.m. to get ready for work at 5:00. One particular morning, I was putting some bark and pieces of wood in my potion, as usual, when a woman came up behind me and said: "Oh, Guru, Guru! You have surely been sent by the angel. I have a stomach pain because

I haven't had a period for twenty years, and tonight an angel told me to come to you, Guru, and ask you for a coconut shell of the potion you would be preparing. Then my ailment would go away." I gave her a full coconut shell of my potion. She returned to her cabin, which was located diagonally from mine. The next day she told me that blood gushed out from her womb making a *pooh* sound, and the pain was gone. I was acquiring a reputation as a healer, although I had had no training, and had made no claims of expertise. It may be that, when you reach this level of desperation, you seek out anything or anyone that might have healing powers, and your own faith is what heals you. I've heard that in the West, you have a tradition of "faith healers"—maybe this is a related phenomenon.

After two weeks, we asked permission from Comrade Saon, the chief of my group, to move, because our cabin was inhabited by a spook. At least that's what we thought—an inordinate number of small snakes were slithering along the roof poles. They would drop off and land on us while we were sleeping. We felt that they were a manifestation of an unnatural presence.

When we moved, a Comrade Keng, who lived two cabins from mine, also moved, to a cabin across from ours. I suspected that he was stalking us. Our cabin was raised on stilts, of course, and one night, when my mother-in-law rolled back her mat to pee, around midnight, she heard someone under the cabin say "It's urine!" Who knows what they thought they would learn by skulking around under our floorboards.

One day my mother-in-law was hungry for chicken. I had three chickens at the time, which were supplying us with eggs. She had helped keep our family together, and I wanted to do something to repay her many kindnesses, so I asked permission from Comrade Saon to prepare chicken for my mother-in-law. He said, "O.K.!" so that night I boiled some water and prayed, "Oh, God! Please don't punish me! I'm going to slaughter these three hens (smallish by Western standards) for my mother-in-law, not myself." Then I grabbed each chicken, snapped its neck, and skinned it. My mother-in-law cooked them and enjoyed her feast. I buried the feathers and skins a foot and a half deep, north of my cabin, and built a latrine on the site. The next morning Comrade Keng asked me where the three hens were, and I told him that I didn't know. He reported them missing to Angkar Chheang, but he never suspected what really happened.

I was assigned to fertilize the paddy fields a half mile away, at Phtdowl. Every morning at 4:00 a.m., I would load cattle dung on my oxcart and hitch up my buffalo. I named the male Fat Guy, and the female, Short Horn. They were very gentle. But when I attempted to plow with them, they were so incredibly slow that they held up everyone behind me, creating a kind of rural traffic jam; consequently, they assigned me to work alone, on the fertilizer, where our pace was irrelevant. The paddy fields at Phtdowl extended over an area of twenty hectares. I made four trips from Sre Pring to Phtdowl a day—two in the morning and two in the afternoon. At night we were assigned to pestle rice that was husked by women during daylight hours. Meanwhile the rice seedlings at Sre Pring were turning green, so the slave laborers were moved to my work area at Phtdowl, to transplant rice there.

One day around 10:00 a.m., I released my buffalo to graze. After lunch I went to fetch water for my mother-in-law to wash herself because she was having trouble walking to the river. At 3:00 p.m. I went to get my cattle to pull the oxcart, but I could find only Fat Guy. When I asked him where Short Horn was, he raised his head and looked toward the bushes to the east. I vaulted onto his back, slapped him to a gallop with my feet, and searched behind every bush, in the ponds, and along the river. I rode back to the cabin to ask my boy whether he had played with her, but I couldn't find him either. I went to the common kitchen to ask my mother-in-law whether she had seen Proelung. She hadn't. I thought perhaps he had mounted Short Horn and taken her to graze somewhere, so I ran into the jungle, wading in water up to my hips, crying for my son. I finally returned to my cabin, and there he was, playing on the ground in front of the cabin.

When I asked Proelung if he had seen Short Horn, he said he had been here playing with "them" the whole time.

"With who?" I asked my son.

"With *them, here!*" he answered, pointing to the ground in front of him. I had no idea what he was talking about, but I was so happy that I'd found my son that I gave him an orange that had been given to me as a special ration that morning. I watched him eat it slowly, while I blocked out thoughts of my imminent execution.

I reported this incident to my chieftain of the group, Comrade Phea, who had replaced Saon. He did not say anything immediately, so I went back to work. That night, while I was pestling rice, a comrade named Chhin yelled out in the darkness. "Old Man Sowann's water buffalo mowed down two acres of rice shoots!" The Angkar sent militia with lighted torches to check the area where Chhin had claimed my water buffalo was running wild, but they didn't find anything.

Next thing I knew, Chhin was in the shed with me, pounding rice in a giant mortar with a pestle. After learning of Chhin's accusation, a friend of mine "accidentally" dropped his pestle on Chhin's head with a resounding *whack*. He fell unconscious.

The next morning around 9:00, I was called to the common kitchen. Angkar Chheang told me that I should sit down and eat before I went off in search of the water buffalo. He said it would probably take some time—the water buffalo was from Coeung, which was located somewhere in the middle of the jungle, and she was undoubtedly making her way home. A hefty young man took the place opposite me as we sat to eat. He wore a rope coiled diagonally from his left shoulder under his right arm. When he sat, he placed a large knife on the table. He gave me a sorrowful look. As we ate, I remembered that he had once worked with me.

Three dishes sat on the table: stir-fried pork, three grilled fish, and a large bowl of soup. As I ate, I kept a clear, blank mind. The field kitchen chief and two women working there looked at me with pity. But the food was tasty, so I ate as much as I could. Just as we were down to the very last morsel, Short Horn showed up, poking her head around the corner of the field kitchen. Everybody broke into laughter. Some exclaimed: "Was Old Man Sowann *lucky!* He was almost sent to the White Bone Village!" I pretended that I didn't hear anything they said; I was determined to finish the first good meal I'd had in three years.

It was not uncommon for the Khmer Rouge to serve a "last meal" to one destined for execution. I knew this at the time, but I simply did not let that knowledge curb my appetite. If I was going to go, I would go out in style. As it turned out, I wound up with the best of both worlds, at least within that little bit of hell on earth—I was given a great last supper, yet lived to tell about it. It is ironic, of course, that on one hand they would go through this kind of formality, but on the other hand, when they were ready for the execution, they would often club people to death with a shovel to avoid wasting bullets.

After the meal, I hitched up my buffalo to the cart and transported the cattle dung to Phtdowl as usual. Along the way, I chanted the traditional introductory passage for thanksgiving:

Namo Tassa Bhagavato Arahato Samma Sambuddhassa
Praise be to Him, the Blessed One, the Fully Enlightened One

I also thanked God, Preah Intda Kosei, and many others—I cried out all the names of those I regarded as being involved in sparing my life.

When we finished transplanting rice at Sre Pring and Phtdowl, Angkar moved us to Chrawlk Marah at the foot of a mountain twenty miles west of Sre Pring. This time I was assigned to plow the fields but with a different brace of oxen, who were more cooperative. My wife was also moved to the same area to transplant rice, but we weren't allowed to stay together. I was in the men's platoon and she was in the women's brigade. We hardly ever saw each other. Proelung and my mother-in-law stayed at Sre Pring.

One day, when I came down with a high fever, the Angkar of my group permitted me to go to the resting shed at Sre Roneam. I had to walk through rattan bushes, with a ballot to carry my plate, spoon, and mosquito net. Halfway there, I collapsed and fell unconscious. Fortunately a base person happened to be driving an oxcart that way, and found me half-dead. He lifted me into his oxcart and drove me to the resting shed. I was in a coma-like state until past midnight. When I opened my eyes I saw Syna sitting beside me, and heard a hard rain pounding on the roof. Syna told me that the man who had brought me to the shed had come to her to tell her that I was dead. Incidentally, it was rare that Angkar gave someone the opportunity to care for a dying spouse. But when she arrived, she found me vomiting and defecating until there wasn't a thing left in my body. People told my wife that *that* was my last breath. But she wrapped porridge in her checkered scarf and placed it on my belly button, and stayed with me for three days, until it became clear that I was going to make it. Ultimately, I stayed at the resting shed for a month to recover.

While I was there, I got to know a man called Yea, who stayed in a cabin next to the resting shed. After lunch I would sneak out to see Yea. He was a blacksmith at Sre Pring and why or how he ended up there I don't know. He sculpted a small Buddha statue out of a broken tusk for me, and somehow I've managed to hang on to it—I still have it after all these years. At first it seemed as if I'd made a friend, but I soon discovered that Yea was duplicitous. He was always trying to get information out of my son, asking him whether he had seen my glasses, or if I had any diamond rings—signs of learning or wealth.

I wasn't working, so while I was at the resting shed, they starved Proelung. This was a way of punishing me indirectly. He lived on whatever he could scavenge—mushrooms, crabs, snails, and wild leaves—for that entire month. Finally, he asked two other boys to accompany him to find his mother at Chrawlk Marah. Coincidentally, Syna had been missing him so much that same day that she had burst into tears. She worked up the nerve to ask permission from Angkar to visit him at Sre Pring, and surprisingly her request was granted. Syna and another woman who had gone along were about halfway there, when, in the thick of the jungle, they heard children's voices—she heard Proelung's voice! But Syna thought she was hearing ghosts. She and her companion started to run, but to their mutual relief, Proelung came out of the bushes and caught up with her. Even under such circumstances people can feel joy. Together they went on to Sre Pring, where Syna was allowed to spend the night with Proelung and her mother.

After recovering from the ailment, I returned to our cabin at Sre Pring, but a new assignment came quickly. This time Angkar ordered me to transport salt from Sre Roneam Camp to Kratie City, about twenty-three miles west on a one-lane asphalt road. On one return trip to Sre Pring, with a full load of salt in the oxcart, I'd only reached the halfway point, when night fell. It was so dark that I couldn't see a thing, and before long I fell asleep. My water buffalo, Fat Guy, led me up hills and down through muddy creeks to Sre Pring, safe and sound. If the ox had banged the oxcart against a tree, spilling the salt, it would have meant my death— waste and ineptitude, particularly in combination, were not tolerated. I released my buffalo and unloaded salt at the granary and built a fire to warm up. Even though I transported salt, I had none in my cabin—I had made a vow that I would remain honest, no matter how desperate the situation might become.

The next day, the Angkar assigned a militiaman to help me transport salt. While returning from Sre Roneam, he saw a beehive on a branch of a tall tree. He asked me to keep an eye on his cattle—which were hitched to the cart—while he climbed up the tree and broke open the beehive. Bees swarmed all over me and stung me many times. My face swelled up like a balloon. It was five days before I looked normal again.

One night soon after that, Angkar Chheang summoned me to his office. When I arrived, he was sitting on a chair facing north, toward the common kitchen. It was night and it was dark. A small petroleum lamp cast shadows in the room. The lamp had a glass bulb to shelter the flame from the wind. He asked me to sit down and started to ask me about my relatives as far back as seven generations. I told him I did not know who they were—I knew only the names of my father and mother. I gave him those and he wrote them down in a notebook. He asked me how many older and younger siblings I had. He asked me politely, and I answered him in a relaxed manner. Chheang did not use any torture techniques. He wrote very slowly, and after he got the five names of my older siblings, he got drowsy and dismissed me.

The next morning, Angkar Chheang assigned Comrade Soan, chieftain of my group, to go with me to gather rattan near Kratie City. I drove one oxcart, Comrade Soan drove another. I wondered why Angkar had assigned me to gather rattan since I didn't have the slightest idea what it even looked like.

When we arrived at the base of Sre Roneam Mountain, we released our oxen, tied them to trees, and spread straw for them to eat. Comrade Soan showed me how to identify and gather rattan—cutting it at the base, then using the back of the cleaver to clean out the cork. I was slow, but caught on eventually. Around 3:00 p.m. Comrade Soan sent me to cut green tramng fronds (only the center frond from each palm tree). At 5:00 p.m. he started looking for me so that we could return to the camp, but I had gotten lost in the jungle. Every tree looked exactly the same. I no longer had any sense of direction, and I couldn't hear him calling. When Comrade Soan finally found me, the sun had already set, but we hitched up the oxen and drove our carts back to the camp.

In my absence my son had come down with a high fever. My mother-in-law told me that Proelung had cried out for me, and had screamed at Angkar Chheang: "Where did you take my father? Bring back my father! Bring back my father!" Then he had vomited. Fortunately his fever broke as soon as I returned.

In the morning, I went to see Comrade Soan, but he wasn't anywhere around. I asked Comrade Keng where Soan had gone, and he said that Angkar had sent him to education camp. When I met him some days later at Sre Krao Camp, he was sitting at the base of a tree looking distractedly at the ground in front of him; he had been beaten. I later learned that Angkar Chheang had punished him because he was supposed to execute me on our rattan-gathering expedition.

The second night, Chheang asked me my date of birth (March 24, 1936—true), my place of birth (Moeun Chey, Romdoul, Svay Rieng—fictitious), and my name (Sowann was the name I used during the Pol Pot era—they never seemed to ask about family names). He asked me about my education, and of course I told him I had none. When he asked me what I did when I was young, I told him that I tended water buffalo, working for a rice farmer. Then he dismissed me again. I was terrified.

The next morning, Comrade Sarin came to my cabin and asked me for some tobacco to smoke. As he squatted in the threshold, he smiled and said, "Last night Comrade Keng, the new Angkar and I invited Chheang to a meeting. When he got there, we dragged him away, and killed him. Don't worry anymore about your biography—we took all those papers to use as rolling papers for our smokes! Now, Ta, just give me a fistful of tobacco to present to the new Angkar, San."

We weren't aware of it at the time, but this was characteristic of the frequent purges within the Khmer Rouge; someone in command one day might be condemned the next—the rules changed constantly.

I slept like a boulder that night. Later my mother-in-law told me that Chheang had lured my son into his office, gave him a professional-quality haircut, and a banana and some sugarcane to eat. Then he asked Proelung about my position back in Phnom Penh. My son told my mother-in-law what he'd said to Chheang: "My dad didn't do anything. But when he went out to take a walk, three soldiers with submachine guns always followed behind him—that's all."

My mother-in-law was shocked. "Why did you tell him that, *Chao* (grandson)?" Proelung said he lied to get a banana to eat. Since Comrade San was the new Angkar, it didn't matter, as it turned out, but my son's innocent flight of fancy had brought me close to the edge of a dangerous precipice.

One day while I was harvesting rice paddy at Phtdowl, Yea approached me and then harvested right next to me. He told me strange stories. He told me that he had been a White Scarf Captain under a Lon Nol commander. He told me about his trip to the Cave of Five Thousand Mountains to see Grandmother Sacamng. (The Cave of Five Thousand Mountains got its name in the late 1860s, when Po Kambo, a rebel against the French colonial government, was pursued by government troops into these mountains, where he disappeared, along with 5,000 of his followers. Grandmother Sacamng is the guardian of Buddhist texts that had been written on scrolls made of beaten gold.) Yea claimed he found Grandmother Sacamng and asked if he could take one of those texts. When she told him that he could not have any, he said he left. He then told me that he had met Hitler at Five Thousand Mountains. He showed me a little booklet written in Khmer by Hitler, he claimed. I just glanced at it. What could one make of such wild assertions?

*   *   *

The method of harvesting paddy rice was to hold a sickle handle in one hand, lift three or four thickets of rice plants with the other hand, then cut the rice plants about halfway up the stalks. Angkar allotted new people an area three yards wide and one hundred yards long as their quota. We had to walk sideways as fast as possible while bent over, leaving no trace of rice stalks behind.

At night, after our porridge of pestled rice, we had a life meeting for the purpose of self-criticism, and then we threshed grain. At night, we had to thresh everything we'd harvested during the day. One night I was exhausted and fell asleep.

While I slumbered, my subconscious mind wandered eastward. In my dream I came upon a shack low to the ground. Inside
I found two old men sitting face-to-face. One played a long-
stringed guitar while the other sang the following song:

> The night deepens, the tide comes in, the cock crows.
> Husbands stretch out their hands to caress their wives.
> Dew weighs down the branches of the trees. But husbands
> are separated from wives, children from their mothers.
>
> Look at the horizon, beyond our powers of sight—
> Desperation is even farther away than that!
> Oh, children, oh, children, when will you see your mothers?
> The three wildernesses have no islands, no shore.

I was standing at the entrance, and somehow I knew this song,
so I joined in.

> Oeuy—look down on us, oh gods of the land!
> My people, men and women, suffer beyond words.
> They work hard day and night,
> they slurp gruel, yet they still bear further indignities.
>
> Open your magic eyes, God—Father!
> Look at Cambodia! Liberate my people!
> They are in Hell: children, elders, men, women.
> Oh, God, free us from agony and fear!

I sang louder and louder until a huge Chinese roast pig with its
front gaping open, stood up trembling, swaggered around on its
hind legs, and jumped from the silver serving tray where it had
been stretched out. I sang to invoke the almighty gods to save my
people from extinction. And then a rhinoceros rushed from a
great distance and charged the roast pig. The rhino and the roast
pig fought each other ferociously. Finally, the rhino tossed the
roast pig in the air and when it fell down, it landed on its back.
When I woke up, bewildered by the dream, it was almost noon.
But because my job was tending my water buffalo, Angkar hadn't

noticed my absence. My water buffalo had straw to munch on, so they had no complaints. Before I hitched them up, I walked my buffalo to the Chhlong River to bathe them and let them drink.

When I reached our work site, I approached Yea and told him about my dream. He said it meant that it wouldn't be too long before we were liberated, and recited two lines of verse:

> The Year of the Horse, flies swarm our bodies;
> The Year of the Goat, death shall prevail.

I started to transport bunches of paddy rice to be threshed that night. In five days we finished harvesting at Phtdowl camp. Then Angkar moved us to Sre Krao. It took two days to complete the harvest at Sre Krao. The chief of my group, Comrade Phea, gave me two yams. I saved them for my son. In the afternoon we had to return to Sre Pring. I was afraid that someone might have seen my yams so I put them inside my shorts and wrapped my checkered scarf around my waist to hold them. At the edge of Sre Pring I stopped to bathe in order to have time to wash the yams. My penis felt itchy from having the yams rubbing against it all that time, but it didn't matter to me because I was happy to have the yams for my son. When I arrived at the cabin, I gave the yams to my mother-in-law. She cooked them and enjoyed a good meal with her grandson.

In the morning my penis was swollen to the size of my wrist. I took a handful of tobacco to offer to Angkar San who was sitting with both knees up to his chin. Angkar San was happy when he saw the tobacco. He took it and rolled it in a paper and smoked it. He lifted his face and blew the smoke up in the air, then asked: "Old Man, do you need anything?"

"Yes, Comrade," I answered.

"What?" he asked.

"I need to see a doctor about my swollen penis." I asked him to step aside so his wife couldn't see us and I showed him my penis. He exclaimed: "Ahhh!"

"Comrade Sarin, come here!" he called. He spoke in a loud voice, startling everyone in the camp, thereby drawing attention to me. When Sarin came to him, he ordered Sarin to hitch up oxen to an oxcart to transport me to the district hospital at Sre Roneam.

When I arrived at the hospital, a woman doctor, a single woman, asked me what was wrong with my health. She was the doctor in charge, but her title should have been "Director of the Sheds." I told her that my problem was in a secret place. She shouted: "I'm a doctor! There is no secret place in the human body to me." So I showed her my penis. She yelled: "Contagious! Contagious! Put him in isolation! Don't let anyone get close to him! *Cock de Crete! Cock de Crete!"* *Cock de Crete* (French, for cockscomb) is a venereal disease that turns one's penis bright red and puffy, like a rooster's comb. It is not equivalent to any other venereal disease, such as syphilis or gonorrhea. It causes unrelieved itching and they had no treatment for it, other than time. So they put me in a private room.

After I got over the infection, I extended my stay another two weeks by feigning illness. While I was there I had occasion to talk to a number of people who had been officers in Lon Nol's army, including an officer whose name unfortunately undermined his credibility with Americans—Colonel Am Rong, who had actually served as the Khmer Republic press secretary. We talked about the liberation of Cambodia, but didn't have the slightest idea how *we* could accomplish this. Colonel Am told me that he had heard a Radio Hanoi broadcast claiming that Vietnam was going to invade, but that he had not heard a specific date. We didn't care anymore about the fact that it would be Vietnam, as long as *someone* would overthrow the Khmer Rouge.

When I got out of the hospital, Angkar assigned me to harvest at Sre Roneam Camp. Four of us were put to work gathering bunches of paddy rice and piling them up. One afternoon people ran wildly to their respective camps. I started to run after them. By the time I got to our cabin, everyone had already packed their belongings. Syna was somewhere in the paddy fields, while my mother-in-law had stayed put. Uncharacteristically Angkar released everyone from their duties so that they could find their families. Syna arrived out of breath as we were packing. At that time I still had two medium-sized suitcases full of clothes. I put them in two *sangrek* (creepers braided in four strands, tied at the bottom, to balance on a shoulder pole), then balanced them from a pole over my left shoulder and rushed along with the others. Angkar said that Yuons were in the vicinity. It was the dry season—January or February 1978, I'd guess.

We traveled two nights and three days to reach Phum Thmey, which was close to Kratie City. On the way we spent nights on the ground. We carried water in a sealed bamboo tube for drinking. We couldn't spare enough to brush our teeth or wash our faces. We each got half a coconut shell of porridge for lunch and dinner.

At Phum Thmey I chose a cow barn to stay in, while my mother-in-law and son stayed with the base people. Apparently the Khmer Rouge had brought people here from many camps to keep them from being captured, and were putting most of them up in some of the remaining big houses, made of milled boards and covered with tiles.

The Sre Pring common kitchen had been resurrected in the shade of the trees on the banks of a creek. We dug a dike to make mud for constructing ovens. I was assigned to fetch water and wild vegetables. Every morning before going out to look for edible wild leaves, I had to draw water from the well to fill two twenty-liter buckets that I carried by balancing them from my carrying pole. Then I trod from bush to bush to pick up wild *saov maov* leaves, and climbed up tall trees to get *neem* leaves. After a week, everyone from Sre Pring Camp had to return except for the old people. I was assigned to stay with the old people at Phum Thmey. The leaves started becoming scarce, and after two weeks there were none left. So we ate lightly salted porridge. Sometimes I caught tiny paddy frogs, broiled them, and mixed them with figs in a mortar and pestle, to eat with my porridge.

I moved from the cow barn to an abandoned cabin on stilts, which had no walls. One night I was on duty to keep the fire going to warm a woman who had just given birth to a child, and Syna was at our cabin alone. That night she saw a ghost climb down a jack tree headfirst. She was terrified, and began to recite: *"Namo . . . Namo . . . Namo. . . ."* and the ghost disappeared. She had been trying to say *Namo Tassa Bhagavato Arahato Samma Sambuddhassa* but was so terrified that she couldn't get past the first word.

When she told this story to the old woman with whom my mother-in-law was staying, the old woman told us that the owner of the cabin had been slaughtered by Angkar at that very spot and no one since had dared to walk close to it, even during the daytime. So the old woman invited us to share her place. I gave her an umbrella I had purchased in New York in 1974. I remember how pleased I was when I had bought it—now it seemed like an artifact from another planet. Then, I was a delegate to the United Nations, now, I was a peasant of no more significance than an ant. It was Walt Whitman who clarified this moment for me, when I remembered his lines from "Song of Myself":

> I believe a leaf of grass is no less than the journey-work of the
>   stars,
> And the pissmire is equally perfect, and a grain of sand, and
>   the egg of the wren . . .

A few days later, they shipped us all back to the Sre Pring camp. I loaded all our stuff on the oxcart and drove it back; it was easier than running away from the Yuon. When I got to our cabin, I discovered that it was now occupied by people from another camp. We stayed under the open sky for a few days, then they moved us to another camp, where I had to build yet another shack. Our life was in a state of constant change, yet nothing ever changed.

ETHNIC MINORITIES

During the Vietnam War, Americans became acquainted with the Hmong, a people with their own culture but without their own country, who had lived peacefully in the mountains between Laos and Vietnam for centuries. The Hmong became allies of the American forces, and since the war, tens of thousands have immigrated to the United States. The public also learned about the hill tribes of Vietnam, the Montagnards. But these are not the only such groups in Indochina; many other ethnic minorities have long lived within countries that either conquered or encompassed them, much like American Indian nations such as the Lakota of the plains, or the Navajo in the Southwest. Some continue to maintain their own dialect, their own crafts, and their own distinct identity; others are slowly being absorbed into the population, and their languages are in danger of disappearing. Two such peoples in Cambodia are the Stieng and the Phnong.

The Stieng live in the Kratie and Stung Treng Provinces, and in Vietnam. The largest concentration in Cambodia is in the city of Snuol, where they speak a Khmer dialect that is instantly recognizable. Stieng tend to stay in small farming villages in remote places, where they use the ancient slash-and-burn method to clear the forest, then poke a hole with a stick to plant what's called "upland" rice. They're noted for their brocading skills and the music they play on their traditional instruments. Though the Bible has been translated into the Stieng language, like most Cambodians, they practice a mixture of Buddhism and animism.

There was a move to assimilate them in the 1960s. Rebellion followed, and many of the Stieng joined up or supported, first the Khmer or Vietnamese communists, then the Khmer Rouge. On the other hand a number of Stieng became firmly anticommunist, mirroring the same conflict that was tearing the country apart.

After Pol Pot was deposed, the new government created a "Policy Toward Ethnic Minorities" in 1984. Attempts are being made to simultaneously transform the Stieng into modern Cambodians, while encouraging them to speak, write, and teach their own language. Many have been assimilated enough to move to the larger cities, and in a few instances they've entered politics, achieved important positions, and moved into big houses. But with an approximate population of 50,000, they have enough critical mass to survive as a distinct group.

It is believed that the Phnong were part of the great Angkor period about a thousand years ago, but moved east as the empire began to crumble, eventually winding up in Mondulkiri Province where they constitute a substantial portion of the sparsely populated region. They have a distinct spoken but not written language, and experts say it may disappear within the next fifty years.

Somewhat primitive, seminomadic, hunter-gatherers, the Phnong settled in an area that is home to a wide array of rare mammals, including elephants, bears, several species of wild buffalo and deer, leopards, and a few tigers. They have developed their own techniques for capturing young elephants and taming them for work, but in recent times, for economic reasons, they have had to sell off many of them to tourist concerns at places like Angkor Wat. In addition to hunting and gathering, they now grow coffee, bananas, and corn, as well as rice. They have a long tradition of weaving, and a vast knowledge of the forest. They collect honey and resin for sale, and use herbs for medicines that the Western world is just starting to study.

They tend to move every four or five years, after depleting the soil in an area. They live in bamboo-framed thatch-covered individual huts, but they also build longhouses that provide homes for several families. A visitor to one of their communities would encounter a number of people with tribal tattoos, and probably hear someone playing the kuong, an eight-string fretless guitar.

The king and the government are now trying to get them to stay put, to educate them, and help them build more permanent wood structures. When I was a child, calling someone a Phnong was an insult, meaning he was an

idiot, as low as a dog. Attempts are being made to transform such percep-
tions, but things change slowly in Cambodia. Refugees International is
currently raising funds to construct a Phnong cultural center—perhaps
this will lead to an appreciation of this ancient people.

RUMORS OF HOPE & TERROR

Chrawlk Marah, Snuol District, Kratie Province, Northeast Zone: Our Fifth Forced Labor Camp. Although base people weren't supposed to be relocated, there were exceptions to this rule. After the frontier conflict between Vietnam and the Khmer Rouge in 1977, the base people in the Eastern Zone—the provinces of Prey Veng, Svey Rieng, and Kompong Cham—were moved further west. Some of those base people, along with many families of new people, were moved to the labor camp we had been living in, Sre Pring, in Kratie Province. Meanwhile some of my fellow slaves and I were moved to Chrawlk Marah Camp, twenty miles west of Sre Pring.

Chrawlk Marah was at the foot of a hill, in thick jungle. Late in 1977, I was assigned to clear that jungle and build two railroad-car-shaped arbors for sleeping accommodations: one for men and another for women. Sleeping stalls ran along both walls, facing an aisle down the middle. We used the stalks of a kind of bamboo called *kley* in constructing these stalls. During a break, a base person named Comrade Seng (not the one who disappeared after delivering a lecture about Marxism) took me to visit some old Viet Cong bunkers, up in the Sre Roneam Mountains. I observed five—there may have been more, but our time was limited.

Once we completed the sleeping quarters, about seventy families were moved to the Chrawlk Marah Labor Camp, including several from the Stieng minority (a group that included both collaborators with the Khmer Rouge, and those who hated them), and a number of Phnong families. For some reason my mother-in-law mixed in well with the Stieng and the Phnong,

which helped her obtain information, and occasionally supplies.

When my family was moved to Chrawlk Marah, I built a shack
in the shade of a tall tree known as *babea kher*. As soon as I saw it,
I remembered that my Guardian Spirit, Grandpa Suos, had once
sung me a lullaby, and the lyric said that I would someday sleep
under "a roof of long leaves." The thatch was made from tramng
fronds, and the roof was just as I had visualized it when he had
sung to me.

Our shack was set up as a duplex, so Hak (one of the two young
men who ate those forty sticky-rice balls) joined us, along with
his wife and son. Like myself, Hak had been in the armed forces
during Lon Nol's tenure, and I knew that I could trust him. He
liked me, and looked out for me and my family, often finding a
dog to share as meat with my son. (Dog meat had never been traditional food in Cambodia, but these were desperate times.)

I was what you'd call a standby man—sometimes I was
assigned to clear the woods so that they could be turned into
cornfields and paddy fields, while at other times I took my turn
as a producer of compost. My most interesting task, however, was
to straighten houses. In Cambodia, old houses of any size have a
distinct tilt. These tilted houses were located at the Sampoch
Camp, about five miles north of the Chrawlk Marah Camp. I had
no knowledge of how to straighten houses, but fortunately I was
given a partner, a Stieng man named Sok, who told me not to
worry. He said we could straighten up those houses in no time,
but first, we should go find fish.

We found some dead fish in a creek, two miles east of Sampoch
Camp. The fish had been poisoned when people had thrown pestled tramng fruit in the deep water where the fish lived. Tramng
seeds are good to eat, but the fruit is poisonous. (Incidentally,
don't try to look up tramng in Southeast Asian plant identification
books, because it grows only in Kratie Province.) Buddhist monks
used to use tramng leaves upon which to write the Dharma
(Buddhist scriptures). The leaves were dried and pressed then a

stylus made of sharpened bone was used to inscribe the words that were relatively invisible until charcoal mixed with coconut oil was rubbed on the surface by hand. Many of these scriptures have survived for hundreds of years.

The tree resembles a palm, and the fruit is similar to the betel nut. As hungry as I was, I didn't think eating poisoned fish was a good idea, but Sok knew just what to do. We cut a big bamboo tube and put salt in the bottom of it, put the dead fish in, poured in more salt, and then sealed the tube with a banana leaf. Sok explained that the salt would leach out the poison, and that in a week the fish would be safe and tasty, and he was right. After a week, I brought the bamboo tube to my mother-in-law so that she could cook the fish for my boy.

Sok was also reliable when it came time to tackle our assigned task. We had all the houses in Sampoch straightened within a month. We actually could have done it in a week, but Sok told me that the Khmer Rouge didn't have any idea how long such a job would take, and they certainly weren't going to reward us if we finished quickly, so we stretched the job out as long as possible.

When I returned to Chrawlk Marah, I was assigned to cut trees to build a corral. We basically just cut down trees and piled them on top of each other to create a primitive fence that surrounded about an acre. While we were working on this project, a Stieng man approached me and muttered, "Don't be so sad. This regime will not last long."

Another day a young Stieng named Pheav, an elementary teacher in Snuol, invited me to join him to look for fish. He whispered that he would rather starve to death than go to eat at the common kitchen. When we reached a dense jungle area, he asked me to climb up with him into a tree called *cambak*. I was wondering if he was planning to kill me by pushing me off, but when we reached the foliage, he told me that we had to be high so that we could see any Khmer Rouge who might eavesdrop on us. Then he told me a series of obscure prophecies his grandfather had made, which had not only foretold our current disaster, but also indicated that all this would not last long. After Pheav finished telling me about the prophecy, we found a few small ponds, and caught some fish in the shallows.

When the corral was completed, Comrade Phin, the Chrawlk Marah Angkar, assigned me to a plowing battalion. But first I was assigned to join five Stieng men, to claim an area of the jungle and transform it into a kapok plantation. This was known as a "mobile team." We cut down the big trees—some were *trach thunong,* a soft wood used for making houses, the others included *dhmea, chhoeuteal, tbeng,* and *sralao,* used for heavier lumber, like planks for flooring. After clearing the land of trees, we built mounds half a yard high and half a yard wide. Then five kapok seeds were poked into the ground at the center of each mound with an index finger. But the soil was far too sandy. I told them that when it rained, these mounds would be flattened; I might as well have talked to the trees. The Khmer Rouge may have believed that farmers were the only pure people, but in fact they knew nothing about farming, and wouldn't listen to advice from anyone who did.

Angkar told us that Red China would trade a tractor for a ton of kapok fiber or seed. The fiber from kapok seed pods is used as stuffing for pillows, sleeping bags, life jackets, and as insulation, and an oil can be extracted from the seeds and used in foods and to manufacture soap. But did China really offer a tractor in exchange for kapok fiber? It was probably just something they dreamed up. We kept such thought to ourselves, of course. We were never allowed to ask questions, so such matters remained mysteries.

The sum total of my belongings at this time was a pair of water buffalo, a plow with a yoke, a hammock made of cloth, a black-and-white checkered scarf (which signified to the Khmer Rouge that I could be killed at any time), a pair of shorts, a set of black pajamas, an aluminum spoon, an enameled iron plate that I brought along from Phnom Penh, an ax, and a four-pound hoe made in Red China, stamped with their rooster trademark. These items were always within arm's reach, night or day.

Syna was in a planting-and-transplanting battalion, and my son was in a children's platoon. The children had a teacher who had no real education, but taught them rudimentary things like the alphabet and then supervised them in tasks such as gathering edible leaves. For some reason, they never moved my son and mother-in-law while we were at Chrawlk Marah. Under usual circumstances, my mother-in-law would have been assigned to babysit, but she somehow evaded this duty. She kept busy by cutting *chke sreng* leaves into strips and mixing them with tobacco to give to Angkar Phin and to chiefs of the Phnongs, the Stiengs, and other ethnic minorities from the northeast.

I didn't get to see my family very often, particularly my wife, but I usually knew where she was, and that she was safe. On the rare occasions when Syna and I were able to spend the night together, we had no sexual desire—it had evaporated with our exhaustion. We were neither happy to see each other, nor sad at our misfortune—we were numb.

My son was becoming indoctrinated into showing allegiance only to Angkar, and to being prepared to disown his family. He was often indifferent when I visited, but I understood what was going on, and did not take it personally. A few times, when my mother-in-law fixed him something special to eat, he berated her in a loud voice, saying, "You are not allowed to prepare meals outside the common kitchen! I am going to turn you in!" Other times he refused food she offered, saying that Angkar had already fed him well enough. We maintained our love for him despite these outbursts. It was not uncommon, though, for children to expose or denounce their parents.

My routine at this time involved plowing the paddy fields from 4:00 a.m. until noon. After we released our oxen, we were each given a plate of gruel that included wild vegetables boiled in saltwater. Then we began other chores—hacking at trees, building dikes, and digging canals to transform other forests into paddy fields. We worked until dark. After dinner, which was the same gruel we had for lunch, we were ordered to uproot bushes and trees by torchlight. If the moon was bright enough, the devils didn't waste their torches. Pol Pot ordered his henchmen to grow rice everywhere, so more and more paddy fields appeared in inappropriate places, and more and more forests were destroyed.

*   *   *

Around this time, two contradictory rumors began spreading— one of hope, the other of terror. Some of us actually began imagining what we would do when we were liberated. Young people finally seemed excited again, and as I walked to and from work, I could hear their voices.

"When I'm freed, I'm going to gobble duck chick eggs to stuff my stomach."

"I'm going to eat beef noodles until I throw up."

"I'd rather be the tenth wife of the dogcatcher, than to live under the Khmer Rouge."

I had my own plan: to go to the Hundred-Column Temple at Sambor to pay respect to Princess Lotus Bud, and then head to Phnom Penh! Had I shared this plan with anyone, they might have looked at me and laughed at even so modest an ambition. I was just forty-two years old at the time, but after almost four years of forced labor and malnutrition, I was a walking ghost, and probably looked two hundred years old.

But as I said, in addition to talk of the fall of the Khmer Rouge, there was also a terrifying rumor that the Higher Angkars had sent a message throughout Cambodia, from Ta Mok, "The Butcher" (deputy commander of the armed forces), to the Angkars of Chrawlk Marah, Sampoch, and Samrong: this season each camp was to finish harvesting crops early, because in February 1979, Angkar planned to eliminate all new people. Only thirty families of the higher class—illiterates who followed Pol Pot blindly—would survive to run the "cooperatives." Could it be true? No one knew.

*   *   *

Then, in the rainy season of 1978, hordes of people were moved to several newly established camps. Two of these camps were beyond description. One was south of Chrawlk Marah and the other in the open *smac* woods some distance to the east of Chrawlk Marah. (Smac, a soft-barked tree, grows on sandy soil and provides little shade. Its bark is stripped and soaked in resin, then used for torches.) In both of these camps I witnessed both old and young lying in the rain, dying, with no one to care for them. They were mostly women, all completely emaciated.

I was assigned to fertilize the paddy fields in Sre Pring and Phtdowl Labor Camps, but it was difficult to get much work done, because in August, the rain poured in sheets for two weeks, deluging the rice shoots and hillocks.

Comrade Phea and I were housemates in a cabin close to the common kitchen. We both tied our hammocks to the central supports. One dark night Comrade Phea and a Comrade Keng told me to make a fire and boil water for them. I didn't ask questions, but did as I was told. They took off for a meeting, and when they returned they had two roosters with them, stolen from the common kitchen. They dipped them in the boiling water then plucked them, cooked them, and then we ate them. It was raining heavily that night, so no one bothered to come around to our shack. I sneaked two thighs into a small jar I was carrying in my pocket. Comrade Phea asked whether the two thighs had fallen on the ground, but Comrade Keng told him not to worry about them— that he should go ahead and finish the breasts. I didn't eat the thighs—I was saving them for my son.

The next morning I asked Comrade Phea for permission to visit my son at Chrawlk Marah, which would have involved crossing the river at flood stage, at a point where it was five miles wide. Comrade Phea told me to wait two days, and warned me that not even an elephant would be able to cross the river in that rain. I wanted to go right away, but I was grateful for the advice. For those two days, the rain continued to pour down, and no one could work. I already had twenty pounds of milled rice and some salt stashed on my oxcart; as long as we were waiting for a break in the weather, I headed a short way into the jungle, and cut a big bunch of ripe bananas for the trip.

The day we left Sre Pring it was still raining, but not as hard. We drove the oxcarts to the high areas where the water was shallow, then through jungle that was sparsely vegetated, having been recently cut. I had no clear sense of direction, but I followed Phea's lead. In the middle of the jungle we came upon another new labor camp. We spotted a few paddy fields, and shacks built low to the ground, in five straight rows of twenty per row. I didn't see any way that the residents could forage or grow food—it was an absolutely desolate spot. Phea visited with the chief of the camp for a few minutes, and then continued leading us on our journey to Chrawlk Marah.

We reached another river that wasn't wide, but it was quite deep. We had to swim the pots across, as well as the rice and other gear. Then we had to swim the bulls to the other bank. Phea gave me ten pounds of milled rice, took the rest for himself, pointed out the direction I was to take, and then took off in another direction.

I hadn't had that much rice in almost four years, but before I could enjoy it, I had to get the oxcart across the river. The oxcart was heavy—how could I tow it underwater? I prayed to the spirits of the elves to help. I put the front of the chassis on my left shoulder and walked into the water. The cart turned out to be lighter than I'd thought. Essentially I towed the cart underwater, pushed up for air, then submerged and continued towing, repeating this process until I eventually reached the other bank. No person in his right mind would attempt crossing a river in this manner, but I could not abandon that cart. I did what I had to do to survive.

When I finally got to the other side, I stepped into a jungle clearing with no idea of where I was or which way to go. But I let go of my fear, allowed the spirits of the jungle to guide me, and arrived at Chrawlk Marah before sunset.

Once I arrived at the shack, I gave the two thighs, the bunch of ripe bananas, and milled rice and salt to my mother-in-law. She always kept a fire going under her bed, because she chilled easily. Her bed was a full three feet off the ground, so there was no danger of it catching on fire. There was plenty of firewood, and we had kept a fire going perpetually from the time of our arrival, so no one was suspicious. She cooked the rice and warmed the rooster thighs for my son. While we were eating, my mother-in-law told me that she had dreamt that I had been sent to Slong, and that an old man had brought a suit for me to wear to Phnom Penh. Neither of us understood what this meant, so we didn't pay it much mind. Then a week later we were moved once again, after seven months in Chrawlk Marah. It was near the end of August 1978.

RENEWING MY VOWS

Sampoch, Snuol District, Kratie Province, Northeast Zone: Our Sixth Forced Labor Camp. We put the sum of our belongings into the crude backpacks they'd issued us, loaded everything else onto an oxcart, and set out from Chrawlk Marah to Sampoch. It was fortunate that I knew the directions beforehand—when I had been assigned to plow the paddy fields I had walked through these areas, so I couldn't have gotten lost even in the dark of night.

When we passed Sre Roneam Temple, I saw that it had been transformed into a district hospital. Although not even one statue of Buddha out of the more than fifty that had once stood there remained, the two large ashrams were still intact. I drove the oxcart south of the temple, where soldiers who had been killed along the frontier with Vietnam had been buried. These totally untrained soldiers had been sent to the front by the Khmer Rouge, and had been slaughtered to the last man.

Halfway across the cemetery, the oxcart pitched over on its right side, throwing my mother-in-law and my son to the ground. Sharp bamboo stumps that had been cut on the diagonal, stuck out of the ground where my boy landed. One of them grazed his right side, but didn't break the skin. I checked with my mother-in-law who told me that her prolapsed uterus was protruding from the impact of the fall, but that she wasn't seriously hurt.

I prayed to the spirits to help me right the oxcart, and perhaps that helped, because for some reason the cart seemed light, and I was able to lift it alone. It helped that the two bulls attached to the cart were quite gentle. So I hoisted my boy on top of our few remaining possessions, and with my mother-in-law walking along beside the cart, we set out again, laughing about the incident. It took us one full day to get from Chrawlk Marah to Sampoch. I should add that Syna was not with us at this time because she had been sent to transplant rice at some unknown location.

Once we got to Sampoch, Comrade Phan, Angkar of the camp, showed me to a large house that I had helped put back in shape once before. There were already three families staying there. My family and I liked our privacy, so I risked asking the Angkar for permission to stay in a shack we'd passed along the oxcart trail. A base person had told me that a former resident had committed suicide in that shack, and was buried behind it, and that his ghost was so frightening that no one dare approach it at night. I figured that the story about the ghost would guarantee that we'd be left alone. Since no one else wanted the place, Angkar Phan gave his consent. After we unloaded the oxcart, I left my mother-in-law to set up the place, while I went to gather palm fronds to use in remodeling. When I was done, we had a living room, two bedrooms, and a kitchen. My mother-in-law complained about the eaves, which were so low one had to duck to enter the shack, but I pretended I didn't hear her. I felt relieved when Syna joined us about a week later.

Just as we were starting to settle down, my mother-in-law realized that we had left her chili tree behind. The trunk was as big around as my thumb, it was almost as tall as I was, and every tiny branch was thick with fruit. I told Angkar Phan that I needed to make a trip back to Chrawlk Marah. He had been in my resin-gathering unit and was inclined to be kind to me. He said "Hurry up. If you don't, Old Man, you will be in serious trouble."

I rushed back to Chrawlk Marah, dug up the chili tree, put it and a few other items in my bucket, and set out for Sampoch again. I turned and took one last look at our old shack and the yam patch we'd planted out back, which would be harvested by a new family coming in from another camp. I knew that this chili tree could cost me my life, but my mother-in-law really wanted it. As it turned out, we never again harvested a single chili from that tree.

At Sampoch, I was assigned to gather resin in the mountains to be used in producing torches for night work. This was one craft I'd learned from my father when I was a boy—two chhoeuteal trees that produced that kind of resin grew in front of our house on the bank of the Vaiko River in Thlok. But I hoped to pick up some tips from my partner, an old Stieng who was regarded as a base person. But the problem wasn't that he spoke very little Khmer, it was his sneaky, secretive nature. After observing him from afar for awhile, I figured out a few new tricks. And eventually even my mother-in-law wound up working with me in what, under different circumstances, would be called a cottage industry.

I was equipped with an ax, a spade with a metal blade, a ten-liter bucket, three bamboo tubes (which I'd made myself), and an oxcart. Each morning we hiked up a narrow mountain trail covered with thorny bushes, looking for chhoeuteal trees. We chopped wedges into the trees, and partly burned the exposed areas with a torch. Next morning we'd find resin collected on the flat part of the wedge that protruded out of the tree, and scrape it off into a bucket or bamboo tube. Then I'd return to camp, hitch up the oxen, and drive them to a field of *breal* plants. I'd cut enough breal leaves to fill up the cart, then return to camp and soak them in resin that had been scraped into empty bombshells. My mother-in-law took over at this point. She removed the resinous leaves from these makeshift molds, wrapped them in palm tramng leaves, and tied them. We produced about thirty of these a day, but that wasn't enough, apparently. Angkar Phan informed me that we needed to step it up to fifty a day, so we just reduced the size of the torches.

In two months we exhausted the supply of resin on our side of the creek so I had to wade across to find more. The creek was narrow but the bank was steep, and there were lots of leeches. They were tiny, almost invisible to the naked eye, but when I'd step on them they'd somehow jump up to my privates, prompting me to itch, and when I'd scratch, I'd start bleeding. I had to apply resin to my hands and everything below my waist to repel the leeches. Fortunately there were lots of chhoeuteal trees on the other bank. As I approached them to begin the process of pounding in wedges, I spotted a lighter someone had left on the ground. When I went out to make resin I normally had to take along an ember from a fire to light the torch we used to coax the resin out of the tree. Trying to keep the ember going while crossing that creek was cumbersome to say the least. Now I had a lighter—a simple thing, but under the circumstances, it seemed to be a treasure that God had dropped before me on the trail.

But gathering resin was only my daytime job. At night I was assigned to guard the rice paddy from marauding beasts. The paddy fields were in the jungle about a mile from our shack. While watching the fields, I kept my eye out for little rice frogs for Proelung. Rice frogs have a really pleasant taste. My partner on guard duty was another Stieng man. To signal each other, we tapped a bamboo tube—*tock, tock, tock.* The Stieng actually built a little shack right out there on one of the dikes crossing the paddy fields. I chose to frequent a termite mound, which Stiengs and Phnongs considered a residence of bad spirits. Frequently, I'd offer sticky rice with fish paste to the spirits and plead that they guard the rice paddies from the wild pigs and other roaming animals. And I *needed* their help, because after answering my partner's signal, I'd return to our shack for a few hours each night.

Not long after she arrived, Syna got sick. She was sent to the subdistrict field hospital at Sre Roneam. It wasn't really a hospital, because there were no doctors or facilities; it was just another place where they sent people to die, more often than not. During the day, while gathering breal leaves, I caught a mud fish the size of my big toe. On the sly, I grilled it, and when the night deepened, I sneaked out of the camp and brought Syna a canteen full of *bye sruoy* (hard cooked rice) along with the grilled fish and some green tamarind fruit. The sky was black, but full of stars. I made my way by starlight to the dispensary sheds. Syna was semidelirious, but she recognized me. I handed her the canteen and exited the shelter right away so I could get back to the rice paddy. When my guard shift was finally over and I returned to the shack, Proelung wasn't there. It was too dark, and too dangerous, in terms of our situation, to search for him. But deep in my gut I knew that he was safe. Sure enough, the next morning he returned dragging a sack of peanuts he'd found in one of the nearby fields.

On occasion, I drove the oxcart to another camp, Sre Krauv, to visit an old woman I used to know when we were at Sre Pring Camp. The old woman welcomed me to her cabin, which was ten times as big as our shack. She offered me cold rice and fish. We discussed a range of topics, never quite connecting on anything. I took the opportunity to walk around the camp and saw new families who had just been moved from other camps. They were living in small palm frond lean-tos. Most of them were sick and emaciated. They had no rice, and what they had scavenged and cooked was indigestible. These people had actually been Khmer Rouge supporters, but when the Vietnamese encroached on the Cambodian border, Angkar Mok, "The Butcher," turned on his own, and denounced the local base people—even the women and children—as traitors.

At about this time, the terrifying rumors I'd heard earlier in the year resurfaced. When last I'd heard the rumor, the Angkar was telling the chiefs at the group, platoon, battalion, and brigade levels that they must finish ahead of time, because next February, they would kill all but thirty families from each cooperative. Only now I was hearing that number had been cut in half—only fifteen families would live. They were planning to kill almost the entire population of Cambodia. My sense of desperation was reaching fever pitch.

I knew that I could not escape death, but while I was still alive I wanted to do something good for all the inhabitants of Cambodia, including the people, wild creatures, and plant life. In a dream, my Invisible Sister, Bido Mean Roeuddhi, had once advised me that if I wished to communicate with the higher realms, I should pray on the night of a full moon, at ten o'clock. I decided to take her advice, and began to make preparations to renew my sacred vows to bring democracy to our land.

During my resin-gathering assignment, I began collecting ingredients to make incense. Working in our shack, I took krasamng bark and ground it in a mortar and pestle until it was in powder form. This powder is quite aromatic when burned. Then I went through the same process with kapok leaves, which served as an adhesive when mixed with the powdered krasamng bark. For the sticks I took foot-long coconut leaf ridges, soaked them in water, then rolled them in the sticky, aromatic mixture that I spread on a plank. I repeated the process until they reached the thickness I wanted.

As the full moon in the month of October approached, I began to prepare an altar—a flattened termite mound about chest high, located in the shadows underneath a tree with an enormous amount of foliage. The preparations took almost two weeks, working bit by bit, to ensure that I would not be disturbed or discovered. Whatever the risk, I was obsessed with the idea that it was my mission to salvage my country and my people.

When the day of the full moon arrived, I picked some mountain flowers, while fulfilling my resin-gathering responsibilities. That evening, as I began my guard duty, the golden disk of the moon rose through the trees of the jungle, spreading its light over Sampoch Labor Camp. The wind ruffled the golden rice paddy from north to south, from east to west, like nymphs performing celestial dances. I was entranced by the fragrance of the rice. The only sound was the wind ruffling the rice paddy.

Before I headed into the jungle, I wanted to make sure I signaled my partner, to make him think I was on the job. I tapped three times with my bamboo tube, but got no response. I didn't trust him completely, so I walked over to his shack to see if he was there. It was empty. Was he spying on me secretly, or was he using this time to visit his family or hunt for food? No matter. The moon was floating higher than the tallest trees. It was time. I tapped the bamboo seven times, meaning I was leaving my post, then I walked along the dikes to see if any Khmer Rouge cadres had come to eavesdrop.

Then I returned to my altar. I stood there in the moonlight until my shadow was a yard in length. My guardian spirit had told me that flowers represent hope, candles and torches symbolize enlightenment, and incense sticks are message transmitters. She also told me that a prayer from the top of a termite mound will reach any realm with which you wish to communicate. So I set my tiny Buddha statues that were always in my hidden pocket on the highest step of the three-stepped altar I had sculpted. I placed the flowers on the second level, and the incense sticks on the lowest step. I lit the twenty-one sticks of incense with my torch, set it on the altar, and squatted to recite the *namusacar*: Namo Tassa Bhagavato Arahato Samma Sambuddhassa (Praise be to the Enlightened One, the Blessed One), three times, while bowing. Then I renewed my vows:

O, God in His Highest Form   higher than the Universe,
the King of Angels,   the Great-Grandmother of Deities,
my Mother and Father   on Heaven Island
     I pray to all of you!

O, Great-Grandfather Raja   Great-Grandfather Suos,
all the local deities,   O, King of the Sacred Cobra,
deities of the six directions,   deities of the mountains and the seas,
     bless these benedictions.

Drive the evil atheists,   those foolish devils
out of Cambodia.   May Khmers
have peace!   May Khmers be emancipated!
    May Khmers be respected and free!

Please banish all devils!   Please blow away
all supernatural devils   beyond the horizon!
Please scour Cambodia!   May democracy
     prevail in Cambodia!

When Cambodia is independent the people free from fears,
I promise to offer   alms to my fathers
at Angkor Wat   to lift the curse
     from this land.

May Great-Grandmother Cobra and the King of the Mountain Country
witness my Sacred Vows.   After I have crossed
these three wildernesses,   after I have reached
     the shore of genuine Freedom,

I will invite the monks   more than five hundred of them
to present Buddhist discourses, to bless
all the people,   to celebrate
     the rebirth of my beloved Cambodia.

Even though the night was quiet, I was still nervous, fearing that the chieftain of the camp might eavesdrop, or that other members of the Khmer Rouge might notice the light on top of the mound. I returned for three nights to pray for peace, then I destroyed the altar.

A month after praying for peace and freedom, just past midnight, I heard someone walking around outside my shack, circling it seven times. I started shaking, thinking that someone had found out about my altar and was there to escort me to my death. But then it was silent again, and I dreamed my way through the rest of the night. In a dream, I heard voices saying "Grandchild, stay here overnight . . . the liberators will come in due time." During the same night, my wife dreamed of rivers of people walking northward, right by our shack. She recognized many of them, but we were not part of the procession.

In the next few days the sounds of heavy artillery came closer and closer. Pol Pot's Angkar intensified our harvest efforts. We were working night and day, but for some reason they sent Syna to another paddy field. One morning shortly after she left, a commander of the women's brigade came snooping around to make sure that Syna had actually gone as ordered. Instead of my wife, she saw my mother-in-law taking her morning meal of hard rice and part of my ration of pork they gave me to take along while I was gathering resin.

"I think we have capitalists here," the commander shouted.

"I think in a few days the soles of your feet will become white with fear," I responded. Something must have come over me, to abandon caution like that.

"We'll see about that!" she sneered, as she left hurriedly.

I put the balance pole on my shoulder, to carry the bucket and bamboo tubes to the mountains to gather resin. I remember looking at my mother-in-law, and looking down at myself, our clothes nothing but tatters. I was just leaving our shack, thinking that we had all become so emaciated, we couldn't possibly live much longer, when suddenly the chief of the field kitchen ran by me with a wild expression on his face, shouting "Stay where you are! Yuon are coming! Yuon are coming!"

I put down my gear. Three planes swooped in low from the east. Two bombs exploded: *Boeung—! Boeung—!* Then another: *Boeung—!* The third one was dropped on a cemetery where soldiers who were killed fighting the Vietnamese in 1977 were buried.

I waved my checkered scarf at the planes: "Drop more bombs! Over here!" Another plane veered in my direction. *Boeung—!* A bomb exploded fifty meters east of me. A piece of shrapnel the size of my thumb hurtled in my direction, landing near my feet. I picked it up and displayed it to the pilot: "Thanks, liberator!"

The shrapnel was hot. I was holding it between my thumb and index finger, standing just a few yards from my shack, when a group of youngsters who had been lollygagging in the shade nearby ran past me shrieking, frightened to death. Some fell down prostrate, others rolled up into fetal positions. The old women yelled for their children with panic in their voices. After watching this display, I raced to our shack to check on my boy and found my mother-in-law hugging him tightly. Suddenly I felt my body temperature shoot up, and I fell unconscious.

I lay there, out of it for most of that day. But in the late afternoon, soldiers swarmed around our shack. They pointed AK-47s at us and ordered us to pack up our belongings and move out. By then I had just enough control of my body to stumble out and hitch up the oxen. The soldiers yelled "Pack stuff for Phnom Chi!" The field kitchen chief ordered me to give a crippled old man a lift. My oxcart was piled up with bundles and three old people.

I noted that it was, once again, the night of the full moon. I began driving my oxcart northward from my shack, but just as I was getting started, soldiers ordered me to stop. While I was waiting, one of the new people, a woman with a shrapnel wound on her left cheek, asked me to give her a lift to Sre Krauv Camp. By then I was very sick, throwing up every ten minutes, and could not respond to her plea. As she stumbled forward into the night, I was ordered to move again. I was delirious and at the point of not really caring what was going to happen next, as long as it brought an end to our ordeal.

THE WHEEL TURNS

We knew the Vietnamese were coming, but we didn't know precisely when or what would happen to us when they arrived. All we knew was that we were on the road again, on our way to a place we had never heard of before, Phnom Chi, or Fertilizer Mountain. Tributaries of people from many directions flowed into one river, but it was slow going because the Khmer Rouge were terrified of the Vietnamese troops, and repeatedly ordered us to hide in the woods. We followed trails through the woods for two weeks and during that entire period my fever never abated. The only medicine available was neem leaves, but on one occasion, to speed my recovery, I overdid it and chewed up too many, turning my stomach inside out. Neem leaves are bitter, resembling quinine's taste, with similar curative properties.

Angkar Phan saw me retching and said, "Sick, Ta? Better get well. If not, we'll have to leave you here." This fellow's eyes made my skin crawl—I had come to refer to the Khmer Rouge as "The Red Eyes," and this man's eyes had a particularly reddish-yellow cast. Rumor had it that the Khmer Rouge made a practice of sneaking up behind young virgin girls, killing them with axes, then removing their livers, grilling them and eating them, and swallowing the bile raw. They believed that this gave them immortality. It also turned the whites of their eyes permanently red-yellow. I have heard that there are instances, on every continent, of warriors eating the livers of their adversaries to gain power. I have met several of my countrymen who admitted doing this in wartime. To this day, I can spot someone who has eaten the liver of another human being—their eyes remain permanently discolored. This all sounds so warped, but there are many other practices in this world that make just as little sense.

After this devil's warning, I somehow struggled to my feet, with a boost from the Almighty, and staggered along behind the others. I had no oxcart now, and was barely conscious of where I was going. That night, I stopped somewhere in the jungle to rest. My sickness intensified, to the point of climax. And I witnessed a remarkable sight—two beautiful girls, shrouded with white veils, were dancing atop a mound. At just that moment my fever broke.

Again our keepers ordered us forward, and again I begged God for mercy as I staggered along. After wading through rivers and crossing islands, I began to lose all sense of direction. (This disorientation affects me even today—I might notice that the sun is setting, but internally, I still have no sense of where I am or what time of day it is. Sometimes it can be frightening. It's one of a number of lingering effects of those terrible years.) Finally we reached a place called the Five Hundred Rice Paddy Camp. Actually, there were five camps numbered 101 to 105, each with 100 paddy fields. The slave laborers who cleared these fields had been Sihanouk's armed forces, civil servants, teachers, monks, and doctors captured by the North Vietnamese in April 1970. The only reminders of them were falling-down cottages.

There were people from everywhere, all directions, crammed together in this place, with almost no rice to sustain us. After the Sampoch contingent was herded to one of the nearby fields in Camp 101, I cleared some bushes, leaving four big plants to act as the posts for our shelter. I spread a plastic tarp to form a makeshift roof and piled bushes to make our walls—primitive, but it was home for the next two weeks.

I was assigned to flatten a paddy field so that it could be used as a rice threshing site. The procedure was to take fresh cattle dung, stir it in a bucket of water, and then splash it on the flattened ground. When it dried it was as hard as cement.

In two weeks, we moved again, this time to Camp 105. Syna was assigned to work at the field kitchen, harvesting yams and digging up manioc bulbs.

One night, around 10:00 p.m., some 200 people were rounded up to be taken to a "special project." As they filed by me, an acquaintance of mine called out to me "Ta Gold, go with us." I told him I was about to get some gruel, and would rather wait. I'm sure he had no idea what I was implying, but I knew they were doomed. And indeed, they were taken to a mass grave and executed in the moonlight. I never saw the graves and do not know the means of execution, but I am positive that this is what happened. All those shanties that were bustling with life the day before were now empty.

Today, a visitor to the Killing Fields at Choeung Ek outside Phnom Penh will get a clear sense of how haunted a place can be, particularly standing in the depression where hundreds of bodies were buried, while schoolchildren recite their lessons at the nearby community elementary school. Their young singsong voices give hope, but they cannot drown out the moans of the dead. There are thousands of such places in Cambodia. A medium, or someone sensitive to spirits, would probably go crazy in short order. In Siem Reap City, for instance, there is a crocodile farm, and some of the older crocs were around when the Khmer Rouge threw live victims to them. You step more carefully along the bridges, knowing they have tasted human flesh. And you also feel the presence of those poor souls who were thrown to them. And you wonder how long it will take the land to cleanse itself of this carnage.

The Red-Eyes moved my family, but I stayed put, as we once again took up the task of clearing the forests to transform them into cornfields. As I worked, I remember having fleeting thoughts of the fields of Iowa—mile after mile of neatly planted corn. The

paintings of Grant Wood idealize that Iowa landscape and that's
the way I see it in my mind's eye. I know now that nothing is as
simple as that. I know those Iowa farmers have their own strug-
gles. But those Iowa cornfields continue to wave peacefully in my
imagination, where time stands still.

I fell ill again. The air was perfectly still; not a single bird song
could be heard, not a single solitary insect chirred. The authorities, for some reason, left me alone in my shack, where I lay in
wait for my visit from Death. But I remained in the protective
shadow of my sacred vows; a small boy got me to my feet, pushed
me onto an oxcart, and carried me to my family. Who he was, and
how he knew where to take me, I do not know. As was the case
so many times during those years of tribulation, an angel came to
my assistance.

As 1979 began, they started moving us southwest again toward a
place they called Phnom Chi (Fertilizer Mountain). We followed
the Mekong into Kompong Thom Province. After crossing the
fourth river on that trek, I found myself lying half-dead on its far
bank. The Red-Eyes refused to give me any pestled rice . . . a sign
that they regarded me as a lost cause. That night, Bido Mean
Roeuddhi visited my wife and told her that Phnom Penh had been
liberated. She whispered this to me, but I was so weak that this
news brought no spark of hope or enthusiasm. Only one thing
was on my mind at that moment—God was about to bring me
peace by letting me die.

But the next day the Red-Eyes loaded me on an oxcart and our
journey continued. After one day's travel, we rested in the rice
fields. Our captors slaughtered some cattle and shared the meat,
but not with my family. My son scavenged two front leg bones.
That night he scorched the hooves and ate them as if he were
feasting on the finest fare. He was so happy. I remember, through
my delirium, hearing him tell me that we'd make soup from the
bones tomorrow, but I could barely answer. The next thing I

knew, it was midmorning of the following day and we had stopped on the road to rest. The Red-Eyes left us to scout ahead for Vietnamese troops. I fell asleep in the shade. My son woke me to tell me that the soup was ready. I was weak, but I crawled toward the soup. Suddenly cattle were stampeding everywhere—God forbid! Not the soup! We tried to protect this precious meal, as the Khmer Rouge pitched their AK-47s, B-40s, and all their ammunition into the trees, and vanished like smoke, as they fled from the Vietnamese. When the commotion was over, our soup, like the Red-Eyes, had disappeared.

Although we did not come face to face with the Vietnamese that day, we somehow realized that we were finally free to go home. Although we did not know it at the time, we had once again come close to death. I had believed, naturally, that the Fertilizer Mountain was a place where the Pol Pot clique actually produced fertilizer from animal and human excrement on a grand scale. Since I had become an expert at producing fertilizer, it was logical that they would transfer me to such a place. But some months later several of us heard widely circulated rumors that the Khmer Rouge had a motorized guillotine at the Fertilizer Mountain, and that they were beheading prisoners and rendering their remains into fertilizer, which they were sending to China. This is where the Red-Eyes were herding us when the Vietnamese troops intercepted their scouts. It turns out we were just a few miles from that grisly destination. Like so many other stories of this sort, it has never, to my knowledge, been substantiated, but maybe the facts will surface before the jungle covers all remaining evidence.

So, despite my condition, the four of us began our journey home. Several days into our return, I met an ex-captain who agreed to ferry us across the river to the Hundred-Column Temple at Sambor, so that I could fulfill the vow I had made back in November, but we had nothing to exchange for our fee. When I expressed my frustration to my mother-in-law, she reached in her gown, and pulled out a pouch that she had worn inside her undergarments all through our years in camps. She'd been hiding a few personal talismans, two bracelets, and an American twenty-dollar bill. Our fare was paid.

After he dropped us on the opposite bank, we squatted in the abandoned shell of a house. All of us were starving. I staggered out to see if I could find fish. I spotted a knee-deep pond that appeared to be full of carp bubbling near the surface. I began splashing the water out of the pond with a discarded slipper I'd found. This bailing was interminable, but I kept at it, confident I would be rewarded with several fat carp. Yet not a single fish was there when I got the level down. "O, Princess Lotus Bud, give me a fish," I sighed. But my prayer went unanswered.

Beyond hope, I returned to the shelter. The sun was blistering hot, the earth parched and cracked. I searched for the inevitable rice frogs in the cracks, but found not a one. In a dry pond near the shack I spotted what looked like the head of a carp sticking out of the drying mud. "Is it a spook, Son?" I asked my boy.

"No, it's really a fish, Dad," he told me. My mind had become so addled at this point that I needed this reassurance—I couldn't tell what was real and what wasn't. But the carp was still fresh, and we finally enjoyed a decent meal.

Feeling restored, we went to the tomb of Princess Krabum Chhouk, at the Hundred-Column Temple. The temple had become pretty shabby during Pol Pot's reign, but at least it was still standing. (Today it has been restored to its former magnificence—one of the projects for which Hun Sen's administration can justly take credit.) I burned nine sticks of incense and recited "Namo Tassa Bhagavato Arahato Samma Sambuddhassa" three times, and then intoned the following verses:

> Praise be to you, my Princess Krabum Chhouk!
> I pledged to come, now I'm here in front of you.
> May our journey home be safe;
> May someone befriend us on the way;

may our land be free; and may our people be happy.
Praise be to You, Machah Bong!
May Human Rights be respected!

If my lot is to be of no use to this land of ours
may Machah Bong expel me.
Praise be to You, Princess Sister!
Let me dwindle away for as long as my life will last.

As I look at those words, they sound as if I were close to drowning in self-pity. But I was so weakened that my body was actually starting to digest itself, and my attitude, which may have already been somewhat fatalistic, was now absolutely resigned to whatever was to come.

That evening, sitting with my face to the sunset, I contemplated a whirlpool in the river. I wondered what had brought the princess to this spot, to perish because of the desire of the Crocodile Prince. The forest was a brilliant, almost surreal green, and the horizon was crimson behind it. The birds of the forest flew energetically to and from their nests. A sense of peace washed over me. I looked at my boy and words started bubbling up from deep within me. "We are free from tigers, Son!" referring to the Red-Eyes. "Let's go home! We are liberated! We are Free! Free! Free! Let's go! Go! Go! Let's pick wild fruit; let's pick wild vegetables; let's fish, let's catch fish—choose the biggest one. Let's cook! Let's eat! Let's sleep! Let's dive into the water; let's take a swim, Son—swim to freedom! Freedom, Son! Freedom!" I began to laugh and cry at the same time. My son's eyes got big—I guess he was afraid of me, knowing the state of my body and my mind. But he must have realized that this burst of hysteria was just the release of all those days and months and years we had just survived together, because he began to laugh, too. We jumped in the water and began splashing each other, and then I took him in my arms and the two of us wept together.

That night, it was so cold that I made a fire to warm us. Some time after midnight there was a *Pok! Pok! Pok!* on the door. "What the hell . . . who's knocking at this hour?" I shouted.

"Open the door or I'll shoot it off the hinges!" a voice screamed. I quivered like a skinned frog dipped in salt. I opened the door. A Khmer Rouge soldier entered, pointing his gun at me. "Who gave you permission to light this fire? Tomorrow you'd better leave . . . if you don't, you'll be executed." Oh, God, when would I finally be free of this torment?

But next morning, there was no sign of the Red-Eyes. Just as the sun rose, we left the Hundred-Column Temple, and balancing our bundle of possessions on my head, we stumbled slowly along the road. Although the bundle had hardly anything in it, and my own weight was down to nothing, my body felt as if it weighed three times my normal weight. We simply had to stop every two or three miles.

To sustain us, I went fishing in the Mekong, with a line and one hook. I caught nothing, of course, but I did find a cow's head, discarded, no doubt, after it had been slaughtered. We cut off the flesh and made soup—it was wonderful soup, no matter how close to putrefaction the meat may have been. It was getting dark, so we moved on, hoping to make another two miles before we stopped. We dragged the rest of the cow's head along with us.

That night, we again squatted in an abandoned house. I could hear other villagers muttering and milling about nearby, but they steered clear of us. In the morning they told us that the house was inhabited by very aggressive spooks. I was long past the point of being afraid of ghosts—after all, I was a walking ghost myself. I lifted the cow's head. Everyone stared at me as we walked along, wondering why on earth I was balancing the remnants of a cow's head on my own. When I finally caught on to this, I pitched it into the bushes. Instead, we picked some wild vegetables, and dug some roots, and begged three small salted fish from some base people along the way.

There were hordes of people everywhere—most of them in oxcarts. All we could do was walk. In a few days, however, almost everyone had disappeared and we were alone on the road. I put together a two-wheeled cart from parts I salvaged from broken carts we found along the way, and loaded what remained of our possessions into it. This made traveling much less taxing.

Suddenly a Yuon emerged from the woods and searched my body and our bags at gunpoint. He robbed the few remaining keepsakes I had saved from the U.S. Since I was too exhausted to be afraid, I asked him: *"Toi sin coeum ma chuck?"* (Do you have rice? May I have a little rice?) Another soldier gave me a crust of cold rice. *"Cam oeun,* thank you!" Speaking in Vietnamese and in English—an indication that I had been educated—would have been grounds for the Khmer Rouge to shoot me. But the Vietnamese soldier merely gave me a hard look and let our group move forward.

We arrived at Kratie City, capital of the province, late in the afternoon, set up camp under the open sky, and prepared dinner. In the morning, an ex-professor who recognized me called on me to discuss the turn of events. He was from a nearby village, and asked us to stay at his house with him. And the day after that, we happened upon Nuth Dara, my former working partner at both the Boh Leav and Sre Pring labor camps. He invited us to stay with him and his family. But we wanted to get back to Phnom Penh.

Since we were all terrified of the Khmer Rouge, we set out for Phnom Penh together as a group. Nuth Dara joined us and soon we were fast friends again. We passed by Boh Leav, the third labor camp where we had worked together—not a single shack remained.

At Prek Ta Am, we stopped at the house of one of the women who had been responsible for killing our twins, but I was too weak to take revenge. Syna spoke with her briefly, but I could muster only a feeble attempt at a smile and just walked past; my anger had no place to go. You will find that Cambodians often smile or even laugh at the most distressing life events—maybe this is cultural, or maybe it is just because there is no other appropriate emotion that would allow us to keep going, given the immensity of the feelings and memories inside.

At Wat Prek Dambok, I became sick again and fell into a swoon. A healthy bull, owned by Dara, was standing next to me. It fell dead on the spot and seconds later my fever broke. When they slaughtered it, I asked for some of the liver. But when I ate the liver, I fell sick again immediately. Dara didn't quite understand what had happened, but he was upset, and used the incident as an excuse to leave with his family and strike out on his own.

That night, on the edge of Wat Prek Dambok, we stopped at an ashram that had been abandoned. Nearby was a dead krasamng tree. I remembered passing by that tree in 1975. It was green and flourishing, and bore fruit that all the villagers used in their soups. At the start of the Pol Pot "experience," people had gathered around this tree as a kind of refuge. Now, four years later, it had withered and died. When I approached it, I noticed that the thorns of the tree held strands of fine hair, and that the bark was darkened in places, as if stained by a thick substance. Then I saw the skeletons of at least fifteen babies scattered around the base of the tree. Their skulls had been smashed. I was already quite ill at the time, but this sight caused my knees to buckle and I fell to the ground and howled. When I found my wife Syna, I told her what I had seen, but urged her not to go there.

Although I have never met anyone who witnessed what happened there, my presumption is that the Khmer Rouge *Utapats* (The Unbelievers) had rounded up the babies and murdered them because they had become a burden. I further presumed that the tree had died because of the concentration of blood that had soaked the ground—all that salt was too much for the tree to survive. The Khmer Rouge were fond of saying "To annihilate grasses, uproot them daily!" This was an application of what they meant. What sin had the grass ever committed, I wondered?

We climbed to the second floor of the ashram and stretched out to sleep in pitch darkness. I could not sleep, because I heard the moaning voices of the murdered children, begging for explanation. That night, the smell of blood permeated my consciousness and I slept only fitfully.

At dawn, I went downstairs to find rice husks spread over blood a yard deep—the smell of blood was more than just in my imagination. There had been a massacre there very recently, of monstrous proportions. But there was no evidence of bodies, and there was no one to ask what had happened. As I recount these atrocities, they seem hard to believe, even though I saw them. They were like a medieval nightmare—something out of a painting by Hieronymus Bosch.

As I walked out the door of the ashram, I saw the krasamng tree outlined against the morning sunlight, and I could hear its choked voice, drowning in the blood of infants. The voice was very faint, and its meaning indistinguishable. The Utapats had killed the fruit of the tree with the fruit of our countrymen and women. Neither the tree nor those babies had had any chance of escaping their fate.

I have never been back to Wat Prek Dambok and am not sure whether I ever want to go there. I no longer have nightmares about what I saw and heard, but I don't want to take the chance of opening up those memories. On the other hand, perhaps such a visit might bring closure. When my friend Ken McCullough went there with Syna in December 2000, they found what was most likely the stump of the krasamng tree—it had been dead those many years and had finally been cut down. According to Ken, the ashram, on the outside, looked much as I had described it. It was now inhabited by young monks, and in a photo Ken took, I could see their freshly washed saffron robes draped on the railings. The sun shone through the cloths, giving the interior of the building a purified cast. The head monk at the local temple said he had never heard the story about the babies being killed or the massacre, but a local farmer Ken met near the stump of the krasamng tree showed him a well that had been poisoned because the Khmer Rouge had bashed the heads of a number of people against its winch, then thrown their bodies down into the water. Ultimately, some of these stories will be corroborated, but many never will. Through the vigilance of people such as Mr. Youk Chhang, director of the Cambodian Documentation Center, these stories are still being sifted through and some semblance of the truth will emerge. As to the outcome of this research? There is a balance between forgiveness and justice, but it takes a superior being to know where that balance is. Perhaps it will be found someday.

*   *   *

We hired an oxcart belonging to a man we knew named Ong, just to carry rice and my mother-in-law. Of all that stuff I'd brought with us when we'd left Chbar Ampeou, we had only one dented pot, and as we walked along I flung it into the bushes because even that weight was too heavy for me to carry.

By nightfall, I couldn't even crawl, nor could I speak. Lying motionless on the ground, I could neither see nor hear anything. A spirit named Grandpa Ang Phim possessed a medium, who gave my wife some medicine wrapped in a lotus leaf. She washed my face with it, and dripped some into my mouth. I came alive, and in the morning we continued our trip to Wat Khplok, east of Phnom Penh. At the pagoda, I found an old bathroom scale and stepped on it. My weight was down to sixty-eight pounds; I was close to becoming a spirit myself.

OUR NEW COLONIAL MASTERS

For the first few months after the Vietnamese invasion, we never knew when we were going to suddenly bump into a small group of Khmer Rouge forces on the run. And when we did run into them, we never knew if they were going to rob us, kill us, or ignore us. Eventually most of them were chased into the western mountain region by the Vietnamese, but I still didn't dare get close to my house. We stayed about eight-and-a-half miles away at Prek Eng, with the sister-in-law of a general I had known from the Khmer Republic years—another victim of Pol Pot. During our stay I suffered another malaria attack, made worse by malnutrition.

Somehow our host found ripe bananas, eggs, boiled chicken, and steamed rice to help my recovery. Fortunately, despite all she'd been through, my wife Syna was in relatively good health, and so was our son. Even my mother-in-law had come through.

After I began to recover my strength, we decided to move to Auntie Yen's house in Koh Norea, slowly moving closer to our house, like a timid cat slowly approaching its eventual target, pretending to be disinterested. We'd heard that Auntie Yen was still hiding out. It felt comforting to stay in her house, but we missed her and her counsel.

I felt as if I had developed an irrational fear of going near my own house. Syna had a great deal of concern, too, but she put on a brave face and volunteered. She discovered that Chbar Ampeou had been blocked off by the Vietnamese troops. Soon we discovered why.

Once the Khmer Rouge had driven the population out of the cities, they had departed too. But before they left, they stockpiled the wealth—gold, silver, cars, and even personal possessions such as sewing machines—in buildings that were located near highways. This practice was repeated throughout the country in every town of any size. Now the Vietnamese were looting these caches. When the Vietnamese invaded, the Khmer Rouge abandoned the rice that had just been harvested. This too, found its way back to Vietnam. As "aid" to Cambodia they shipped back spoiled rice, fit only for pigs.

Most of what had been taken from homes in our neighborhood of Chbar Ampeou had been stored in the buildings around the market. Now they were loading it into trucks and transporting it southeast, down National Highway 1, to Vietnam. When everything of any value was gone, they let us return.

When we finally arrived at our old home, we discovered that five families were staying there, all from the same forced labor camp in the Eastern Zone where we had been. They were among the few I had trusted, like Nora, for example, who had been a professor of English at Lycée Sissowath, and his wife, who had been a nurse. In the camp, I had told them that if they survived Pol Pot, they should offer a little food to the elves that inhabited the forest around the camp, and then they were welcome to go to Chbar Ampeou and stay at our house until they found another shelter.

Once we arrived and exchanged greetings, I looked around for items I had hidden in the walls—statues of Buddha, military ID cards, certificates—but the house had been stripped bare. The structure was pretty much intact though, except for the bathroom, which either the Khmer Rouge or the Vietnamese had broken up, looking for concealed gold (that didn't exist). They had ripped down the ceiling, which had been easy enough, since it had been made of plywood. I had hidden my crystal amrita, our Zenith radio, and a Canon camera up there, along with three sacks of rice, and a few books I hadn't had the heart to burn—all were gone. On the floor, however, I did find one page from one of my old books—it was a poem by Emily Dickinson. For many years afterwards I kept it in a safe until very recently, when I asked Syna to send it to me here in the U.S. I carry it with me, tucked into a manuscript of my poems, hoping that that one page will somehow transfer its power to my own work.

The survival of that page seemed miraculous at the time, and I showed it at once to everyone who had been camping out in our house. They were suitably impressed, and asked about my background. Even though we had all talked a bit during our labor camp years, none of us ever disclosed too much about our past. It was safer that way. When they discovered that I had been a National Assemblyman and a member of the Khmer Republic United Nations delegation, they felt a bit intimidated, and by evening, they had all gone to find new shelter. It was as if Emily Dickinson, who had always treasured her own privacy, had helped us regain ours.

We were home, but we had no idea what would happen next. The nation was in a shambles. Phnom Penh had been deserted for years. Suddenly goods and services were back in demand, but guard posts manned by Vietnamese soldiers dotted the landscape, and blocked every route, including the Monivong Bridge into Phnom Penh. We were back to relying on our survival skills.

After we obtained some medicine, and my health began to improve, I returned to a primitive way of life. I woke up at 3:00 a.m. and walked three miles southeast to a place called Monkeys Have Hidden Their Pets Lake where I fished for shrimp. When I had about three pounds, my mother-in-law took most of my catch to the market to trade for milled rice. We got five cans of rice for a pound of shrimp. We still wore rags, but we enjoyed those meals as if we were millionaires. Everything's relative.

As it began to get hot, the water in the lake evaporated, and so did my brief career as a fisherman. Next, Syna, my son, and my mother-in-law went to the countryside to glean paddy rice left over after the last harvest, but the little they found wasn't worth the risk of running into a skirmish between retreating Khmer

Rouge and Vietnamese troops. Then Syna remembered that she had actually buried some gold in our yard, unbeknownst to me. And it was still there. That gold kept us fed, while I tried to figure out who was going to pick up the broken pieces of a nation and how they might try to reassemble them.

I was also trying to find out about my family. I knew my oldest brother, Sa Em, had been killed, but what of the others? There were no phones, there was no mail, I had no way to learn about their fate. But one day in June, my youngest brother, Sa Lorn, arrived from Svay Rieng. Like many of us, Sa Lorn had changed his name during the Pol Pot years, and to this day he has continued to use that new name, Un Buntha, instead of returning to his given name and family name, as I have.

Buntha told us that our older sister, Touch, her husband, and all ten of their children had survived (they still live in Svay Rieng, our native province), but no one yet knew anything about Sa Mouth, our oldest sister, or our youngest sister, Chin. Nor did Buntha have any information about our other brothers or their families. Then he hesitated, and with tears in his eyes, he told us that out mother had died of starvation in 1977. It would be five years before we would find out the final toll:

My father had died in 1970, but my mother died of starvation during the Pol Pot years.

My sister Chin was killed, along with one of her children. Her husband and the other two children survived.

My sister Sa Mouth, her husband Mam Sam, and their son were killed, but their two daughters survived. One still lives in Cambodia, and the other lives in New York.

My brother Sa Em, his wife Mey Thol, and all twelve of their children were killed.

My brother An, his wife Long Van Thet (who had served in the National Assembly), and their son were all killed.

My brother Sam Ul, his wife Ray Yana, and their son were killed.

And of course our own twin daughters were strangled at birth.

Somehow my brother Sun Ly, his wife Nith, and their seven children all survived, along with Buntha, his wife, and their five children. Half of our family, wiped out. This was an all-too-common story throughout the country.

I continued fishing for a few more months, while I regained my health, my strength, and a little bit of my sanity. But I couldn't hide out forever. The Khmer Rouge had devastated a generation of educated people. As one of the surviving Cambodians with a college degree, I had an obligation to make a contribution to the task of rebuilding the country. But that meant approaching a government in a state of chaos and paranoia. Although we were all relieved that Pol Pot had been overthrown, we had to face the fact that we had been invaded by Vietnam, and they were intent on taking over the same role that the French had played, but with less élan. We had never been happy about being colonized by a distant European nation, but it was far more humiliating to be taken over and "lorded over" by a neighbor with whom we had been fighting for more than a thousand years.

After World War II, the Soviet Union had installed puppet governments in Eastern Europe to give those conquered countries the illusion of self-rule, while Moscow dictated policy from afar. The process was about to be repeated. Vietnam claimed they were planning to allow Cambodia complete self-rule, but everyone knew who was really in charge. So if I were to make my contribution to the rebuilding of our nation, I was going to have to work within this government-with-strings-attached that they called the Revolutionary People of Kampuchea.

Having studied in the United States and served in our U.N. delegation, it seemed appropriate to apply for a job at the Ministry of Foreign Affairs. And so in early July 1979, I went to the Ministry, picked up an employment application card, then went out for some air. I wanted to take the time to read the application carefully. A few minutes later, Hun Sen came out, crossed the street, and approached me where I was standing under a tamarind tree. A tall, thin, gregarious man, he was serving as head of the department at the time. He seemed like a young man on his way up, but no one could have guessed that he would eventually outlast all his enemies and become prime minister. On the other hand no one would have guessed that I had any legitimate professional credentials had they looked at the long unkempt beard on my face that day. He asked me about my background, and I told him that I had a master's degree from the United States, and that I'd like to help rebuild the country. "Yes, yes, yes," he said. "Come back tomorrow—but first cut your hair, shave your beard. Clean yourself up and come back." But I didn't. I reentered the building, completed the application, gave it to the office manager for the chief of the cabinet, went home, and back to fishing. Two weeks later a new Peugeot pulled up in front of my house, with a driver and three soldiers, two armed with machine guns. One soldier got out of the car, and while looking at our house, called, "Old man . . . come out."

The neighbors began to commiserate. "He survived Pol Pot, and now the Vietnamese are going to arrest him and kill him." The fear and despair in the air was palpable. I came out to ask what was going on. The soldier didn't explain; he just told me to bring my wife and son. Only my mother-in-law was allowed to stay. We got in the car and they drove us to the Ministry of Foreign Affairs— the former Buddhist University, which had been built on the west bank of the Mekong River. We were told we had to undergo indoctrination before I could work for the government.

We stayed there for a month, waiting for the indoctrination to start. Buntha was there at the Ministry of Foreign Affairs at the same time, also waiting for the next indoctrination, but he got bored after about a week, and took off toward the Thai border. He had a scheme: it seems he had gotten some gold that he had hidden on the family property in Thlok. At the Thai border he exchanged the gold for what we call *BiCheng* (monosodium glutamate), which was used in almost every Cambodian dish at that time. He did well, and has succeeded in almost every venture since. He is now a prominent bureaucrat and businessman.

At mealtimes they gave us a wide variety of food to choose from, cafeteria style—entrées plus two bowls of rice and one bowl of *trakuon* soup. Although they offered us many choices, Syna was afraid to take more than she needed to survive. My son didn't stay too long. He got tired of eating trakuon every day, and left to stay with his grandmother, where he could get food more to his liking. She loved taking care of him, and he loved scavenging mangoes, guavas, and watermelons for her. They had reestablished schools by then, and Proelung started going to classes in September, at Wat Unalom. He was ten years old, a smart kid, but had received only rudimentary schooling during the Pol Pot years. We registered as U Bunyaroeuddhi, a name of his own choosing.

In some ways the indoctrination period was a kind of "reunion of the educated." I saw many of my former students from the University of Technics, some of the other teachers I'd met during my brief stint there, and some of the people I'd served with in the National Assembly. I met other intellectuals I had heard of, and discovered they had heard of me as well. If not for the requirement that we all write autobiographies each week, it would have been an entirely enjoyable time. They watched us carefully to make sure that we did not discuss what to include and what to leave out of these documents. The Vietnamese were particularly interested in what I did during Sihanouk's regime, the Lon Nol period, and during Pol Pot. I maintained the same story every time: I had been technical manager of the fish canning factory at Koh Kong, and had been trained as an English teacher.

The autobiography is one of the classic tactics employed by communist regimes everywhere. Each person in a group is required to write an autobiography on a daily, weekly, or monthly basis. Sometimes the autobiographies are read aloud, or by other members of the group, and sometimes they are reviewed by the "higher-ups." People are given an incentive to be critical of each other, even to turn in a former friend, creating an overwhelming atmosphere of distrust. And of course the autobiographies are kept on file. If the government becomes suspicious of someone, all of his or her autobiographies can be reviewed for inconsistencies, to aid in an investigation, and later, an interrogation. A "mistake" in an autobiography meant certain death during the Pol Pot years. Under the Vietnamese regime it sometimes meant death, but it usually meant six months of "reeducation" and a demotion in rank.

After the month of waiting for indoctrination, I was assigned to take care of cattle, and grow trakuon at Ta Khmao, far to the south of Phnom Penh. Word of my assignment spread to some of my relatives who worked in a soft drink factory, and they approached me and urged me not to go. They were convinced this assignment was a ruse; they believed someone who was jealous of my past achievements had plotted against me, and that when I arrived at Ta Khmao, I would be killed. They urged me to join them in the factory where they worked. The factory was situated just a few blocks from the Ministry of Foreign Affairs, north of the Royal Palace.

I decided to heed their warning, and went to Hun Sen to plead my case. My plan was to exaggerate an existing eye condition. I bowed to him three times, and told him that I couldn't read, that I was almost blind because of cataracts. He asked me how I expected to work in a factory if my eyesight was that bad. I told him that I was a skilled mechanic, that I knew the machinery by touch. He gave the O.K., then presented me with eight yards of cloth, and thirty pounds of milled rice as gifts. He also offered us a car, and even a villa, but Syna and I both thought it would be inappropriate, and possibly dangerous to accept such gifts.

So we headed back to Chbar Ampeou, and in mid-August I started work at the soft drink factory: Le Brasserie Glacière de L'Indochine. I took care of the machinery, showing the workers how to lubricate the machines and run the generator. I also organized a program to gather raw materials to keep in storage.

But in America I know you have a phrase that says that no good deed goes unpunished. The progress we were making came to the attention of Nuon Saret, the new vice minister for industry. (The former minister had been arrested after giving a speech protesting the way the Vietnamese were hauling off our forests and other natural resources. He was not the first, nor would he be the last to be arrested for this "crime.")

Nuon Saret was an ethnic Khmer who had grown up in Vietnam. He could read and write in Vietnamese, but his knowledge of conversational Khmer was limited, and he couldn't read or write in our native language. Despite his lack of education, he was a capable man, and over the next ten years, would frequently act as my ally. Our relationship began when he asked me to organize a union in the soft drink factory. I must have given a fairly persuasive speech because they elected me to serve as president. I enjoyed working with my relatives in this low-key operation but I was only there for a few months.

In November, Nuon Saret appointed me general manager of a bicycle factory in O Roeussei, just a fifteen-minute walk from the soft drink factory. Keep in mind that bicycles weren't just for kids or for adults who wanted to get some exercise during their leisure time. Fewer than ten percent of Cambodians own cars—even today, our people get to and from most jobs on bicycles, while freight is still carried in oxcarts. Getting new bicycles manufactured was an important step in getting our economy moving again. In other words, this was an important assignment.

The factory was manned entirely by peasants, with an elementary school teacher as manager. I immediately identified two problems. First, we had almost no raw materials, and in the aftermath of the war, no easy way to procure any. Second, nobody knew how to run the machinery in the factory. So I divided the staff into three groups, one for administration (including finding the day-to-day necessities for the workers), one for procurement of raw materials, and one to learn how to run the equipment.

Considering the transportation system, and the general chaos every business found itself in, I decided to divide my procurement staff into two groups: one to search the streets for discarded materials—nuts and bolts, chains, chrome, and other metals, and rubber; the other group sorted and labeled the materials for later use. Before long we had enough materials stockpiled to keep the factory moving right along. While my procurement people were searching for raw materials, I trained the manufacturing team, teaching them not only how to use the machinery, but how to keep it clean and well-lubricated, to eliminate breakdowns. By the end of December we were turning out two hundred bicycles a month, and delivered them proudly to the Ministry of Commerce, which found ready customers for them all.

During my stint at the bicycle factory, a Vietnamese "consultant" on an inspection tour started shouting, yelling, and banging the table in my office with his fist, because he believed I was recruiting only women workers. I should have let him blow off steam, but after keeping quiet during the Pol Pot years, something in me snapped, and I responded with equal vehemence. "They're not my workers, they're yours," I shouted. "It wasn't my choice to hire only women—you forced the decision by killing all their husbands—now what can I do? I have to feed them." The interpreter broke into a sweat. He recognized that my behavior could land me in prison. But suddenly the Vietnamese expert started to laugh, and I joined in. I was lucky that time.

I didn't realize it at first, but Nuon Saret was keeping his eye on me, and was praising me highly in periodic reports to the Ministry of Industry. And so as January 1980 dawned, I discovered that I had been promoted to the position of director of technics, in the Ministry of Industry. I was back in the government again. It was gratifying to be recognized for the good work I had accomplished, but I had a feeling that working for this government, with its Vietnamese "consultants," would be neither safe nor satisfying.

DR. MAK

During the mid-1980s, we went through a very trying period in my son's life. In June 1984, Auntie Yen was at our house and spontaneously went into a trance. Indta Kosei, the King of Angels, my Father from the Second Realm of Heaven began speaking through Auntie Yen. He told me that he had just returned from making a tour of Cambodia, and that he wanted to put an end to our wars, and that he had noticed that many treasures had been stolen from Vihea Preah Keo (The Silver Temple in the Royal Palace, Phnom Penh) and replaced with counterfeits. Then he said something very surprising—he reprimanded me for letting Roeuddhi play with a poison-ous snake when he was about two years old. "A snake," he said, "that had red stripes and a small head. That snake was half cobra and half sang-soeur. Its venom has now reached his heart, liver, marrow, and even his brain. There is no possibility that a human doctor can heal such an advanced condition. There is only one doctor who has the ability to treat my grandson's ailment—that is Kuma Petya, the Angel Doctor, or Thornvorntrei, in Pali." This was the doctor's title, but my Father did not mention his name.

He told me that he would order the doctor to prepare usatha (medicine), but that it would take a year before it would be ready. Then he told me that when peace prevailed in our land, he would return to recite the true history of Cambodia to me. As he left Auntie Yen, there was a strong wind that whirled the coconut fronds and the leaves on the mango branches. Auntie Yen had no memory of coming to our house, and was surprised to see us.

My son became weak, but he still managed to go to school. I went to the Department of Technics, where I worked as director, without paying any attention to what Indta Kosei had promised. Doctors working at the

Ministry of Industry where I worked prescribed antibiotics of all sorts for my son, but nothing seemed to halt his deteriorating condition.

I had to go to India for several months that year. When I got home in December I found our boy pale, and so skinny that he'd become almost humpbacked. I tried every means to find a cure for his condition, from traditional to allopathic, from free-of-charge to the most expensive Chinese potion. Nothing worked. And still I ignored what Indta Kosei had told me—maybe I was skeptical that there was such a thing as an angel doctor.

During the next year we continued to try conventional and unconventional medicines, to no avail. I sought out a woman who read tarot cards, who told me that when my boy was healed he would never get sick again. I went to my office as usual every day, beside myself with worry. By February 1986, my son had become very weak. His skin had the yellowish color of a rotten saffron bulb.

One weekend, a medium, my wife's great-uncle, told me that I should beseech Grandpa White Horse to cure our son. I had no idea who this was, but lit incense and prayed to him. I thought he was the spirit of my great-great-great-grandfather from Svay Rieng, but I found out later that I was mistaken.

I was sitting by myself after lunch that day and had a vision in which two elves appeared, each with an arm across the other's shoulder. They were wearing nothing but black shorts. I conversed with one of them, bargaining about the fee for healing my son. The other remained silent. The boy told me that I should pay after my son recovered.

I immediately sought out Syna and told her about my vision. She said it might be Dr. Mak, a legendary healer from the spirit world, who had appeared to her relative in similar form some years before, and the woman had been cured of her cancer. She said Dr. Mak was the one who spoke, and the other elf was probably his brother Mek, a kind of pharmacist. Mak was the only one allowed to converse with humans, but both of them could change shape. In American Indian stories there is a character known as Trickster, who is often depicted as one kind of animal or another, such as Coyote or Raven. He sometimes does outrageous and even stupid things, yet he also solves problems. Dr. Mak is such a being.

The next day we went to Auntie Yen's house. Syna went in first to talk to her, while I waited at the foot of the stairs to the house. I heard a conversation, and a voice that sounded like that of a drunkard. I entered in time to hear Dr. Mak order Syna to drink a cup of hot water he had poured from a kettle on the stove. She was afraid it was too hot, and at first refused. But when he insisted, she drank the water down.

I immediately bowed and said, "Thank you for coming, Ta Mak."

"Don't call me that!" he said. "Until you address me by my title, I can do nothing!"

"Very well, Thornvorntrei. I will do as you say," I replied. At that moment I noticed a complete transformation in his bearing, from drunkard to guru.

"From this very moment your son is cured," Thornvorntrei exclaimed.

My wife laughed. "What in the world are you saying? All I did was drink everyday water. How can that heal our child, who is miles away?"

"Wait and see." said Thornvorntrei.

A handful of people were in the room, and they told me they too had drunk hot water in this manner and their children had been healed. Thornvorntrei then gave a few drops of his potion to Syna to take home to Roeuddhi. My wife complained. "Buddho! Why does Thornvorntrei give me so small an amount of his potion? How can this potion heal my boy?"

He told Syna, "You can boil as much water as you like and pour the potion into it—then you will have a huge amount. Note that this magic potion will heal your son only and no one else. If anyone else drinks this potion he or she will be drinking nothing but water—the medicine will stick to the bottom of the glass."

At that time, my son had no idea that we had gone to see Thornvorntrei. But he knew the moment Thornvorntrei began to operate on him. My son said that he saw a needle fly through the air and pierce his chest. Suddenly pus came pouring out from deep inside. In a week's time, Roeuddhi could eat again; his appetite was ravenous. We treated him by serving him young roasted chicken.

What had happened was that Thornvorntrei had pumped the pus from Roeuddhi's liver. According to Roeuddhi, a group of surgeons started to operate on his heart and brain. He heard them urge each other to hurry up—if not the patient was going to die. Then they removed his heart to flush the pus from it and to cut away some matter that had built up on its surface. Then they put the heart on one side of a scale and the brain on the other to see if they weighed the same. When they were satisfied, Roeuddhi heard one of them say "Quick, quick—put the heart and brain back. We're running out of time! The patient is going to die!"

Thornvorntrei told me that after my son's internal organs had healed and his heart and brain were functioning again, the only major problem left was that his clavicle was broken and his back was all humped up. But he promised to plane off the hump until it had a normal shape.

Wherever Auntie Yen showed up to be possessed by Dr. Mak, she always had a gaggle of people in tow. I welcomed them all, which meant that I had to offer food to all of them. But I had no complaints, because in two weeks my son had recovered to a remarkable extent.

In return for all his good work, I paid Thornvorntrei 2,000 riels. He then turned to my mother-in-law and said, "Grandma, I've heard that you like to offer alms to the monks. Is that right?"

"Yes, Chao!" she answered with deep respect.

"Here are 700 riels to give them. Is it enough, Grandma?"

"Oh, yes. Thank you, Chao!" Her hands shook as she extended them to receive the twenty-riel bills. She was seventy-three years old, and until that moment had never handled that much money—she trembled with excitement. Thus everything was settled, and all parties involved were satisfied.

My son recovered from his long and life-threatening ailment. The elves continued to appear to him on occasion, to let him know that they were looking out for him. Thornvorntrei was assigned to Roeuddhi as his Big Brother, his own one-on-one personal guardian angel. Dr. Mak assured Roeuddhi that he would stay close to him for years and years to come. He was, indeed, the Angel Doctor, of whom Indta Kosei had spoken.

CHAPTER TWENTY-FOUR: 1980-1987

GOVERNMENT WORK AGAIN

Before I continue my personal narrative, I think it's important to provide a political picture of Cambodia in the early 1980s—at least to the best of my knowledge. One should bear in mind that at that time, we had no independent daily newspaper—only a weekly, published under government supervision. The government also controlled the radio stations. We had no "open meetings" law, or Freedom of Information Act. And so some secrets from that period may never be revealed, some rumors will never be proved true or false. But one thing is clear: Cambodia was a little country caught in the middle of a geopolitical struggle between three giants: China, the Soviet Union, and the United States. The story of David and Goliath is very popular, but in real life, the little guy usually doesn't get the best of such a struggle, and we were no exception.

The Khmer Rouge had always looked to China for financial support, for political support, and for weapons. Vietnam, always nervous about its northern neighbor, had long looked to the Soviet Union for assistance, and in return, it supported Russia on all United Nations votes. During the Khmer Rouge era, as the death toll began to reach catastrophic proportions, disillusioned members of the Khmer Rouge and members of the Khmer Republic Army that managed to escape joined other Cambodians in Vietnam, and began to assemble a new political faction, and a small army.

The December 1978 attack on the Khmer Rouge was conducted by a joint Cambodian-Vietnamese army, using weapons and ammunition from the Soviet Union. By January 1979, the Khmer Rouge and Pol Pot were on the run, ultimately settling in the northwest provinces, along our 500-mile border with Thailand.

They were joined by two other groups: a royalist party that wanted to reinstate Norodom Sihanouk as king, and a republican party—led by Son Sann, an old-timer from the independence movement of the 1950s—that wanted to create the kind of representative government we had once hoped the Khmer Republic would become. (Note: The names I have used for these parties are for the convenience of the reader. These parties actually used ludicrously long names, and even some of the acronyms, like FUNC-INPEC, seemed to go on forever.)

On January 10th, an interim government of the newly named People's Republic of Kampuchea (PRK) was announced, with Heng Samrin, an old guard communist from the 1950s, as president, and Pen Sovan as chairman of the party. During the next two years they maneuvered for position in this government-in-the-making, while they worked on a constitution. The constitution was finalized a year later, in January 1981. National Assembly elections were held in May, the constitution was ratified, and Pen Sovan was elected prime minister in July, while Heng Samrin continued as president. Chan Si, Chea Sim, and Hun Sen were named deputy ministers.

On the page, it all sounds ideal: a National Assembly, a president, a prime minister . . . almost like a Western European government. But this was not a democracy, it was a communist government, propped up, overseen, and dictated to by the ever-present Vietnamese "consultants." To keep their offices, not to mention their heads, everyone in the Heng Samrin administration had to appear as if they were acting on behalf of Cambodia. But in fact, they allowed Vietnam to raid our natural resources at will, and they established trade agreements that were designed to keep our nation permanently dependent on Vietnam.

Meanwhile, the Khmer Rouge, headed by Khieu Samphan (who replaced Pol Pot), Sihanouk's royalists, and Son Sann's republicans publicly continued their effort to form a coalition, while privately each one tried to gain dominance over the other two. Eventually they realized they needed each other, and announced an alliance known as the Tripartite Government, which continued to rely on China for funding and weapons.

So we had the Heng Samrin government supervised by Vietnam, which in turn received backing from the Soviet Union. And we had the Tripartite Government, which was backed by China. And off in the distance, the United States was using Cambodia to play the two communist giants against each other.

The atrocities of the Pol Pot era were starting to come to light at this time, but the United Nations (and the United States) maintained that the Khmer Rouge had been ousted by an invading Vietnamese army. According to their charter and their principles, they couldn't endorse a puppet government that had been installed by force. In spite of the cataclysm we had just survived, and in spite of the fact that the Heng Samrin regime controlled ninety percent of the country, the Tripartite Group was recognized as the legitimate government of Cambodia, and retained control of our seat at the United Nations. That certainly provided the government in Phnom Penh and our Vietnamese "consultants" with an excuse to maintain a constant atmosphere of paranoia.

That paranoia led the highest-ranking Vietnamese ministers to form an umbrella organization called B-68. Not unlike the Soviet KGB, they had investigative authority over everyone in Cambodia. I knew I was in favor at the moment because the workers I had supervised were efficient, and I had gotten impressive results with few resources. But I also knew it was easy to fall out of favor. Sometimes they announced that someone had been "promoted," and had gone to Hanoi to learn the new position. And sometimes that person was never heard from again. This was the fate that terrified me—I would be sent to Hanoi for training, I would be forced to rewrite my autobiography, and then I would "suffer a heart attack," or simply disappear.

When I first ran for National Assembly in 1972, my dream of a true democracy in Cambodia seemed within reach. Even when it became clear that the Lon Nol regime was riddled with corruption, I believed we were experiencing the kinds of growing pains other countries had gone through during the transition from monarchy to a representative form of government. Now I was entering the bureaucracy of a communist government, supervised by another communist government, and we were still fighting the remnants of a previous communist government. With illusions gone, I just hoped to serve my country and stay alive. However even those modest goals proved difficult to achieve.

At that time, each ministry had five departments: Planning, Finance, Accounting, Administration, and Organization. The Organization Department combined the responsibilities of a personnel department with the tactics of a secret police force. They had the right to transfer anyone from one department to another, or to have anyone within their purview arrested without question. Sometimes one worker would try to get ahead by informing on another, and the accused rarely had an opportunity to present a defense. Desk clerks and high-ranking administrators alike would suddenly be assigned to cut trees in the jungle— a fate I hoped to avoid after all I'd been through. My intent was to keep my head down and get my work done without being noticed. But I wound up making a bitter enemy within my first six months on the job, an enemy who plotted against me for the next ten years.

We had to resurrect an economy in complete disarray, and develop a long-range plan for industrial development, without catching the attention of the Vietnamese consultants. And before we did anything, we had to procure a variety of raw materials and finished goods from the outside world. Lubrication for machinery, raw material for producing soap or mosquito nets, band-aids for the health department, hoes for farmers—all of that went through my office.

But I was more than a bureaucrat. I had to draw on my practical skills to resolve on-the-spot dilemmas as they occurred. For example, the government bought tractors from Moscow, and they thought the tractors came with all the attachments. When they read the fine print, they discovered that all they'd gotten were the basic machines. We didn't have the money to order more parts, nor could we afford to have a planting season go by with these tractors out of operation. So I drew up designs, oversaw the making of the dies, and manufactured all the parts for plowshares, discs, and the other attachments necessary to make those tractors a worthwhile investment.

When I took the position in 1980, we had an entire country, an entire population that had essentially lost all personal possessions and household goods. We had to produce a real hodgepodge of items to fill immediate needs, before we could begin putting together a long-range industrial plan. For the moment, everyone who wanted to start a small factory came to me for an application. I had to consider whether there was a need for that item, and whether the applicant had the knowledge and resources to implement the proposal I was reviewing. I approved permits to manufacture slippers, shoes, bicycle inner tubes, spoons and forks, aluminum pots, pans, plates, band-aids, clothes—everything that humans needed for everyday use.

But naturally some people expected me to rubber-stamp their application without any scrutiny, especially other government officials. That's how Sok Issan, the director of the Organization Department in the Ministry of Industry, became my enemy. He came to my office with an application for an ice depot, a very profitable business in Cambodia. I didn't say no. I didn't even give him a suspicious look. I told him I was sure it wouldn't be a problem, and asked him to leave the application on my desk and I'd look it over later. Well, apparently he had a highly-developed sense of entitlement, and thought it was outrageous that I hadn't approved his application immediately. He said he was going to sue me. He said he knew I had studied in the United States, and that

I had been a captain in Lon Nol's regime, and that he would find a way to use that information against me. At first I thought he was just venting his emotions, but I soon learned from my subordinates that he was spreading rumors about me behind my back. I couldn't believe I'd made an enemy that easily, while just trying to quietly do my job. Then again, deep down I knew I was swimming against the current.

Regrettably, many policies and practices were decided upon from afar, while we were put in the uncomfortable position of having to enforce their implementation. For instance, every factory was required to grow its own produce. Then government inspectors showed up, took the produce and livestock, and gave back some paltry commodity such as textiles or agricultural implements. There was a yearly plan: each province had to produce a designated quantity of rice, let's say 20,000 tons. A certain percentage went to the central government and what remained was for the people in the province—something like the relationship between medieval lords and serfs. That would have been bad enough, but the provincial governors wanted to remain in office, so they routinely promised more tonnage than they could deliver, thereby impoverishing the working people. Just as in the days of the Khmer Rouge, families often had to go out and forage for enough edible leaves to stay alive. During this period the Ministry of Industry was tightly controlled by Vietnam—all we could do was carry out their orders without question. And I was determined to do exactly that.

In spite of my customary caution, I became involved in several issues over the next few years that forced me to speak up. The first occasion was imposed by outside forces. In recent years, Fidel Castro has allowed large numbers of Cubans to immigrate to the United States, but immigration officials discovered that Castro had emptied the prisons and hospitals and sent his dregs to Miami. Similarly, in mid-1980, the Vietnamese emptied their hospitals and asylums and dumped patients and inmates in Phnom Penh—as if we needed more problems. These people couldn't be ignored. They wandered around the city, begging, stealing, and in some instances dying on the street. Without some kind of plan, they could have represented a significant health hazard.

But when Pen Sovan recommended that we starve them and turn them into fertilizer, many of us heard echoes of the Khmer Rouge. During the debate that ensued, I began to formulate a plan that not only addressed this issue, but had possible wider ramifications for the entire economy. And in the process of presenting my ideas, I gained a key ally—Keo Chanda, the minister of information.

Keo Chanda argued that we should temporarily quarantine these unwilling refugees, and group them—syphilitics with syphilitics, lepers with lepers, the lame with the lame. His plan was to move them to an island, feed them, heal them, and turn them into productive citizens. That's when I spoke up.

I suggested that Keo Chanda's plan would prove more successful if we built them looms and taught them to weave, or to make baskets or other such items to trade for a living. Keo Chanda was then minister of industry, the mayor of Phnom Penh, and the minister of information. I had made a very influential friend, and I had come up with the beginning of a plan to revitalize the economy.

I believed that we shouldn't invest in new factories. I argued that we needed to find the raw materials necessary to get the factories that had survived the Pol Pot years up and running, and eventually make use of their full production capacity. And I also believed that we should balance that effort by encouraging the development of cottage industries. As I explained to Keo Chanda and Nuon Saret, five family members working in their home or in a small garage could produce goods as diverse as slippers or bricks more cost-effectively than a new factory with a load of debt and high overhead. Meanwhile we could begin to educate a new generation of young people to help the country enter the modern world. They both agreed with me, but the Vietnamese consultants didn't like this policy. They wanted us to haul our raw materials to Vietnam, where they would manufacture consumer goods and sell them back to us at huge profits.

I also got involved in the transition to a new printed currency. It was a controversial move. We had always used the riel for currency, but it had become so devalued it had practically been abandoned. Cambodians had become used to trading a chicken for a fishing net or for rice. And we had a sense of how much gold it would take to buy necessities we couldn't trade for. But without viable paper currency, it was becoming increasingly difficult to engage in international trade, and it was imperative for us to be able to buy and sell raw materials and finished goods more easily. Eventually the plan went through. Even though the new riels were printed in the Soviet Union on plain paper, without gold deposits in the international banking system to back them up, the new currency proved effective internally, and internationally.

For some time, a steady stream of colleagues flowed into my office at the Ministry asking me if paper currency would be safe, if it would be effective, if it would be efficient. They regarded me as an expert because I had studied in America. I began to get irritated, but finally understood that the officials who were asking my advice simply wanted to give the appearance that they had the consent of the people, in case the new currency failed. We held a big public meeting, and I gave a speech explaining how paper currency would make international trade possible, and that people would adjust to it quickly. I was flattered when everybody applauded, until I realized they were just waiting for the speech to end so they could start partying. The business people were backing paper currency, and they'd supplied free food and liquor. The drink of choice at the time was Bayon, distilled right on Grandma Penh's Hill. It was eighty proof, a pinkish concoction of rice wine and other ingredients so strong that one shot would make you burn from one end to the other.

This scene was typical of the Pen Sovan regime. The administrative committees of the approximately one hundred factories in Phnom Penh took turns sponsoring similar parties. Ministers from each ministry showed up and danced with the women on the staff. They would kill maybe two cows for one of their parties, or they might have two tons of fish delivered—and then they'd invite everybody in the factory to come and drink. Meanwhile, in the country, the farmers continued to struggle. And in the northwest, the Tripartite Government was taking advantage of the instability and corruption to spread dissension and extend their influence.

With the increase in Khmer Rouge activity, rumors proliferated within the government that the Vietnamese would have to find someone to blame. In December 1981, Pen Sovan went to the Ministry of Industry to investigate corruption reported by my nemesis, Sok Issan, the director of the Department of Organization. Unfortunately a conflict had developed between the two people who backed my economic ideas, Nuon Saret, my immediate superior, who had risen from machine operator to the position of vice minister of industry, and his boss Keo Chanda. Maybe it was because Saret was from the south, and Chanda was from the north. Maybe it was because Chanda had become an outrageous flirt, and was known for dispensing exit visas to Thailand in exchange for a kiss (although I never heard of him actually trading visas for sex or money). Their feud had come to the attention of outsiders, and contributed to this visit from the prime minister.

When Pen Sovan arrived, we were all ordered to come to an auditorium to hear him speak. He talked to us about the glory of the communist party, which had fought with bare hands against the Khmer Rouge and the imperialists. He said our closest hegemony was China, and the remote (yet foremost) imperialist entity was the United States. He said that now we were the masters of our future, and we had to unite and work together to move the country forward. He preached at us for almost two hours without saying anything concrete.

When he finished, he asked anyone who had an opinion to come forward and express it. I was the first one to the podium. I told him that I wished to thank him, the great professor, for enlightening us with his philosophy of life. Then I presented some of my ideas about rebuilding the country. I talked about cottage industries for adults, and high-quality education for young people. I talked about the time and rigorous training required to produce a new generation of intellectuals, engineers, and technicians.

Under some circumstances a speaker can get carried away by the sound of his own voice and forget to notice that the audience is no longer paying attention. But when Pen Sovan pulled out a pistol and put it on the table, I knew it was time to conclude my remarks. As I wrapped things up, I could see him leaning over to ask Nuon Saret for details about me. Convinced I was going to be arrested, I looked up at the sky and prayed.

After I spoke, one of the youth leaders came to the podium and supported my proposals, until Pen Sovan stopped him and said the meeting was adjourned. But before sending us away, he responded to my contention by saying that it was easy to make engineers; it was just a matter of minutes, that's all. I thought it was just a matter of minutes before I would be on my way to Hanoi.

I was not experiencing post-traumatic stress syndrome—the Ministry of Industry, at that moment, was actually surrounded by tanks. I don't know why I had opened my big mouth—I should have known better. As this thought ran through my mind, rain started pouring down—a driving rain. Pen Sovan announced that we would continue this discussion the next time we gathered, and left. I was positive that I would be arrested before the next day dawned, but as it turned out, both Pen Sovan and Keo Chanda were arrested that very night; Keo Chanda was sent to South Vietnam, Pen Sovan to Hanoi.

When I got word that my mentor, Keo Chanda, had been arrested, I ran into the swamps and stayed there for two weeks.

I didn't know that Pen Sovan had also been sent away. I didn't show up at my home or office. I didn't tell Syna where I was going. I just left. Syna heard about Pen Sovan and Keo Chanda, but my name was not among those arrested, so she suspected that I was hiding out somewhere.

Once I learned that Pen Sovan had also been whisked away, I took a risk and returned. Nuon Saret pretended nothing had happened, and so did I. I just went back to work. Later that year, Keo Chanda was released, and returned to the Ministry. But Nuon Saret and Keo Chanda, who both backed my ideas, never got along with each other. It was just one of many frustrations I faced on a daily basis.

Pen Sovan's imprisonment marked the beginning of a whole round of arrests, which included two of my friends: Um Bunna, an engineer educated in France, and Chhay Neth, a fellow graduate from California State. And then the authorities started to investigate me intensively. On a daily basis they would place paper in front of me and tell me to revise my autobiography. I told them that I'd written it many times already, and had never changed it. I asked why I should write it again. One day I got so angry (I may have been a little drunk, too) that I told them to go to hell. I didn't want to be prime minister and I wasn't going to write my autobiography one more time. Within half an hour everybody in the Ministry had heard about the incident. I don't know how I managed to get away with that outburst, but nothing came of it.

After Pen Sovan and Keo Chanda were arrested, Chan Si became prime minister, while Heng Samrin continued as president. Chan Si had undergone military training in Hanoi in 1954, and had most recently served as minister of defense. He was very popular, and for a time, it seemed as if Cambodia might be headed in the right direction. During his term in office, a little of the distrust that kept us all on edge seemed to dissipate. And when the Vietnamese consultants urged him to cut down trees—

supposedly to improve the roads—Chan Si resisted. The secret
code name the Vietnamese used for this was K-5, and their real
plan was to clear the five-hundred-mile border all the way from
Koh Kong to Laos; the plan wasn't fully implemented, however,
until Hun Sen came to power.

In 1984, the Ministry of Industry sent me and Ken Vath—one of
my classmates at California State—to Hyderabad, India to be
trained in the promotion of cottage industries at SIET (the Institute
for Small-Scale Technology). We spent four months in comfortable,
air-conditioned accommodations, along with participants from all
over the world, representing a wide spectrum of vocations.

In November of that year, Prime Minister Indira Gandhi was
assassinated. Our classes were suspended and no one was
allowed to walk the streets. I had an appointment with an eye
doctor, however, because I was having vision problems. On my
way back I was arrested—the police thought I was a Sikh (I had
let my beard grow out). But when I showed them my passport
and explained what I was doing, they released me.

We took many field trips. In particular, I wanted to find out how
they produced butane from cattle manure, energy from windmills,
and how they extracted oil from rice bran. One day on our lunch
break, our guides took us to a nearby park, where they distributed
box lunches and Pepsis. Suddenly a group of people identified as
"untouchables" surrounded us, begging for food. To get away from
them, one Cuban participant climbed a tree and ate his lunch up
there. I wasn't very hungry so I decided to share my lunch with the
untouchables, but they wanted all of it. I left it for them to fight over.

During one field trip to New Delhi, I approached an Oxfam
officer to get some information about how to reach the U.S.
Embassy. But when he told me that the U.S. Embassy was directly
across the street from the Vietnamese Embassy, I abandoned my
fleeting notion of defection.

Then one night, about a month before our stay was over, I had
a dream that a female water buffalo had climbed up the stairs to
our house. Such spirits are called *preay*—they live in trees, and

appear to be surrounded by a ball of luminescence. This seemed like a terrible omen. At the time my son was ill, and I had not yet sought the help of Dr. Mak, so I wanted to get home.

In those days, all flights to Phnom Penh went through Bangkok. I considered walking out of the terminal to immigration and applying for political asylum, but when I thought about my family, and of all the risks involved, I let go of my fantasy. When we arrived at Ho Chi Minh City, my vice minister and his cronies were there to meet us. Resigned to my fate, I took a spot in one of the cars ferrying us home. Even though escape had been on my mind unceasingly, I had still bought many useful books for the Ministry of Industry, to convince them that I was serious about my work.

A few days later, three years after he took power, Chan Si released my friend Chhay Neth, who had been accused of corruption, and threw a party at his own residence, to which I was invited. We all sat in a big room, all the cadres, the ministers, the directors of the departments, and they served us a banquet of great food and Johnny Walker. I sat across from Chan Si's wife, a slender Montagnard from the north of Vietnam. Whenever I looked at her, she looked away, so I chugged my whole glass of Johnny Walker. Then she would look back at me, notice my empty glass, and pour me another. It went on like this. She must have wondered why my glass was always empty, but she just gave me an enigmatic smile. Actually I was a bit on edge at the time. I was worried that somebody at the party knew that I had been an assemblyman and had fought against the communists during the Lon Nol regime. To put my mind at ease, I just sat there, downing drink after drink.

In the morning Chan Si was sent to Hanoi by our Vietnamese consultants. They told him that they had recognized he had worked very hard and was loyal to the communist party, and that it was time for him to take a break—to have a routine checkup in Hanoi. He departed in high spirits—a strong man, bright and charming. When it was reported that he had gone to Hanoi for just a week, I had no premonition that something was going to happen to him.

In early January 1985, every factory had a conference. Reports on planning, production, and the need for unity were presented by the committee leaders. A banquet with dancing and music usually followed such conferences. I was with Klaud Randy—one of my superiors at the Ministry of Industry—at one such party that year, when we ran out of booze around ten o'clock. I was just telling Randy that I would treat him to a case of Heineken beer, when we heard a radio broadcast that Chan Si had died in Moscow. His body was to be flown to Phnom Penh the next day.

Everyone was depressed by this news, so we dispersed. Now that Chan Si was dead, we were afraid that there might be a massive shake up of personnel, and possibly a new round of arrests. The next day was declared a day of mourning. Individuals from every level were assigned to place wreaths at the funeral. The Royal Palace was chosen as the site where the coffin would lie in state. The authorities said that Chan Si had been struck down by hemorrhagic fever, but everybody suspected that when he had reached Hanoi they had injected him with the appropriate microbe.

The funeral was prepared as if a member of the royal family had died. They mobilized the whole country, the governors, the chiefs of districts, the cadres, to honor Chan Si. At the place of cremation, they dug three yards deep in the ground, and they built a stupa, more beautiful than for a king. But they cremated the body underground. No fire, no smoke. Once they had reduced it to ash, they popped it up to the surface where it was surrounded by beautiful sculptures. My distant uncle, Po Neang, was in charge of these proceedings. He said that it was just like being inside an oven, the fire underground, and that there was no way for the air to get in or out. He himself was almost roasted. But he considered it a great honor. (He is still alive today, living in Chbar Ampeou, taking care of our house.)

I know that historians will tell you that Chan Si really was sick, and that the Vietnamese had nothing to do with his death. Some say my contention that the Vietnamese had him killed is just an urban legend. But I was there. I saw Chan Si before he left Cambodia, and he didn't look sick to me. Many who agreed with me at the time have since changed what they say, which is easy to do because the tongue doesn't have any bones and can waggle easily.

Two weeks later, at the age of thirty-three, Hun Sen came to power as prime minister, though he was the youngest of the heirs apparent. Somehow he had curried favor with Mien Ga Tite, the Vietnamese director of the Cambodian Bureau, whose mission was to manage Cambodia's political direction. He recommended Hun Sen to Le Doc Tho, the Vietnamese prime minister, and suddenly it was a fait accompli. A driven, ambitious man who lost an eye fighting for the Khmer Rouge, he eventually became disillusioned with their genocidal policies, and fled to Vietnam. He was imprisoned at first, but after being released, joined the December 1978 attack against the Khmer Rouge that led to the overthrow of Pol Pot. Hun Sen's administration began in January 1985, with runaway economic growth, a revival of the war against the Khmer Rouge, and the beginning of the devastation of our forests.

Hun Sen promoted small-scale industry, as I did, but he believed in letting the people manage their own businesses with minimal government oversight. I believed that a country like ours, with a history of large-scale corruption, required a little more supervision. Sure enough, thousands of small industries sprang up in Phnom Penh—a tire factory, a fibro-cement plant, a paper factory, a factory for producing pots and pans, factories for dishes, shoes, inner tubes, bicycles for children, and so on. Some of them were on the up-and-up, but many of them were producing shoddy goods, and others took orders for items that would never be produced. I was invited to put my name on the list of boards of directors of many such businesses, and was promised lots of money if I would lend their schemes an air of integrity. But I saw the whole thing as a breeding ground for greed, and kept out of it.

Of course the change in administrations and the rapid growth of corruption led to heightened rumors about the return of the Khmer Rouge. K-5, by now, had become a primary focus. The K-5 committee ordered the Ministry of Industry to produce iron booby traps to kill the enemy. They were weighted in such a way that wherever they were thrown, they landed with the three points down and one pointing up. The booby traps were constructed by taking two rods, bending them, and then welding them together. I estimated that it would take 2,000 tons to produce them. The K-5 minister ordered a million tons of iron rods from the Soviet Union—everything always seemed to involve excess. They put these traps all along the border with Thailand, from Koh Kong to the border with Laos—wherever the Vietnamese thought Cambodian resisters might infiltrate.

After that we had to make antitank bomb casings. One factory produced these shells. I was adamantly against this, and said so in a meeting with the council of ministers of industry, but was ignored. I was ordered also to produce hoes, hammers, and axes, in cooperation with Czechoslovakia. We could do this kind of thing well, but we didn't have time. The bombshells and the booby traps had priority. I went around from factory to factory to determine our supply needs. Then I met with a number of nongovernmental organizations (NGOs) such as the Mennonite Central Committee and Catholic Relief.

Of course the Khmer Rouge fought back in every way they could. And they forced the inhabitants of the northwest region to house and feed them, and worked hard to convince them that the Tripartite Government, headed by Sihanouk, represented the best interests of Cambodia. In late 1985, because of my speaking ability, I was assigned to travel throughout the war zone to present the ruling government's case to the people.

The last time I had barnstormed around the country, I was denouncing communism on behalf of the Khmer Republic. Now I was speaking on behalf of one communist government against the previous communist government. At times it was difficult to determine if I really was supporting the lesser of two evils.

Prior to this new offensive, the Khmer Rouge had terrorized the people. But just before I headed to the region, the Vietnamese had conducted their own purge. They arrested most of the local government officials, from midlevel bureaucrats to the governor of Siem Reap Province. They arrested people whether they were pro-Sihanouk or not. Half the province disappeared. I was told that if the Vietnamese were convinced of someone's guilt, they buried the suspect up to his neck, kicked off his head, and then booted it around like a soccer ball. Needless to say, the people I spoke to had long ceased to trust anyone representing either side of this conflict.

Our leader, Duong Chhum, had been trained in Hanoi and Beijing, where he had specialized in communications. I was a member of his group of seven. The others were mostly my subordinates at the Ministry, so we all got along. I had brought my Buddhist scriptures with me and chanted every day, memorizing them. One day Duong Chhum saw me chanting and gave me an exasperated look. "We came here to explain to the people that the Tripartite Government is going to take over the country if we don't fight against them, and you waste your time with Buddhist texts?"

"Well, this is one way to convince the people we're on their side, because *they are* Buddhists," I responded. That shut him up temporarily.

I've always been convinced that Sok Issan assigned me to the front to get me killed, and his plan almost worked. At one point, Son Sen, the Khmer Rouge defense minister, deployed 700 men armed with AK-47s and B-40s within twelve miles of our headquarters in the Kulen Mountains. A scout reported to Duong Chhum that Son Sen's troops were well-supplied with canned food, and that they rested in green hammocks like bats—too many to count. Duong Chhum ordered our group to dig trenches and build bunkers. At night, I put on my white meditation outfit, burned three sticks of incense, and prayed. Eventually we made it to Siem Reap City, where we stayed for more than two months until all the other barnstorming units finished their duties and joined us. Then, in early 1986, they flew us back to Phnom Penh in a Soviet bimotor plane.

Hun Sen and the Vietnamese used the revival of the war against the Khmer Rouge as a rationale to move forward with another aspect of K-5—the destruction of our forests. The forests, they claimed, gave the Khmer Rouge too many opportunities to capture supplies, too many places to hide. They began a campaign to mobilize everyone to cut the tress and bushes. They started along the Thai border, from Koh Kong to Laos, then they tackled National Highway 4, the U.S.-built highway from Phnom Penh to Kompong Som. Actually, the Japanese offered to cut a kilometer-wide band on each side of the highway—they wanted the timber themselves. In exchange they offered to build a new road and refurbish the port of Kompong Som. But the Vietnamese just mobilized the Cambodian people to cut down the trees, and they transported all the good timber to Vietnam.

Aquatic bushes around Tonle Sap were burned to ashes. Similar undergrowth near Phnom Penh was cut back to a distance outside the range of heavy artillery. Many who served during this time, particularly along the border that became known as the K-5 battlefield, died from mine explosions, malaria, or were paralyzed from gunshot wounds; it was, in essence, a death sentence that went unnoticed. If anyone spoke out against this policy, he or she was arrested or executed.

Keo Chanda was one of the few leaders who dared to protest. We both agreed that this plan had no real military value. "When we destroy our forests, we destroy our wealth. We destroy our whole country," he said, over and over. But no one listened. There were thousand-year-old trees along the sides of the mountains. The authorities ordered even those venerable beings cut down.

To this day, during the monsoons, the southwest wind just blows straight through to Vietnam. There are no trees to stop the wind, no trees to stop the clouds to give us rain. Right now there are drought conditions in Cambodia, and this is one of the reasons why.

A few months after I returned from my barnstorming assignment in the northwest, in July 1986, I was promoted. I was now the director of the Department of Economic Cooperation with Foreign Countries, another division of the Ministry of Industry. For the next three years I communicated with representatives from Vietnam, and from international business interests across the globe. Mining companies came to look for gold and gems. Other companies came to build new factories, power plants, bridges, and buildings. I was a sort of middleman, but I wound up having food, liquor, and other gifts thrust in my face. I also had to listen to a lot of harebrained schemes. One character wanted to build a broom handle factory—why a factory when you can just cut a length of bamboo? Another thought Cambodia needed to get into the laser beam industry—in a nation that still hauled freight in oxcarts.

Of course all someone had to do was mention laser beams and rumors began to spread. During a periodic exchange of technicians with Hanoi, one of our people began bragging that he was an expert in producing laser beams, and the Hanoi engineers got worried. "Gee, Cambodia has an engineer who can produce laser beams—that's dangerous!" So went the rumor. A month later they sent some of their engineers to Cambodia to research this man's laser technology. He showed them a little contraption that looked like an oven, that the Chinese used in the production of needles. The top engineer from Hanoi just shook his head. For the rest of the year we took pleasure in the knowledge that at least one crazy guy had scared the hell out of Vietnam.

With the new job and the new responsibilities came increased scrutiny. Before long Sok Issan had me writing my autobiography again, over and over. Negotiating international contracts was new to me, but I had been negotiating my way through political land-mines and quagmires for a long time. I was beginning to wonder if my guardian spirits could continue protecting me much longer.

BRAINWASHED & BRUSHED ASIDE

One of the reasons for my promotion was my ability to speak Khmer, French, and English. After my years in the forced labor camps, where such knowledge could mean death, it was tremendously satisfying to use my language skills to communicate with people from different parts of the world. And I didn't mind the free food and liquor that always seemed to facilitate the process when terms of contracts were being discussed.

Since we were finally reconnecting with the outside world, our neighbors were taking a closer look at us. The Association of Southeast Asian Nations (ASEAN) was exerting continued pressure on Hun Sen, the Tripartite Government, and the Vietnamese to enter into negotiations for a final peaceful settlement in Cambodia. Time after time, just before a scheduled meeting, one of the parties would back out. But the Vietnamese began to see the inevitable—in order to normalize relations with other nations, they would have to find new techniques to maintain control of Cambodia. They selected brainwashing and immigration.

While peace talks dragged on during the next few years, Hanoi stepped up its campaign to complete the "Vietnamization" of Cambodia. During this period it was prohibited to teach history and geography in Cambodian schools. According to the Vietnamese, we didn't need history and geography; we ate rice, not books. As long as they had us directly under their thumb, they continued to bombard us with misinformation. They actually tried to rewrite history, claiming that Cambodia had once been part of Vietnam, and that they had been the major power in Indochina a thousand years ago. And Vietnamese was introduced into the entire school system as a second language.

Of course they knew they couldn't reeducate the entire population, but they were determined to inundate everyone who worked for the government with these ideas, including the directors and deputy directors of all the departments in the ministries of Cambodia, the committee directors of the factories, the deputy governors of all the provinces, the chiefs of police, the deputy chiefs of police, judges, attorneys, high school teachers, and professors. To that end, in 1986, Hanoi opened the Political College of Phnom Penh. Everyone I knew called it Brainwashing School.

They held six-month courses, preliminary in nature, which were primarily for rank-and-file officers. They sent officers with greater leadership potential to Vietnam. They planned to train some for two years, others for four. Those who exhibited a marked predilection for the Vietnamese philosophy were sent to Hanoi for training, while those not as zealous were sent to Ho Chi Minh City.

In July 1987, I was enlisted for a six-month course. Our situation in Phnom Penh was similar to boot camp, in that there were no ranks, and we lived together in barracks-like buildings. Each ministry had its own room. Ours accommodated the ten of us, in two rows of five single beds—no mattresses, just mats.

Every morning at 5:30 a.m. someone banged a large cauldron to wake us up, and off we went to grow trakuon for an hour. Humbling well-educated government workers with menial tasks was typical of communist reeducation centers, but after the Pol Pot forced labor camps, I didn't want or need any additional humbling. Their goal may have been to make us realize that we were no better than the lowliest farmer, but as far as I was concerned, all they succeeded in doing was to increase my resentment.

After a breakfast of rice porridge, we filed into a huge auditorium that seated 700. For the next hour our ears were assaulted with slogans:

Marxism-Leninism is Permanent Forever Until Doomsday!

Wherever there is Marxism-Leninism, there is no Buddhism!

Victory to the Revolutionary Party of Kampuchea!

Glory to the Republic of the People of Kampuchea!

Jaiy-yo! Jaiy-yo! (Viva! Bravo! Viva! Bravo!)

We not only had to listen to this nonsense, the slogans were posted on banners everywhere the eye could see, in letters as bright as freshly spilled blood. After listening to slogans shouted at us with exaggerated zeal, we dispersed to classrooms to hear lectures on a wide range of subjects, all from Hanoi's perspective.

In their Marxist interpretation of evolution, apes came down from the trees to walk on the ground because of the nature of their food-gathering activities. First they lived on fruit; then they became carnivorous. After a long time, primitive people discovered fire. Then they evolved from living in extended family units to something more complex known as primitive collectivism. In primitive collectivism, people were equal. But later, the strong came to dominate the weak, and slavery came into existence; feudalism and capitalism inexorably followed.

Under capitalism, we were told, the workers were exploited by the factory owners. If a pencil takes an hour to make, the worker should receive a wage equal to the value of what is produced; the system of capitalism, however, forces workers to produce ten pencils in an hour, without an increase in wages. In effect, they explained, one pencil went to the worker and nine pencils to the factory owner.

These lecturers stuck their noses into every aspect of our lives. They told us that we as Cambodians should allow Vietnamese families to live with us—that we should "integrate." They told us that Cambodia should operate on a strictly agricultural basis, while Vietnam should produce industrial goods. Whether exporting or importing, in their ideal world all merchandise would go through Vietnam.

In the political arena, they let us know, in no uncertain terms, that we should keep Heng Samrin's proclamation of January 1979 paramount in our consciousness: "The waters of the Mekong may dry up, the Lam Son Mountains [in Vietnam] may be flattened, but the solidarity between Vietnam and Kampuchea will never be shaken for ages to come."

Regarding religion, they made it clear that under Marxism-Leninism there was no room for Buddhism. When this was being discussed, my fellow participants asked me to go to the podium to express my views on the subject. In front of all 700 participants, I said that religion is an abstract entity. And that even though Pol Pot had smashed statues of Buddha, killed Buddhist monks, and destroyed Buddhist temples, Buddhism still remained in the minds of the people. There was silence in the auditorium, followed by an undercurrent of whispering. Once again, I escaped any consequences for speaking out, but I knew that somewhere, someone was keeping a file on me.

There was actually an approved party method for doing everything. Under the aegis of "international protocol," things became quite absurd. They taught us how to get into and out of a car! First, we were told, you open the car door, and then you put your foot in and slide onto the seat. When getting out, we had to swing our legs to the side, put the left foot on the pavement, and then exit. They assumed that we had been living in a vacuum all our lives, so they taught us everything from square one.

Some people with limited knowledge were completely converted. Others, with limited ability, who had never had the opportunity to move to a higher position, paid bribes to be accepted as communist cadres. Once they were in the party, they had the chance to get a house, a car, household appliances, and even simple food supplies at outrageous discounts. I got good grades, but I certainly wasn't converted. I just jumped through the hoops like a trained dog, without deviation.

Not all the participants were so lucky. One of them, Ong So, had been a communist before Lon Nol, during Ho Chi Minh's early days. He bragged that he had stacks of books from South Vietnam and had learned everything about Marxism-Leninism. He couldn't stop talking about it. This guy was also sexually out of control, probably because he always drank too much rice wine. One night he happened to get chummy with one of the girls who cooked there and dragged her away from the kitchen, got caught, and was reprimanded by the board of the school. He shot off his mouth in one class after another. At some point during my stay, Ong So was sent to South Vietnam for a "checkup," and returned in a coffin—to no one's surprise.

People knew that I passively resisted the nonsense we were going through, and as a result, some of them confided in me, such as Lang Nget, the director of a lumber mill. He dreamed that everybody in the Brainwashing School was standing along the road from Pochentong Airport to Phnom Penh to welcome Sihanouk. Next morning he told the dream to the wrong person, and in no time he was summoned to the office, where they threatened him. "There's no Sihanouk coming," they warned him. "Cambodia is now a province of Vietnam!"

Terrified, Lang Nget told me about his dream, and the response of the authorities. I told him not to be scared, that I had had a similar dream and had written a poem about it. But in truth, I too was starting to feel panicky. I dreamed I had seen Sihanouk in the sky, a symbol of deification. Readers may wonder about this nostalgia for a king. Certainly many of us had tired of Sihanouk's film festivals and his other excesses during the 1960s. But he had also helped us gain our independence from France, and we had taken pride in his neutral stance during the Vietnam War. As Americans might say, his stock was starting to rise again. Once more, the old fox was becoming a symbol of national pride. If it had wound up in the wrong hands, my poem about seeing Sihanouk in the sky could have put me in jeopardy; nevertheless, I decided to take a risk and let Lang Nget read it. He felt relieved to learn that he was not the only one dreaming about the days when Cambodians ruled Cambodia.

During my stay in Brainwashing School it felt as if the world outside had ceased to exist, but in fact change was in the air. Earlier that year Sihanouk had taken a "one-year leave-of-absence" from the Tripartite Government, which helped distance him from the Khmer Rouge. Recognizing that it was difficult to get all the interested parties together for a formal conference, a "cocktail party" in Jakarta was proposed, to give Hun Sen and Sihanouk an opportunity to talk without any expectations. Although the cocktail party never actually took place that year, Hanoi began hinting that if Hun Sen and Sihanouk could work out an arrangement, and if the Khmer Rouge agreed to disarm, they would leave Cambodia by 1990. Neither the Khmer Rouge nor China were happy with the way things were developing; nonetheless Hun Sen and Sihanouk finally did meet in a village northeast of Paris in early December, during the time when I was completing my session in Brainwashing School.

And as it turned out, I was part of the last graduating class. As our group was getting ready to go home, they announced that they were closing the school for good. It must have been part of the peace negotiations. By the time we started pouring celebratory drinks, I felt as if I were out of my mind, literally and figuratively. During the closing ceremony I bowed before pictures of Lenin, Karl Marx, and Ho Chi Minh, and said, "I am scared of you three, so from now on, let's not see each other ever again!" After that "toast," I walked out the door with a few friends, and together we stared at the night sky, drinks in hand. Suddenly bats appeared in great numbers. They flew from the four directions, and circled over the four affluents of the river, blackening the sky. Huge numbers of crows were crying *kwak kwak kwak*. To many of us this was a clear omen that the king would soon return. The festivities lasted all night. And in the morning they just let us go.

When I got out of the Brainwashing School, I returned to Phnom Penh with their slogans still echoing, like a bad dream:

Communism never changes.

The closest hegemony is China. The remote enemy is American Imperialism.

We have to fight forever.

Other countries moved from an agrarian society to capitalism then to communism. Cambodia will move to communism without any transition through capitalism.

I may remember their "lessons," but the school didn't affect my thinking. I took their classes in economics, but I knew the real story. Bulgaria, Hungary, Poland, Czechoslovakia, the former Soviet Union, Vietnam—all those communist nations were borrowing from each other and paying each other with worthless promises. Goods changed hands, but the books never got balanced. Their economies were just castles in the sand, waiting for a big wave to wash them away.

By June 1989, the wave arrived, and Soviet bloc nations *were* washed away, one by one. Before long, the Department of Economic Cooperation with Foreign Countries had no countries with which to cooperate. So they closed down the department, and gave me a new assignment: official consultant to the Ministry of Industry. I was responsible for bringing modern technology to our power plants, textile plants, and construction companies. I reported directly to the minister.

In keeping with the trend sweeping communist nations around the world at the time, Cambodia wanted to change from a state economy to a market economy. That meant we had to sell every factory, and to privatize them. In theory, that might have given some upstarts an opportunity to bring fresh ideas and spirit to our economy. In practice it meant that we had to distribute land to everyone in the upper echelons of the government. The top officials all rushed to acquire every piece of land they could, by whatever means. They evicted the poor farmers, confiscated their land, and sold their houses. Everything was in a state of chaos.

In the middle of this chaos, the tens of thousands of Vietnamese troops, who had scattered all over Cambodia, began preparations for a mass withdrawal. Knowing that their time in our country was drawing to a close, they accelerated their previous effort to strip our nation of what little wealth remained. In part, they were stealing from thieves. Most of the officials in charge of distributing humanitarian aid that came in from other nations actually sold the goods on the black market, bought rotten moldy rice, rice bran, and corn, which they distributed to the factory workers, and pocketed the difference. The Vietnamese found stockpiles of good grain, and stashes of gold, and transported it all to Ho Chi Minh City.

Finally, at the appointed time, U.N. officials showed up at all the border towns to formally observe the troop withdrawal. All government employees were ordered to stand along the roads to salute the departing Vietnamese army. It was a rainy September day—disappointing, actually. By then, the main body of troops had already departed. But we all stood, holding two flags, the Cambodian flag and Vietnamese flag, as a few sick Vietnamese soldiers with broken guns rolled past in rattletrap cars. We waved and called, "Good-bye, good-bye, good luck, good luck." We stayed all day, and then we went home.

In 1990, Sihanouk, Son Sann's Republican Party, and Hun Sen met and agreed to form a new government. A new constitution was drawn up calling for a Supreme National Council that represented all major parties. We changed our name from the Peoples Republic of Kampuchea to the State of Cambodia. And Buddhism was once again recognized as the state religion, although it was not to be imposed on anyone. For instance, the Chams, another ethnic minority in Cambodia, were once again permitted to freely practice Islam. (During the Pol Pot years, Cham communities were brutally destroyed, and in many villages every man, woman, and child was killed.)

While all this was going on, official spokesmen continued to maintain that communism never changes, and that Cambodia's government would never change. We would remain communist forever until the Party took over the world. In universities in America, France, and many other countries, intellectuals love to theorize about communism. If all you know about it is what you've read in books, communism can be made to sound like a utopia. But until you have lived under constant surveillance, until you have lived in fear of saying the wrong thing to the wrong person, until you have lived in fear day and night, day after day, year after year, you don't know what it means to live under communism.

I had been living cautiously for a long time, keeping my thoughts and feelings about the government to myself. I didn't even talk to Syna about my anger and frustration, although she understood what I was going through. Finally I started writing poems again, without any expectation that anything would come of it. I even wrote a letter to the University of Iowa, asking them to send me a copy of the poems I had assembled for my master's thesis. Once I started writing, my feelings began pouring out. In 1988 I began work on a poem I called "Neo-Pol Pot," but the impetus for completing it was this so-called withdrawal of Vietnamese troops in September 1989. For the next nine months I continued to fiddle with it, changing a word or a phrase every now and then. It spoke of the sorrows of my country, and of my longing for democracy.

I suppose the new constitution, the privatization of industry, the new religious freedom, made me overconfident, because I kept a copy of this poem—which spoke not only of Pol Pot but of the puppet government Hanoi had imposed on us—in my desk at the Ministry. I should have known better. Some things may have changed, but Sok Issan, who had been promoted from director to vice minister of the Organization Department, was still the bane of my existence. I mentioned earlier that when I had heard the radio report of Chan Si's death, I had been drinking with another staff member at the Ministry, Klaud Randy. I had always thought of him as a friend, but all along he had been spying on me for Sok Issan.

In June 1990, while I was inspecting a factory that had recently installed new equipment, Klaud Randy searched my desk and discovered a copy of the poem. He confronted me with it upon my return that afternoon, and accused me of treasonous behavior, before turning the poem over to Sok Issan. I asked myself if I should resign. I had no idea what would happen next, but I felt too old to hide in the swamps again. Some spirit must have seized me, because I suddenly threw all caution to the winds. For the next few days, as I walked into the Ministry, I stood in the middle of the lobby and chanted the following verses before going to my office:

> Being a poet, my words from the source,
> I tell my people the truth.
> I was born into peasantry.
> Now I'm a traitor for loving my nation too dearly.
> They've propped up a commoner as king
> and even the *chrach* grass has become expensive.
> The learned ones, savants and poets,
> confronted with fear of reprisals
> have all run away, away,
> all run away from Cambodia!

At noon when I came down to lunch, I chanted those verses again, while walking through the lobby. I knew that Sok Issan could hear me. I repeated this every day. "One more time, one more time, Grandpa," people shouted. I knew *my* time at the Ministry was nearing an end.

A few days later, I went to work early. It was a fine morning, not too hot. As I approached the Ministry, a man named Peou, a minor functionary, came out on the steps and yelled to me from a distance: "Old Man, stop where you are! We don't need you any more! Sok Issan will be sending a secretary to your house with your letter of resignation. The waves farther out from the shore will roll over the ones close in!" I turned around and went home.

I didn't even bother to clean out my desk—there was nothing there I needed.

After receiving Peou's mocking taunt, I didn't leave the house for a week. Then, sure enough, a secretary from the Department of Organization for the Ministry of Industry arrived at my door, shoved the letter of resignation at me and ordered me to sign it. I did. And I never showed up there again. I had been at the Ministry for eleven years. Overnight, I had become persona non grata.

I experienced a certain feeling of dread, not knowing what the future would bring. But I must admit that I also felt relieved to be released from that life of duplicity—like the sparrows one can purchase at temples and set free from their cages. So I stayed home and revised my poem, "Neo-Pol Pot," and began to write others. Aside from my family, I began to lead a solitary existence. That is, after all, what the life of the writer is, for the most part. It has its rewards, but in some ways facing one's inner self can be more difficult than facing an oppressive regime. I thought about Walt Whitman, who had been fired from a job at the Department of the Interior shortly after the Civil War, when poems were found in his desk. I had always thought of him as my "Captain," but I had never expected this parallel in our lives.

MARKING TIME

When I was eight years old, I was given the responsibility of keeping our family's water buffalo out of the rice paddies. Since that time I had worked for my father, I had been a student, a teacher, a factory worker, a soldier, a politician, a diplomat, a slave laborer, and a government bureaucrat. Now I was unemployed, and very much at loose ends. I stayed home watching Chinese Kung Fu movies, and movies about the monk-adventurer Tang Chheng, who went to copy Buddhist scriptures in Sri Lanka. I looked again at the "human rights" section of the Declaration of Independence, which I had once memorized as a young student at Georgetown:

> We hold these truths to be self-evident, that all men are created equal, that they are endowed by their Creator with certain unalienable Rights, that among these are Life, Liberty and the pursuit of Happiness. —That to secure these rights, governments are instituted among Men, deriving their just powers from the consent of the governed, —That whenever any Form of Government becomes destructive of these ends, it is the Right of the People to alter or to abolish it, and to institute new Government, laying its foundation on such principles and organizing its powers in such form, as to them shall seem most likely to effect their Safety and Happiness.

After the failed attempt to create the Khmer Republic, the Killing Fields, the overthrow of Pol Pot, the Vietnamese-installed puppet government, and my last eleven years in the Ministry, those words had a special resonance for me. I recited them on the veranda overlooking my backyard. I walked back and forth, from east to west to east, howling so that everyone could hear my English, whether they understood or not. No one did, but children congregated below, peeping up at me, listening to my recitation with their mouths open. From what I know of the Bible, I must have seemed like an Old Testament prophet crying in the wilderness. Sometimes I recited Whitman's "O Captain! My Captain!" which may have been more pleasing to their ears. Over and over, I delivered these "scriptures" from my "pulpit."

Some afternoons I went to the rice wine shack. A small place, five people could just squeeze in, sitting cross-legged on the shredded bamboo floor. It was basically just an open stall, not like a bar or tavern—it was bare bones basic. After one or two shots of rice wine, we began reminiscing about our lives during Pol Pot. The stories were often harrowing and bizarre, sometimes amusing. One man talked about his hardships while herding cattle. There were too many cattle for the available forage, so they slaughtered one or two and buried them, preserving them as if they were in a refrigerator. Every few days they dug up a portion to feed their families. "You were lucky," I told him. "In my forced labor camp there were thorny bushes and hardwoods." To some extent, we were trying to outdo each other with our tales of woe.

The first few times, we spent an hour or two together, then we dispersed. But as time passed, we became companions. We had no rank or position; we were rice wine drinkers. Each of us had some poems to chant. Most, who had grown up in villages, chanted Kram Ngoy's poems, and such classic pieces as "Chbap Srei" (Buddhist code of ethics for women), "Chbap Broh"(another selection of Buddha's teachings), "Trei Neth" (an epic about a character named "Three Eyes"), and "Tom Teav" (an epic hero), while some sang love songs.

One night I dreamt of seeing American airborne troops parachuting onto National Highway 1, within 500 yards of my house. I saw seven of them with parachute outfits jump from a huge helicopter.

Was I clairvoyant? The next day I told this dream to my companions, but they just shrugged their shoulders.

During 1991 a hot debate took place between Hanoi and the United States regarding the organization of a general election in Cambodia. In honor of this debate, I treated everyone to a round of rice wine one afternoon. I raised my glass and said, "Let's toast freedom and democracy!" Then I chanted a poem I had just written. Try to imagine the faces of my compatriots, and the ambient chatter in the rice wine shack that afternoon as I let my inhibitions fly with my words:

THE ENTRÉE CONFRONTS THE WORD KEEPER

Roosters crow   the sun tears the sky
clearing Asia.   It's blindingly bright.
We can see men and women   walking briskly
           to work.

Their physical senses   experience their circumstances clearly
but their minds   do not grasp what's really happening;
I see clearly, though,   from one day to the next
           till the sky closes its door.

They say: the economy develops—no one dare criticize.
A lot of goods, but no buyers, imported, but secondhand;
they rot and rust,   for these goods
           are used goods.

Quasi-Cambodians   don't even have to be born here—
every morning they crowd   at Chbar Ampeou;
they are born with gray hair   broken teeth—
           just born, they are old right away.

(My audience was with me now, egging me on.)

Very honest, very loyal,   our leaders trade our resources for
                                                          worn-out junk

to quell the war   "Look at me now!
Ideal business   without a hitch;
          I can return by sunset.

Why should you hesitate?   If you want to know how . . .
I'm not scaring you, am I?   I've seen with my own eyes
those high authorities   at noon and evening—
          the magic food sits on their table,

Hennessy Whiskey—   all are Chinese gifts.
Entrées of all kinds   jump over the fence
get into the house   anything imaginable
          in exchange for their signatures."

This poem may seem a bit obscure, but my audience understood my references to the graft and greed that surrounded us.

A week passed. I returned to the rice wine shack. This time I brought a photocopy of my poem "May Peace Prevail in Cambodia," which had been published on April 13, 1967 in *Kampujea*, owned by the head of state, Norodom Sihanouk. My fellow imbibers were not impressed that the poem had been published. I chanted this poem for them, nonetheless:

MAY PEACE PREVAIL IN CAMBODIA

O, Cambodians, do not change your minds.
Please think it over well—
if our home is enchanting and prosperous
why be fed up with Peace?

If the water in our pond is still transparent
please don't try to make it muddy;

do not litter it with trash,
and do not bathe in its waters.

It is true that fire is hot—
everyone knows it well;
we don't need to test it to find that out—
it would consume our bodies for nothing.

(My companions' faces were starting to blanch a little. I continued.)

Just because we are intellectuals
don't think that our enemies
don't want us to be annihilated,
don't want us to fall into the chasm of war.

O, intellectuals, stay clear of pitfalls,
don't trample the green prairies;
while the grass grows green, treasure it—
don't take pride in laying it to ruin.

There was silence. Faces turned away. One by one they left. Alone, I went home and wrote a poem called "Mad Scene," in reaction to their reaction. (Loaded with topical references, it doesn't translate well, but at that time, it was like playing with dynamite.) Three days later I went to the rice wine shack, bought a five-liter jar of rice wine, and invited my old and new friends to share it with me. Because the wine was free, several men came in off the street to join us. After we had all had a few drinks, I chanted my new poem at the top of my lungs. Even some of my "friends" didn't get all the politics behind the poem, so they cackled nervously. But one man understood. He quietly let everyone know that even listening to that poem could endanger their lives. Furtively they retreated into the dusk, one by one. Yet I crooned on, like one deranged, hobbling along on the potholed road to freedom. At least that was the path I thought I was following.

One day, I was at a wine shack owned by the sister of one of my cousins. It was located along National Highway 1, in front of Wat

Nirodha Rangsei. I was sitting alone at a round table in the eastern corner of the shack. After awhile, a stranger about my age came in and joined me. After an uncomfortable silence, he looked up and quietly said, "You are a mature politician. You should know that you can't express your opinions and views without reservation. We, at the temple, fear that you will be arrested. Please, do not put yourself in harm's way." Then he walked across the road, and disappeared behind the temple's doors. The rest of the day I sat there alone. Even my cousin's sister didn't talk to me. I didn't feel that I'd done anything wrong, but I recognized in my gut that my life was drifting farther off center.

But politics went on as usual. The Supreme National Council (SNC) now consisted of twelve members: six from Hun Sen's faction, including Hun Sen; two from Son Sann's republican party (Son Sann and Ieng Moly); two from the Khmer Rouge (Khieu Samphan and Son Sen); and two from Norodom Sihanouk's faction (Sihanouk and his son, Norodom Ranaridh). An endless series of negotiations took place. After each session, Hun Sen returned to Phnom Penh and summoned ministers, generals, commanders, governors of the provinces, and directors of all the departments of ministries to a meeting at the Catamuk Theater. I used to attend these meetings myself, before my "resignation."

One of the bones of contention was chairmanship of the SNC, which Hun Sen had very reluctantly turned over to Sihanouk. From the podium, Hun Sen boasted, "We control eighty percent of the country! Why should we let the Khmer resistance have the chairmanship? I'm just thirty-nine years old; I can fight for more than twenty more years. By then, Sihanouk, Son Sann, and Pol Pot will all be dead. So I must be the chairman, or at least co-chairman." These meetings could go on for an entire day.

But during one meeting of the SNC that took place in Thailand, a dam that had been built during the Pol Pot era failed. A wall of water, higher than sugar palm treetops, poured down from the mountains, deluging all the hills below. Schoolchildren, houses, and agricultural equipment were all washed away. The floods inundated four provinces (Kompong Speu, Kandal, Takeo, and Kampot). Like other communist leaders of the era, Hun Sen believed that the world would be more likely to give Cambodia humanitarian assistance if this engineering faux pas were made to look like a natural disaster. Further, Hun Sen believed that he had to offer the chairmanship to Sihanouk because he was convinced that the world would not be sympathetic to victims on his watch. He knew Sihanouk would present a better public relations facade. Humanitarian assistance did pour in from around the world, convincing Hun Sen that he had been an effective pragmatist. But it didn't wash the sour taste of losing the chairmanship out of his mouth.

The next week I went to the rice wine shack again and treated my fellow workers to a five-liter jar and read one of my poems that included these lines from "Lift Ev'ry Voice and Sing," by James Weldon Johnson and J. Rosamond Johnson, which many people in the United States know as "The Negro National Anthem":

> "Lift ev'ry voice and sing,
> Till earth and heaven ring,
> Ring with the harmonies of Liberty;
> Let our rejoicing rise
> High as the list'ning skies,
> Let it resound loud as the rolling sea. . . .
> Facing the rising sun of our new day begun,
> Lets us, sons, let us sons
> March on till victory is won."

(They had no idea what the words meant, but they were stirred by my enthusiasm; they clapped and cheered, as I sang the chorus):

> "Sing! Let's sing!
> Let our rejoicing rise
> High as the list'ning skies
> And let it resound loud as the rolling sea . . ."

Then we all laughed and drank some more wine together. I was starting to slip into a deep depression.

Political machinations continued, and for me, the wheel turned once again. After offering the Chairmanship to Sihanouk, Hun Sen flew to Beijing to invite him to Phnom Penh to celebrate Sihanouk's birthday on the day of the full moon in November 1991.

As I've mentioned several times, most of the important events of my life have begun on a full moon. This time, it was an offer to serve as political assistant to the new U.S. Mission to the SNC, which had just been established in Phnom Penh at the Hotel Cambodiana. My spirits were lifted—at least I would be doing something worthwhile; at least I was going somewhere other than the rice wine shack—*those* spirits had begun to leach away my soul.

FULL MOON OVER IOWA

My office was a room on the second floor of the Hotel Cambodiana. My immediate superior was Second Secretary Mark Storella, but First Secretary Dirk W. Hutchins, Khmer Affairs Consultant Sos Kem, or Ambassador Charles Twining could give me an assignment to get information at any time. They didn't have computers or cell phones at the time, so field operations were very cumbersome.

One day I would be asked to get information from the Son Sann group, and the next day from the Cambodian Peoples' Party. Every morning and every evening I had to listen to the Voice of America broadcast and write a summary. I also read the local newspapers (by then we had five dailies), and summarized all political news. These summaries were reviewed by the mission staff, and were frequently shared with the new U.N. Advanced Mission that had been sent to Cambodia to establish offices and recruit personnel for the more permanent U.N. Transitory Administration that was expected to arrive in March.

I was assigned to report on politics, social unrest, privatization of the economy, the feud between Hun Sen and Chea Sim, and the management of the government bureaucracy. I was also called on to serve as interpreter because of my knowledge of Khmer, French, and English. Although "political unrest" had come to be the normal state of affairs in Cambodia, I began this new position during a time of renewed tumult, despite the U.N. presence.

The privatization of the state economy was in full swing at this time. The Cambodian Peoples' Party allowed every ministry to lease or sell factories, but the level of corruption in this process had gotten completely out of hand. Ministries routinely sold offices, villas, and land, and confiscated individuals' property to sell to foreigners. To the world at large, Cambodia's warring factions had come to a power-sharing agreement, and it looked as if things were settling down. But old resentments had never been fully aired, and new resentments added fuel to a slow-burning flame that was about to become a conflagration.

The first meeting of the Supreme National Council took place in Phnom Penh in January 1992. The Khmer Rouge faction, represented by Khieu Samphan and Son Sen, had purchased a villa east of the Olympic Stadium. One afternoon, about 1:00 p.m., I saw a big crowd in front of the villa. I asked an acquaintance what was happening and he told me that the people were taking revenge for the Khmer Rouge atrocities. I could see the trespassers climbing over the fences and scaling the building into the residential area, with the obvious intention of killing anyone they could find inside. I saw one group that had taken a suitcase full of dollar bills and was burning some of the money while stuffing the rest into their pockets.

I went back to the office to inform Sos Kem of the situation. He and the ambassador both told me to return to the scene of the debacle and to send periodic reports. When I returned, I saw Hun Sen and his troops on the roof of the villa across the road. They were yelling through a loudspeaker, warning the crowd not to hurt the delegates, but the protesters paid them no heed as they surged forward, looking for Khieu Samphan and Son Sen, ready to rip them limb from limb.

By 3:00 p.m., Sihanouk begged Hun Sen to take Khieu Samphan and Son Sen into custody and fly them safely to Thailand. An armored tank rolled backwards into the Khmer Rouge villa to rescue the two delegates, then they were transported to the airport, accompanied by dozens of troops. Needless to say, the SNC meeting was temporarily postponed.

For the remainder of the existence of the SNC, Khieu Samphan and Son Sen commuted from Bangkok. They were still a presence, but they took their names off the ballot and did not participate in the elections directly. They recognized that Hun Sen was not playing by the rules of the Paris Agreement, but what did they expect?

That evening, Hun Sen appeared on television and said that the people had "the right to protest," even the right to revenge, because the Khmer Rouge had killed so many people.

Later I learned that the incidents were staged. The Phnom Penh regime had set up coffee sellers, bicycle repairmen, motorcycle repairmen, and other groups around the Khmer Rouge villa. On television, bystanders said that the protesters were Yuon.

This new idea—the right to protest—spread like wildfire, or, from the perspective of the government, like an infectious disease. The workers believed that Hun Sen had given them permission to protest against any injustice. It was like throwing a boulder in a still pond—the ripples were significant and immediate. One group of factory workers marched to the Ministry of Industry to kidnap Vice Minister Sok Issan. Obviously I wasn't the only one he had mistreated. He not only acted like a petty dictator when he visited the factories, he hired all his relatives and put them in supervisory positions, allowing them to continue his dictatorial ways. Somehow Sok Issan got wind of the plot and escaped before the protesters arrived.

The demonstration around the Ministry of Industry lasted a full week. While the authorities were dealing with that incident, the bank employees joined the protest when they heard the bank had been sold to Thai investors. The employees staged a sit-down strike, refusing to leave the building. They slept and ate in the bank, both men and women. Finally, they received guarantees that all of the bank's employees would be retained.

The ripples continued when the Ministry of Public Works and the Ministry of Telecommunications both went on strike. These ministries were near the medical school, and groups of students had gathered outside their building to observe the strikers. Hun Sen's policemen broke up the gathering and arrested two of the students. So all the medical students rallied to protest against the police, demanding that their fellow students be released.

Of course the police were convinced that the students were coming to do them bodily harm, so they sprayed the crowd with bullets. It was at this point that the students of the University of Phnom Penh joined the strike, and Hun Sen declared martial law. Sos Kem and I drove out by car to observe the events, but the roads were blocked by newly mobilized soldiers, none of whom spoke very good Khmer—they were probably Laotian.

In February 1992, a religious liaison of the National Salvation Front was kidnapped and slaughtered about fifteen miles south of Phnom Penh. Shortly after that, Ung Phan (Hun Sen's secret operative within the Royalist Party), was wounded in his car, four miles from Phnom Penh. Ambassador Twining wanted to console Ung Phan and asked me to find him and bring him to Phan's residence.

I sought out Phan's second wife, who managed a restaurant northeast of Grand New Market. His wife told me that Hun Sen was hiding Ung Phan at the premier's residence. I returned to the office and asked the ambassador whether he wanted to visit Ung Phan at Hun Sen's house. For political reasons, he wanted to meet Ung Phan at his own residence at 1:00 p.m. It was already past 11 a.m. at that point. I returned to Phan's wife and explained the situation. I wrote a note to him, assuring him that the U.S. Ambassador would guarantee his safety if he returned home. Then Roeuddhi and I went to look over Phan's house for security purposes and to position the furniture for the interview and the photographs the ambassador wanted as documentation of the meeting. Amazingly, everyone arrived on time, and after a fifteen-minute talk, it was time for photographs. They asked me to take charge, but I couldn't figure out how to use their new modern camera, so Mark Storella took the pictures instead.

Even though I was working for the U.S. Mission, I was once again involved in the Cambodian government, and these assignments were awakening hidden feelings that were still smoldering inside me. My next investigation made things worse. On successive days, two people were killed right in front of U.N. officials. Many suspected that this violence had grown out of a feud between Hun Sen and Chea Sim, a deputy minister in the SNC. Ambassador Twining assigned me to look into the matter.

Getting to the bottom of this controversy required that I question innumerable people. I tried to maintain a confident demeanor, but frequently found myself stopping to look over my shoulder, scanning the other side of the street, watching the hands of the person who just rode up on a motor scooter. Before long, I noticed that my own hands were starting to shake, my blood pressure was up, and I was always irritable. In conversation, I was starting to ramble, and at home I was short with my wife, my mother-in-law, and my son. In fact, I withdrew from everyone close to me. I knew that I was coming apart. I'm sure that my bosses at the Mission noticed, and were starting to doubt my stability—I saw it in their eyes. Or was this just my imagination? I had to laugh at myself—I was starting to feel like one of those Cold War spies I had seen in movies, whose life becomes an intricately woven web of dissimulation.

Then, on March 27, 1992, thirty well-armed troops arrived at my premises, and announced that they were there to seize and divide my house and land. I was at work when this happened. When I returned home, my wife told me that had I been there, they would have shot me on the spot.

I went to the U.N. office to get my house back. A Ugandan captain said "Don't worry—so long as I'm here, I'm going to work toward getting your land back for you." He then assigned two Filipino officers to go to my house with me to investigate the circumstances of the incident. When we arrived, the troops made themselves scarce. The two officers poked around my property and took photographs. But when they saw a soldier lurking in the background with an AK-47, they jumped in their car and took off.

I wrote a long letter to the U.N. Human Rights Commission, but nothing came of it.

It turned out that I was actually on a list of people targeted for assassination. In all my activities, I acted in the best interests of Cambodia and my employer, the U.S. Mission. But Cambodians at that time didn't make a clear distinction between the Mission and the CIA. A friend warned me that I was targeted for assassination because the Phnom Penh regime was convinced that I was actually a CIA operative. Given the manner in which the CIA had conducted itself in Southeast Asia and elsewhere, this misperception was natural, though unfortunate for me.

After a year without a job, I had been so elated to be employed by a United States government agency. But after a few months, I had started to feel exhausted—the work was endless. And I received only ten dollars a day, regardless of the hours I put in. The Mission didn't provide me with any transportation. I had to take a taxi to and from work. Now my property had been seized and my life was again in danger. I would like to emphasize that everyone had been pleasant and considerate—it was as if Ambassador Twining and the entire staff treated me as a brother; nevertheless, by the end of March, a little more than three months after taking the position, I handed in my resignation. And once again I fell into a deep depression.

A few weeks later I went to the home of one of my cousins to kill a few hours. A young man who claimed to have royal blood was sitting there. He had been living in the Kulen Mountains, north of Angkor Wat, where he discovered that he was a medium. While my cousin and I were chatting, a deity of some sort possessed the medium. The deity identified himself as Ta Mao from Prasat Bayon. The medium then pounded his chest and his back so severely that I thought he would fracture his ribs. Instead, he spit a little black pearl into his palm. Then the deity spoke to me. He said, "The Empire Deity Congress has convened at Angkor Wat, and unanimously adopted a resolution to release you, Grandson, from this land, and to prevent any physical harm from coming to you. In three months, Grandson, you will receive good news about traveling beyond the borders of this country."

After all that had happened to me, I must have lost some of my faith, because I found it difficult to believe what I had just been told. "How can this small pearl possibly have the power to liberate me from this land of crocodiles and tigers when I don't even have a dime?" I asked the deity. "All the papers needed to leave the country are almost impossible to obtain. If I don't have an approved autobiography, birth certificate, and application for passport in order, the Ministry of Foreign Affairs will not issue me a passport. And furthermore, a passport costs two thousand dollars."

"Just take this pearl and hang it around your neck. You'll see what happens, Grandson!"

The pearl was free of charge, so I took it and wrapped it in a pouch made of cloth as a pendant to hang around my neck.

Sure enough, in July, three months later, Big Brother Sos Kem came to my house and said "Little Brother Sam Oeur, prepare yourself to go to the United States. We just received a fax from the University of Iowa!"

I felt indifferent. I couldn't believe that there was any way that I would ever be able to escape the Indochinese communist circle. But a week later I received a letter from the University of Iowa. It had been sent to the wrong address, but it reached me safely through an acquaintance. The letter invited me to participate in the International Writing Program at the University of Iowa. The stipend was $6,000 for a three-month stay.

Now I was starting to feel a glimmer of hope. I immediately sent a letter to Mary Gray at the Asia Foundation in Washington, DC and asked if I could borrow $300 from her. A few weeks later, her assistant Bob Cannon arrived in Phnom Penh, and handed me a letter from Mary Gray. Dr. Gray said that she was giving me the $300 instead of lending it to me, because if the debt wasn't paid on time, it might get in the way of our friendship.

Once I got the money, I began the process of applying for a pass-port. I picked up copies of the blank application. I wrote yet one more autobiography. When I took my application to the subdis-trict level, the officer in charge told me he wanted a new Khmer-English dictionary in return for his signature. I had no choice—I found him a copy of a Khmer-English dictionary. Then I went to get the applications stamped by the deputy of the municipality—I was lucky that I knew him. My next hurdle was the Ministry of Foreign Affairs. Before going there, I went to see my "Big Brother" Sos Kem, for a letter of support from the U.S. Mission. Again I was lucky. Big Brother Kem wrote a letter saying that the U.S. govern-ment would strongly support my visit as a significant cultural exchange, and that the U.S. Mission strongly urged the Ministry of Foreign Affairs to issue me a passport.

I submitted an affidavit with my application to the director of the North American department, who brought the material to the vice minister, who scrawled "O.K." at the bottom of the applica-tion. The entire process took a little over a month.

A week before my departure, I threw a modest party for several of the people who had helped me through the last few years, including Dr. Gray's young assistants. My brother Buntha paid the expenses.

Syna and I never discussed whether I would try to stay in the U.S. longer than my original visa allowed. My mother-in-law was still living with us at the time, but had little to say about my depar-ture. Roeuddhi was still at home, too, now teaching high-school math. I had the uneasy feeling that if I stayed out of the country beyond the three months, the government would find a way to make life unpleasant for my family, but I knew that it was unlikely that I would return, if I really did find my way back to Iowa.

On August 31, 1992, I went to the airport. I had asked a friend of mine, who was a colonel in the police force, and my youngest brother, Buntha, to accompany me, but neither of them showed up. Before leaving for the airport I went to say good-bye to another friend who was serving as the director of the Consular

Department at the Ministry of Foreign Affairs. I showed him my passport. He opened it and said "Oh . . . the passport isn't signed yet." He signed it and told me to enjoy myself in the States for six months, which was three months longer than I had expected. My son drove me and Syna to the airport at 10:00 a.m. We had what was to be our last breakfast together for some time.

Bob Cannon had bought me a ticket on Thai Airways from Phnom Penh to Bangkok and wrritten a note on a small piece of paper to take with me to the Northwest Airlines office at the Bangkok airport. My flight was scheduled to leave Pochentong Airport at 11:30 a.m. When I arrived at the checkpoint, I stood with my wife, because our son had gone to visit his friend working at the other end of the terminal.

A young man approached me and asked, "Where is Big Uncle going?"

"I'm going to Bangkok."

He took my ticket, checked my luggage (such as it was), and then led me by the hand to the waiting room, bypassing customs and the police. I didn't get a chance to hug Syna and Roeuddhi good-bye. In the waiting room I heard a bullhorn calling out names. I prayed to every deity and spirit I could remember to allow me to make this voyage. It was 10:30 a.m. Then it was 11:00 a.m. Then 11:15. I realized that I had been holding my breath and was about to faint. I hoped that the boarding pass officer would call passengers sooner than the time of departure. By then I was soaked with sweat as I sat there waiting to leave Cambodia.

Finally the announcement came for us to board. As I was walking to the plane, many officers from the Ministry of Industry waved their hands in good-bye gestures. I looked at them, realizing that I was shaking.

Once I boarded and took my seat, I felt a little more relaxed. We taxied down the runway and were airborne. I was doing fine until we approached the Thai border. The guy sitting next to me, from the Ministry of Culture, said, "Two weeks ago there were twenty-seven passengers who flew to Bangkok on this same plane, but the plane turned around and was escorted back by two MIG-21 jets and now they are all in T3 Prison." I started shaking again and I'm sure that I turned an ashen white. But soon the plane landed and I got off and went through customs to the baggage claim area.

I still didn't feel safe yet. After claiming my luggage I went to the Northwest Airlines officer for my ticket. I pushed the cart along until I found the counter. I handed the little piece of paper that Bob Cannon had given me to a young lady behind the counter and she said, "It's not a receipt." She gave it back to me and turned away. Then I was desperate. I wheeled the cart outside to get some air and to think. I stood there for a while then approached the woman again and explained to her that a round-trip ticket was supposed to be waiting for me, and that it had been purchased by the International Writing Program of the University of Iowa, who had invited me to the U.S. She phoned someone, then told me that I would have to go downtown. I told her that I did not have permission to leave the airport. She made another call, to the main office, and told me to wait until 5:00 a.m. the next morning. She said the ticket would be at the check-in gate.

I pushed my cart back to the waiting room. I stayed there from 2:00 p.m. to 5:00 a.m. That night I pushed that cart back and forth from the restroom to the waiting room, where I would sit for a couple of hours, then it was back to the restroom. Now and then I would go into a toilet stall where I would close my eyes for a few seconds.

Finally 5:00 a.m. arrived. I pushed my cart to the check-in gate. There, a young policeman stopped me and asked where I was going. I told him that I was going to the United States.

"Who said you could go to the United States?"

"I was invited by the International Writing Program of the University of Iowa."

"What do you do in Cambodia?"

"I am a poet."

"What is a poet?"

"A poet is a person who writes poetry."

"What is poetry?"

I did not have time to explain poetry to this policeman barely into his twenties, so I handed him the handwritten ten-page manuscript I had with me. He took it to his superior. He returned, apparently having been given authorization to allow me to get on board, because he went about busily slapping stickers on the collar of my jacket, my suitcase, and handbag. When my flight was called to board I saw the same policeman at the plane door. "You're already inspected—go ahead," he told me.

Even after we took off, I realized that I was still very tense. I know Americans used to joke about crazy people who were convinced that Russians were hiding under their beds—to me, it was no joke. I continued to imagine that I was being hunted down by communist agents. When we got to the Tokyo airport I couldn't stop looking around to see if any of Hun Sen's men had followed me.

When I landed in San Francisco, and they stamped my visa, I began to breathe more easily. By the time we reached Minneapolis-St. Paul I knew that this wasn't a fantasy. And then I transferred to another plane for the last leg of the trip—the flight to Iowa.

I was shaky when I got off the plane at the Cedar Rapids airport, the same airport I'd left back in 1968. I hadn't had anything to eat in two days. At first I was desperate—it was 11:30 at night— where was I going to stay that night? Maybe I would have to stay at the airport again until the next morning.

But when I stepped off the escalator I saw my old friend and brother, Ken McCullough, waiting for me. We were both grayer than when we'd last seen each other, and I'd been through three howling wildernesses since then, but it was good to see his smile and it was good to be back in Iowa. I was so happy; I felt that I had been reborn on that day, September 1, 1992.

As we walked into the airport parking lot, I looked up at the sky in anticipation. I was not disappointed. Once again, on the eve of a new stage in my life, a full moon brightened the autumn Iowa night. I was finally free.

EPILOGUE

THE INVITATION TO IOWA

When Phnom Penh fell to Pol Pot, Cambodia became isolated from the world. Phone service outside Cambodia was unavailable. Mail neither entered nor left the country because the Vietnamese wanted to limit our interactions with the outside world. Conditions slowly began to improve in the early 1980s; in 1984, I decided to send a letter to the English Department of the University of Iowa requesting a copy of my thesis.

Although I had been cut off from the outside world, I was not cut off from the thoughts of my brother, Ken McCullough. During the years when we were out of touch with each other, he spoke of our friendship to everyone he knew, and told one and all to contact him if word of me ever surfaced. The executive secretary of the English Department, Felicia Lavalliere, was one of the many people who had heard of Ken's Cambodian classmate; she showed my letter to Ken as soon as it arrived.

And so in 1984, the year of George Orwell, Ken and I renewed our correspondence. We communicated through a labyrinthine process: I gave my letters to a sympathetic staff member of an Australian NGO, who hand-carried them to Bangkok; from there they could enter the conventional international mail system. Ken's letters reached me through the same chain in reverse.

Once Ken knew I had survived the Pol Pot years, he began to look for someone who could help him find a way to bring me back to the United States. He approached Clark Blaise, the director of the Iowa International Writing Program, who took up my cause.

Together Ken and Clark worked tirelessly to find the requisite funding, and to gather the mountain of documentation necessary to bring me to Iowa. They approached a number of foundations before the Dashiell Hammett-Lillian Hellman Fund for Free Expression agreed to sponsor me. (Ironically some foundations had been reluctant because I had not created a significant body of work since leaving Iowa. I had written poems before the Pol Pot years, but I had burned them. I had written since the Pol Pot years, but the first time one of my poems surfaced, I was forced to resign my government job. If I *had* published a significant body of work, I would probably be dead many times over by now.)

During a visit to the International Writing Program, each participant shares his or her work with the other fellows at a series of semiformal readings. When it was time for me to make a presentation, we worked out an arrangement for Ken to read each poem in English—I followed, chanting in Khmer. I admit that I was very shaky that night, finally giving voice to poems I had hidden in my soul all those years. There were many tears among the members of that audience, as several of them had suffered permutations of my experiences. A number of them wept openly. It was hard for me to maintain my composure.

I wish to again express my gratitude to Clark Blaise, and to the International Writing Program. In large part, the presence of this visionary component of the University of Iowa inspired the mayor and city council of Iowa City to officially join the North American Network of Cities of Asylum. The asylum network provides safe havens for writers who are under threat of death, torture, or imprisonment in their native countries. Host cities provide the writers with a monthly stipend, a furnished residence, and health insurance for one to two years. I salute the International Writing Program for long providing a forum for communication among the writers of the world, and now for their work in administering this asylum program. I am honored to have been one of their fellows.

MY FAMILY

In telling my story, I fear I have neglected to give a complete picture of our family. As mentioned, we named our son *Bun Nol* when he was born. During the Pol Pot years, when so many people changed their names, we called our son *Proelung*. In the 1980s, we registered him for school as *U Bonyaroeuddhi*. He was an intelligent boy and in two years skipped ahead to the fourth grade at a school at Wat Koh south of Grand New Market. He found his own way to school—we didn't worry about him. Roeuddhi graduated from Boeung Trabek High School in 1988, and earned his bachelor's degree in math from the University of Phnom Penh in 1992. He taught math at Roeussei Keo High School from 1993 to 1995.

While I was living in Iowa, I met a young woman named April McAllister, who was planning to visit Cambodia. I told her to look up my son while she was there, and I wrote to my son, and told him to show her around. Something must have clicked between them, because before she returned to the States, they were married. He told me later that he had already seen her, in a vision.

Roeuddhi immigrated to the United States in November 1995 to join his new wife. Before long, he changed his name one more time, to James Bonya Ou. He had tried to keep our simple family name—U—intact, but he discovered that airlines will not let you use a single-letter last name. Perhaps this practice may have originally been a racist reaction to names such as Malcolm X. Now, occupied as they are with terrorists, the airlines are unlikely to change this policy.

My son is currently employed as a technical engineer in McKinney, Texas. He has continued his education at night school, studying new forms of technology and engineering. He and April have three sons: Edward, John, and Daniel McAllister-Ou. Syna and I, of course, are very proud of our beautiful grandchildren.

Syna began working at the soft drink factory in 1979 at the same time I did. She worked in a lab mixing salt in a tank of water to produce soda and *okirii* (drinking water). She served as chair-woman of the Women's Association of the soft drink factory for a year. In 1980, she was transferred to the Ministry of Industry, and was sent to a school to study accounting. She was an accountant for three years at the Ministry of Industry. In 1983 she was transferred to the Phnom Penh Health Department, where she was employed for five years. In 1988 they transferred her to the Department of Health at a district closer to home. In this new position, she worked as a nurse, assisting in the delivery of babies. She had acquired this knowledge starting back in 1970 when I was in the Army. Although she never expressed it, I'm sure that every time she helped in a birth, the memory of our lost twins must have passed through her mind. Through all those years, she was an efficient and cheerful homemaker and companion, a demanding but generous mother, and an excellent role model for our son. Friends, neighbors, and coworkers alike were captivated by her ready smile and positive demeanor. We both had determined that if I were to ever return to the United States, that I should stay. She remained in Cambodia for many years, taking care of her aging mother. After her mother's death, with Ken's help, she secured a visa and now lives with us in Texas. Since then she has gotten her green card, and returns to Cambodia whenever we have the money to fly her there. We still have our house in Chbar Ampeou and she continues to run a small business. After all, Cambodia is her home—she has not learned much English and feels somewhat out of her element in the U.S., though she loves her grandsons. And we continue to be devoted to each other, speaking on the phone once a week when she is in Cambodia.

MY RECOVERY

When I arrived in Iowa my eyesight was failing. Cataracts on both my eyes made it painful for me to read for any length of time. But the International Writing Program medical insurance allowed me to have laser surgery on both eyes. During my convalescence

Maggie Hogan took care of me at her house. I would have been a sad case without her assistance. I will be eternally grateful to her for her kindness. If this operation had taken place in Cambodia it would most likely have resulted in blindness.

I also had an operation on one of my eardrums, which had been ruined during the Pol Pot era, when I fell asleep on guard duty and my ears had filled with filthy swamp water. A surgeon repaired the eardrum, and my hearing began to recover. But several months later, when I returned to have a checkup and get my ear cleaned, an intern examined me, and didn't read what the surgeon had written in my case history, nor did he listen when I told him I had had recent surgery. He started probing around and spoiled the progress I had made since the operation. I have noticed that some Western doctors regard their judgment as infallible. They don't listen to their patients, and don't consult with other doctors unless insurance requires it. Maybe some demonstration of intuition ought to be required for entrance into medical school. Yet I am grateful for most of the care I have received here. And at least I can read again.

Several of the churches in Iowa City helped me out financially during this time, particularly St. Mary's and the First Mennonite Church, where I attended services for a while. Pastor Firman Gingerich and Hobart Yoder were godsends. Most people know that the Mennonites are very active overseas, but unlike several other Christian groups they are more interested in helping people than in converting them.

Of course not all wounds are physical. During my first few months in Iowa, every time I heard more than one person clomping down the hall, I was sure the agents of Hun Sen were coming to get me. After I left Iowa, I lived in Minnesota for a few years, and, on occasion, shared my story with people at the Center for Victims of Torture. Sadly, such an organization is badly needed in the world today. They helped me, as they have helped many others. I thank them for their good work.

PUBLICATION AND RECOGNITION

Since returning to the States and regaining my health, I have resumed writing, and the reception I have received has been very gratifying.

In 1993, Ken and I put together a chapbook of eight poems in Khmer with facing translations, called *Selections from Sacred Vows*, and in 1997, *No Exit* magazine published a special edition devoted to my work. When we sold the chapbook and magazine at readings, I would write my signature, followed by the phrase *kavei gocaw*, which means "itinerant poet." I wasn't romanticizing my situation; this is the traditional way of referring to my profession in Cambodia. But, to me at least, there was some measure of irony.

Also in 1993, Ken introduced me to his coworker Mark Bruckner, a composer who had done quite a bit of sound work for theater. During the next few years we collaborated together, first on a performance of my poems, accompanied by Mark's thoughtful and haunting instrumentation.

When Mark began to blend the sounds of traditional Cambodian music with modern atonal jazz, a larger work began to take shape in his mind. Then his partner, Mary Beth Easley, became involved as director, and eventually, a chamber opera entitled *The Krasang Tree* was created, and presented on a number of stages. It incorporated dancers, singers, mimes, and concluded with me walking on stage and reciting my poem, "Lunar Enchantment" in English—the rest of the opera was in Khmer. Those performances were among the proudest moments of my life.

The production in Minneapolis had an added charm for me—most of the cast, and the musicians and dancers were Cambodian. Ken's son, Galway, participated, miming the actions of the Khmer Rouge symbolically from behind a screen, in a spin-off of traditional Cambodian shadow plays. These performances required a large stage, sound people, musicians, singers, dancers, lighting technicians, and ushers—all coordinated by Mark and Mary Beth. I remain amazed by their effort and abilities, and grateful for their friendship.

In 1998, Coffee House Press published the full-length version of *Sacred Vows*, again with Khmer and English on facing pages. Coincidentally, the book arrived from the printer on the same day Pol Pot was found dead. That confluence of events helped gain some initial publicity for the book, but more articles—including a long interview in the *New York Times*—followed. Some unexpected responses came, too; I received a few threatening letters. But they were not as explicit as the ones I received in 1993, which were handwritten, coarsely worded death threats postmarked from Long Beach, probably from the Khmer Rouge contingent there. When we traveled in those days, Ken would often give our contact people false times and places of arrival, just in case.

I have read my work, sometimes accompanied by Ken, at well over a hundred colleges, universities, communities, festivals, and other functions. Probably the most amusing venue was the Nuyorican Poets' Cafe in New York. Ken and I were the warm-up act for the poetry slam. I was a monk at the time and wore my saffron robes. My friend Lang Leang Kulen came with me from the North Bronx Cambodian Buddhist Temple. We got there early, and the cafe wasn't open yet, so we went across the street to find a place to drink some tea and wait. As it turned out, the place we entered was a strip club. We settled in anyway and ordered soft drinks. We drew a few stares, especially me in my saffron robes. When we went back to the Nuyorican, five minutes before our performance, Ken was quite agitated, thinking that we had gotten lost. But once we went on stage, I gave it my operatic best, and I think our part of the evening was a rousing success. One man, who may have been on drugs, came up to me as I left the podium, took my hand and looked deep into my eyes. He said, "Thanks, man . . . tonight I heard the voice of God." Afterwards, we sat and watched the poetry slam. Some of the poems were entertaining, some just plain crass, but all were filled with energy.

A documentary about my life is underway. Mary Ellen Will and her videographer Steve Clary have taped over 200 hours of footage covering my life, and the life and culture of Cambodia. She is currently looking for funding to enable her to complete the editing process.

AFTER IOWA

Since my return to the u.s., my existence has been fairly nomadic. Unlike the character Blanche in Tennessee Williams's *A Streetcar Named Desire,* who depends on "the kindness of strangers," I have depended on the kindness of friends, who, in several cases were actually angels. I arrived in Iowa in September 1992, and for my first few months I lived under the auspices of the IWP. After that I stayed in Iowa City in the home of Maggie Hogan, as mentioned above; with my brother Ken; in Sioux City with Ginny and Mike Duncan; then in the Cambodian Buddhist Temple in Des Moines.

While in Iowa, I was recommended to a group from Taos, New Mexico, and presented my poems at their annual reading for peace. I developed many close friends in that community, and have been back several times. I consider it, after Iowa City, as my third home. Rose Gordon has worked with me in several critical situations, Lorraine Ciancio and Phyllis Hotch have kept me involved, and Mag Dimond and Charlie Strong have saved my life many times over. Others in Taos have been generous to me along the way, including Catherine and Stephen Rose.

In November 1994, I moved to Minneapolis, Minnesota, and lived there, on and off, until September 1999. During those years I stayed with a number of friends, and found a number of ways to make ends meet. For a while I put in sixty-hour work weeks at the Douglas Corporation operating a machine that coated manufactured items with polyurethane. Then I received a Bush Foundation fellowship and a grant from the St. Paul Companies, which sustained me during much of my tenure there. I also returned briefly to the University of Iowa for another brief stint as a writer-in-residence. Minneapolis has always been an incredibly nurturing environment for me. In July 1999, I moved to Texas to join my son and daughter-in-law, and I have lived with them, on and off, ever since. I have attempted to get work, but my age and declining health have relegated me to the position of babysitter for my grandsons, which is, after all, noble occupation.

RESIDENT STATUS

I applied for political asylum on September 24, 1994, and was approved on October 1, 1998. I applied for a green card in 1999, but since then have been shunted through a labyrinth of bureaucracy that would make Kafka feel right at home. I have spoken to many lawyers, and written to many politicians. I have been told that "it's only a matter of time," by many people. I have been told not to worry by many people. But until I have a green card, I will continue to believe that in the middle of some dark night, I will be drugged and whisked off, only to wake up in prison in Cambodia, or worse, in Vietnam.

I continue to hope that some day I will return safely, with Syna, to Cambodia, and that I can somehow assist my country in coming back to a balanced way of life. I know that when I do get there, the flood of feelings, sights, smells, and sounds will be overwhelming. Jimmy, his grandmother, his mother Syna, and I lived through a protracted nightmare, which was followed by an assortment of other bad dreams, but my dream now is to return to Cambodia, to see a glimmer of democracy there—that would be heaven on earth.

MY OWN EFFORTS

To increase the effectiveness of my prayers for peace, freedom, and democracy, I have twice entered the Buddhist Order here in the States: in July 2000, and again in February 2004. This gave me the opportunity to communicate more closely with the Holy Beings. One problem I've observed among stateside Cambodians is that their spiritual connection with Buddhism has been reduced to paying the monks to pray for them, especially for good luck at the casinos. This may sound cynical, but I experienced this frequently during my two stints as a monk in this country.

Young Cambodian Americans, like other transplanted Asians, are working very hard to distance themselves from their traditional language and culture. The only noticeable vestige for some is in their hand gestures when they are dancing to rock and roll music—it's almost comical, but touching in a way. I'm sure that they are not even conscious of the fact that they are doing it. Unfortunately it's not just Khmer that they're ignoring. They're just not reading—but then again, they are simply following the same trend that has left an entire generation of young Americans ignorant of their history and their literary heritage.

I believe that Walt Whitman's work just might be the antidote. Some years ago Ken McCullough and I began translating selections from *Song of Myself* into Khmer. A selection was published in the *Walt Whitman Quarterly,* and we published a larger selection as a pamphlet. I believe that Whitman's expansiveness and cosmic vision, when applied to our traditional forms, will bring Cambodian poetry into the new millennium. His vision of nature, of unity, and of human nature was informed by Transcendentalism, which in turn was informed by both Hinduism and Buddhism, so by inspiring Cambodia, he will be paying his debt to our spiritual legacy. For me, reading Whitman is like reading any other sacred text—when I am receptive, his poems give me answers to the deep abiding questions.

AMERICA AND CAMBODIA

I know that the United States has made grave errors in judgment in Cambodia as well as in other places, and it seems that lately these errors have been assuming more ominous overtones. (If you want a full accounting of the United States's blunders in Cambodia, you should read William Shawcross's *Sideshow,* which is out of print but still available.)

Nevertheless, the United States has had a hand in training the youth of Cambodia ever since World War II, in the most positive way. I feel certain that this flow of energy from the U.S. will continue, and spread to our younger generations. Observing our youth these days, one might be tempted to say that it is rampant consumerism that will most likely spread from the u.s. to Cambodia.

But I know in my heart that it is the goodness of the American people, and the value of hard work, which will help transform Cambodia into its own quirky version of democracy. All my work and all my prayers are dedicated toward making that transformation a reality in my lifetime.

COLOPHON

The text was designed by the publisher, Allan Kornblum, who selected
Iowan Old Style for the body type because the author's years in Iowa
were among his happiest. The Pompeijana Roman used for display,
was adapted from one of the earliest formal Italian handwriting
styles. The resemblance of this Roman hand to Hebrew, and to
Sanskrit (which influenced the Khmer alphabet) would indicate that
all three might have developed from some lost common source, just
as genocide itself seems to have developed from some common flaw
in humanity, a flaw we must all work to overcome.

COFFEE HOUSE PRESS FUNDERS

Coffee House Press is an independent nonprofit literary publisher. Our books are made possible through the generous support of grants and gifts from many foundations, corporate giving programs, individuals, and through state and federal support. This book received special project support through grants from the National Endowment for the Arts, a federal agency, and from the Peter and Madeleine Martin Foundation for the Creative Arts; and from the following individuals: William Golightly; Stephen and Isabel Keating; Seymour Kornblum and Gerry Lauter; Tom and Gwyn Rosen; and Charles Steffey and Suzannah Martin. Coffee House Press receives general operating support from the Minnesota State Arts Board, through an appropriation by the Minnesota State Legislature and from the National Endowment for the Arts, a federal agency. Coffee House receives major general operating support from the McKnight Foundation, and from Target. Coffee House also receives significant support from: an anonymous donor; the Buuck Family Foundation; the Bush Foundation; the Patrick and Aimee Butler Foundation; Consortium Book Sales and Distribution; the Foundation for Contemporary Performance Arts; the Lerner Family Foundation; the Outagamie Foundation; the Pacific Foundation; the law firm of Schwegman, Lundberg, Woessner & Kluth, P.A.; the James R. Thorpe Foundation; the Archie and Bertha Walker Foundation; West Group; the Woessner Freeman Family Foundation; and many other generous individual donors.

This activity is made possible in part by a grant from the Minnesota State Arts Board, through an appropriation by the Minnesota State Legislature and a grant from the National Endowment for the Arts.

 A celebrated Cambodian poet, U Sam Oeur grew up tending water buffalo in the Svay Rieng Province. After studying in the United States and receiving his MFA from the University of Iowa Writers' Workshop, he was elected to Cambodia's National Assembly, and served as a member of Cambodia's delegation to the United Nations. When Pol Pot assumed power in 1975, Oeur survived six forced labor camps by feigning illiteracy and utilizing incredible survival skills. After the Vietnamese forces overthrew Pol Pot, he served in the Ministry of Industry until a pro-democracy poem was discovered in his desk, forcing his resignation. A devout Buddhist and passionate advocate for peace, freedom, and democracy, Oeur is the author of *Sacred Vows*, a bilingual English/Khmer collection of poetry. He now lives in Texas where he is translating the poems of Walt Whitman into Khmer.

Ken McCullough met U Sam Oeur at the University of Iowa Writers' Workshop in the 1960s and was instrumental in helping him return to the United States in 1992. He is the author of six volumes of poetry, including *Walking Backwards*, a volume of stories, *Left Hand*, and the co-librettist for the chamber opera, *The Krasang Tree*, based on Oeur's poetry and experiences of survival during the Cambodian genocide. He lives in southeastern Minnesota and is an administrator at St. Mary's University.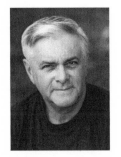